THERE AIN'T NO ———
IN ROCK 'N' ROLL

My Life in the Music Industry

By

Kenny Denton

Copyright © 2024 Kenny Denton Music

All rights reserved. No part of this publication may be reproduced or transmitted by any means, electronic, mechanical, photocopying or otherwise without the prior permission of the copyright owner.

Disclaimer

The events and conversations in this book have been set down to the best of the author's ability, some names and details have been changed to protect the privacy of individuals.

This book is lovingly dedicated to:

My dear Mother, my amazing wife Sue our beloved daughter Natalie and our precious grandchildren Adam, Grace, Ryan, Luchia, Nevaeh and Dexter. It is also dedicated to all the remarkable characters and friends whom I have had the privilege of riding the roller coaster of life with.

I would also like to express my deep gratitude to Ben Matthews for his outstanding work in editing the book and for his invaluable support, patience and unwavering enthusiasm.

Special acknowledgements go to Pat Godwin. Miki Dallon. Louis Elman. Stuart Taylor. Dave Miller. Dave Hunt. Dag Häggqvist. Jack Haley (Bill Haley's son) Caroline Boyce (Tommy Boyce's widow) Neville Crosier. Phil Newell. Harry Ledingham (Ex jukebox records market stall holder East Lane 1960's)

Foreword

I remember the first time I met Kenny; I was sticking postage stamps onto seven-inch record envelopes in the reception area of the small record company I worked at. Suddenly, the entrance door swung open and in walked Kenny - a man of short stature, adorned with thick, curly brown hair and sporting flares contributing to his very distinctive style. His infectious smile, stretching as wide as his lapels, lit up the room, and clearly, everyone was delighted to see him.
It quickly became apparent why Kenny was so well-liked, he possessed a warmth and kindness rarely encountered in the cut-throat world of the music industry.

Fast forward a year or so and fate threw me an unexpected opportunity: the company acquired a recording studio and, despite my total lack of experience, I found myself at the helm of its operations. It was here that Kenny took me under his wing and selflessly gifted me the benefit of his years of experience in studios around the world.

From here we forged a remarkable friendship that endures to this day, punctuated by countless collaborative musical endeavours. During these sessions there was always time for Kenny to tell me a tale or two from his incredible past adventures, each narrative a masterclass in comedic timing, that never failed to leave me doubled over in laughter. With each anecdote, my appetite for more grew insatiable and Kenny, ever the raconteur, obliged without hesitation.

In the midst of uproarious laughter, I'd often jest that Kenny ought to immortalize these tales in a book, their brilliance too potent to remain undocumented. His response was always tinged with a knowing smile, as if the notion had crossed his mind before.

I am delighted to declare that the day has finally arrived. Within these pages lies a treasure trove of anecdotes, offering a rare glimpse behind the curtain at some of the music industry's most iconic figures. Prepare to be enthralled, amused and perhaps even astonished, as Kenny's chronicles unfurl in all their glorious detail.

It's worth noting some of the names of the people involved have been changed to protect the guilty.

Ben Matthews

Preface

Introduction

Chapters:

1. The Beginning
2. Then There was Music
3. Pye Studios
4. Isle of Wight Festival 1970
5. Back to the Studio
6. De Lane Lea
7. Fate Calls Time Out
8. A Welcome Return
9. The Music Centre and Clients
10. Bill Haley and the Demise of Early Rock 'n' Roll
11. Hercules the Bear
12. Louis Clark
13. The Sonet Recordings
14. Nashville and Jerry Foster
15. My Cajun Adventure
16. Alisha's Attic
17. Fleetwood Mac's Peter Green
18. Anthony Newley
19. Sir Thomas Hicks OBE AKA Tommy Steel
20. How to Sign an Exceptional Record Deal
21. Vic Maile Engineer and Producer
22. A Few Gems I Picked Up Along the Way
23. Epilogue

Preface

For over 40 years I had the privilege to work with some of the most amazing, talented, crazy and often deluded people in the world of music and movies.
I've spent endless hours stationed behind the mixing desk, orchestrating the recording and production processes for a diverse spectrum of artistes.
From the remarkably gifted to those whose creative spark may have flickered less brightly, I've navigated them all.

It began in 1969, at Pye Studios in London, where I was fortunate to learn the art of recording from some of the most acclaimed engineers of the time. I subsequently moved on to De Lane Lea Studios, an expansive state-of-the-art facility acclaimed as the world's largest purpose-built studio.

Both Pye and DLL functioned as my educational institutions for mastering the intricacies of sound recording. Significantly, they also served as platforms for me to immerse myself in the realm of record production and song writing, where I gleaned insights from the luminaries who frequented the recording studio and consistently topped the charts.

Throughout the years, I've regaled friends and family with countless anecdotes from this captivating journey. As moments turned into memories, the notion to preserve these tales began to crystallize, prompting a profound appreciation for the intricacies of the human mind. It's a marvel that commences its workings long before one's birth and doesn't stop until the moment one sits down to write a book.

Coming up with a name for a book is a crucial task and I needed something both attention grabbing and sales worthy. My initial ideas, "Sold Over 5 Million Copies Worldwide" and "The Number One Best Seller," both certainly have a catchy, attention-grabbing quality to them, but they might not accurately reflect the essence of the book's content.

Compiling an accurate timeline of my narratives became achievable through consulting my diaries. Spanning from 1971 to 2009, I consistently maintained these journals, not out of any historical intent, but merely to log the sessions I worked on and the overtime hours I accrued. Unexpectedly, they have emerged as indispensable references, furnishing precise dates and contextual details to my various escapades. Reflecting on my experience within this captivating industry, I've arrived at a simple realisation:

You may have been in the business for 5 minutes or for 20 years, you could be very gifted or have no talent at all but to achieve success you must remember one crucial thing

There Ain't No Rules in Rock 'n' Roll.

Introduction

As a young child, my imagination was my playground, I believed that no dream was beyond reach. As I grew older, I came to understand that achieving those dreams would require surmounting numerous challenges and obstacles. Nevertheless, throughout my life, I've been fortunate enough to conquer many of these mountains and reach their summits. Yet, to my surprise, the view from the top was never quite as I had imagined.

Now, semi-retired, I am finally standing on the summit I had always dreamed of. The view before me matches the vision I had always imagined. Yet, in a twist of fate, this seemingly perfect sight soon transforms into a daunting realisation: there are no more mountains on the horizon, no more challenges to overcome.

Determined not to let complacency settle in, I set forth on a new quest creating a new mountain to climb. The following pages represent that quest.

Amidst the multitude of books dedicated to the music industry, this one stands apart, offering a different perspective through captivating narratives.

Join me as I take you on my personal journey, traversing the glorious heyday of the music business and revealing the transformative shifts that have shaped it into the industry it is today. Through the pages of this book, you'll encounter a colourful cast of characters who have graced stage, film and studios, leaving their mark on the musical landscape. From legendary artistes to unsung heroes, their stories intertwine with my own, creating a vivid tapestry of experiences and observations.

Hopefully with a touch of wit and humour, I'll share anecdotes that span generations, from the golden era of the past to the ever-evolving landscape of the present. As you delve into these pages, you'll gain insight into the highs and lows, the triumphs and tribulations that define the music industry's complex tapestry.

Together, we'll uncover intriguing tales and captivating moments that will hopefully linger in your heart and mind. Get ready for a memorable adventure filled with passion, creativity and reinvention that defines this ever-changing landscape. Let's embark on this unforgettable expedition and gain a deeper understanding and appreciation of the music world's soul.

Kenny Denton
April 2024

Chapter 1

The Beginning

I was born in the early 50s, the last decade in which the world appeared to exist only in black and white.
Among my family, I was the youngest of three siblings. There was my older sister, Roberta, who married and left home before I could even grasp her presence. Then there was my brother, Harry, who boasted a ten-year seniority over me. Regrettably, I never had the opportunity to know my father; his passing occurred shortly before my birth. This event left my mother, a true angel, pouring her heart into loving me with every breath she took.

In the summer of 1956, at the tender age of four, I encountered an extraordinary sound coming from my brother's bedroom, this sound would forever alter the course of my life.
I discovered a peculiar box in his possession which he would activate by turning a handle on its side. Once wound up, he would delicately place a weighty arm onto a black, circular object. Intrigued, whenever he went out, I would sneak into his room and copy the process and listen to the sounds it made over and over again.
Sometime later I found out that this "magic box" was called a Phonograph Player Turntable, which played 78 rpm records and was the forerunner of the record players that followed the introduction of the seven-inch vinyl single, EP and LP. I was too young to know how to read the record labels but I could easily remember the words from my favourite sound:

Well since my baby left me,
I found a new place to dwell,
It's down at the end of Lonely Street,
At Heartbreak Hotel

After each clandestine session, I meticulously returned everything to its original position ensuring my brother remained unaware of my intrusions. But it wasn't long before I overheard him confronting my mother, expressing frustration that I had been in his room, engaging in unauthorised record-playing escapades. How he managed to uncover my careful covert endeavours was a mystery to me.
Eventually I found out that there were small needles on the end of the arm that needed replacing after every few plays. From then on, my brother locked his room each time he went out, so my desire to play music was curtailed for the time being, but my first addiction in life had begun.

In 1962, my mother used to take me shopping every Saturday to East Lane market, just off the Walworth Road in South London.
At the market's entrance, there was a stall that sold new records, including singles, EPs and albums. They also owned a shop on the Main Street called The A1 Stores. It was a fantastic place to listen to many of the latest recordings. Unfortunately, the prices were beyond our means.

Towards the end of the market, there was another record stall. This one sold a few albums but mainly dealt in ex-jukebox records - previously used and often no longer holding their chart positions. These records were sold at a fraction of the cost of new ones. Just browsing through the records brought me pure joy. Occasionally, my mother would have enough money to treat me to a single, making it the highlight of our Saturday shopping outings.

Every week, I would ask the stall holder, whom I had come to know as Harry, if I could work for him. Being only ten years old, the answer was always no.

Two years passed before I heard the magic words - Harry agreed to let me work with him on Saturdays in exchange for payment: two or three singles.

For the next three years, I never missed a Saturday. In fact, after the first year, I started working on the stall on Sundays as well. With each passing month both my record collection and my musical preferences were steadily growing. Although I would usually pick chart singles, I also started to collect and listen to artistes as diverse as Dinah Washington, Johnny Cash and Peter, Paul and Mary.

In addition to the pleasure of immersing myself in music all day and broadening my musical preferences, I gained valuable insights into the intricacies of market life. I interacted with a diverse array of individuals and navigated through various situations unique to the market setting.

There was a stall situated opposite owned by a Mr. Rubenstein, he specialised in selling women's clothes. Throughout the day, I would frequently hear his catchphrase: "I'm not here today and gone tomorrow, I'm here today and gone tonight."

I am immensely grateful to Harry Ledingham for introducing me to a diverse array of musical genres and for sharing his delightful sense of humour, coupled with an exceptional approach to engaging with people.

After working at the market every week for about a year, I noticed something interesting happening in South London: wherever I went, people would greet me with a cheerful "Hi Kenny, how are you?" It was a bit puzzling because I didn't actually know most of them. It dawned on me that they must recognise me from the market stall.

School Days Adventures

Growing up, I was far from a model child. Like most kids in my area, I was invited to help the police with their enquiries on several occasions, but I was lucky enough never to be charged with any misdemeanours.

During the mayhem of puberty, I was chosen by my school to become a choirboy for Southwark Cathedral, why I agreed I would never know.

The choirboys were all very upper-class snobs who I had nothing in common with whatsoever and the choirmaster was always telling me off for extending my notes longer than anyone else during the services. I did this so I could hear my voice lingering throughout the Cathedral. This also upset the rest of the choir and made me about as popular as a condom on the Pope.

After six months and a couple of bouts of fisticuffs with my choirboy cohorts it was mutually agreed that I should leave.

Quite a few of the kids I went to school with had fathers or uncles who were involved in criminal activities.

A good friend of mine at the time was a boy called Louie Humphreys, a very popular lad at school. He had a fondness for donning fashionable clothing and always seemed to have a large variety of porn magazines in his possession, one of the reasons he was so well liked by the other school kids. Everyone wondered where Louie used to get all this adult material from, but he would never say.

He also got things rolling with my first ever introduction to a 'Jamaican Woodbine' - oh how we laughed!

Some years later, it came to light that Louie's father was the West End club owner and notorious pornographer King Jim Humphreys. His mother was Rusty Gaynor, an exotic dancer, the queen of SOHO and the best-known stripper of the 1960s. Louie's father happened to be the individual whose disclosures about corrupt police officers sparked Scotland Yard's most significant corruption scandal after the war. This scandal ultimately resulted in the imprisonment of around 12 detectives who had accepted substantial sums of protection money from him.

Another classmate was nicknamed "Billy the Kid" to his friends or "Mad Billy" to his enemies, his father went by the name "Colin the Con".

Colin became the stuff of legends due to an incident in which he purchased 1,000 commemorative coins from the Exchange & Mart, the old-fashioned paper version of eBay, for just a shilling each. These coins hailed from an obscure country that nobody had previously heard of.

He soon realised that they were worthless, so he went to see a good friend of his who owned a jewellery shop in Bond Street. He wanted to ask for a favour and place four of these coins in the front window of the store at a price of ten shillings each. His friend pointed out the obvious, they were worthless, but Colin begged him to leave them in the window for two weeks, which he reluctantly agreed to do. Colin then set about advertising them in the most popular local newspaper, The South London Press, for five shillings each.

A few days later a punter came along, took one look and said, "Five shillings? You must be mad! These coins are rubbish, you should throw them away".

Colin told him. "They may look like rubbish to you mate, but they're selling them in Bond Street for ten bob each. The punter immediately took a trip to Bond Street to confirm the story, having seen them in the window at ten shillings each he quickly returned to Colin and bought the lot.

Colin the Con told his son Billy, "If you appeal to people's greed you will always make money."

On Saturday nights my friends and I, with our teenage hormones raging, would venture into Soho in London's West End where we would encounter photographs of semi-naked girls decorating the doorways of several strip clubs, tempting the casual passer-by to enter.

On one occasion we decided to chance our luck and asked the doorman of one of these clubs how much it was to go in.

He first asked our age, the oldest was a kid called Mickey O'Grady who was almost 16 but looked 12, the rest of us were 15 but looked 14, so we all replied in unison "18". To our complete surprise he told us the price and promptly let us in. We paid at the little kiosk and eagerly rushed down the staircase into a small dark room.

There were about 20 people facing a brightly lit stage, where we just caught a glimpse of a naked girl's bum as the curtains closed.

Like a herd of raging bulls charging at a Matador we pushed our way to the very front of the stage just as the music started playing "Big Spender" by Shirley Bassey. As the curtains parted, they revealed a girl who didn't quite match the standard of beauty I had in my teenage imagination. Mickey leaned in and whispered to me, "If being ugly was a crime, she'd do life."

She was scantily dressed as a cave girl, carrying a polystyrene club. After strutting up and down this small stage a couple of times, flashing her breasts, she stopped right in front of Mickey, tapped him on his head with her club and said, in a loud voice, "Does your mother know you're here?" The audience roared. As the laughter subsided Mickey shouted back, "Does your muvver know you're here?" The place erupted with cheers and laughter.

Her act finished with us seeing very little of what we came for and when the curtains closed, we were all quickly escorted off the premises.

As I continued to learn the lessons in life from the streets, I took on various part-time jobs to help support myself. One of these jobs involved taking phone bookings whilst working the night shift at a minicab office on Blackfriars Road.

At this time there was an all-out war going on between the Black Cabs and minicabs. Black Cabs were furious with the mini cabs taking their business and were doing everything they could to curtail what they believed was an attack on their livelihoods.

Such were the times that I don't recall ever being phased by a brick crashing through the office window, or by the phone calls from anonymous callers threatening to beat up anyone who was working for the company.

In fact, during that period, none of the things I observed struck me really as out of the ordinary. When your exposure is limited to your immediate environment, everything appears to be just part of the norm. It's only now that I realise that I witnessed many events that would be considered unthinkable today.

I left school when I was 15, graduating with ten "no-levels" after failing my maths exams more times than I could count. Fortunately, this was of little significance as you'll discover in the subsequent passages. For the previous few years, I had been devoted to pursuing my aspiration of starting a band and becoming a huge success in the music industry.

Soon after leaving school, I took a part time job working in a small newsagents shop on the corner of Braganza Street and De Laune Street in Kennington. The proprietor, Roger Puree was also the manager of the band I had formed.

Roger possessed a formidable presence, his closely shaved head and partially scarred face added to his tough appearance.
He was a member of the notorious Richardson gang, a well-known criminal group operating in South London. His wife Mary was the sister of George Cornell. Ronnie Kray had shot and killed George Cornell in the Blind Beggar Pub a year earlier, so the violence between the Krays and the Richardson's gang was prevalent.
Frequently, Mary would phone me at around four a.m. requesting my presence at the shop to help label the newspapers. This need usually arose because Roger hadn't returned home, often due to his involvement in some altercation with the Krays gang and requiring him to need stitches on some part of his body.

Under Roger's management, our band faced no difficulties securing gigs and receiving payment became even smoother. Although he was quite affable as a friend, Roger's charm didn't extend to individuals he didn't have a positive connection with or those he was unfamiliar with.

In this tiny shop, he would casually settle into a chair, propping his feet up on the counter. This strategic seating allowed him easy access to the cigarette shelf situated behind him and the cash till positioned beside him, all without exerting much effort.

His interactions with customers were notably devoid of charm. For instance, a customer would ask, "Could I have a pack of cigarettes, mate?" As he grabbed the pack, he'd toss it onto the counter and said, "That's two shillings and eightpence and I'm not your fucking mate."

One Saturday morning an individual entered the shop, not with the intention of making a purchase, but rather to express a personal grievance he had with Roger. While the exchange was pretty heated, things remained manageable until the man made a derogatory comment about Mary's brother, George.
In a single bound, Roger vaulted over the counter and forcefully pulled the man outside onto the street, proceeding to deliver a series of punches that left him nearly unconscious. Afterward, Roger casually returned to the shop and informed me, "I'll be upstairs in the flat if you need me." The onlookers who had gathered outside began to disperse gradually, while the disoriented man stumbled away from the scene.
Approximately three hours later, four imposing individuals entered the shop. The largest among them inquired, "Is Roger here?" My stomach churning with unease I shouted up the stairs for Roger, informing him that there were people downstairs who wanted to see him.
Roger and Mary came downstairs and, to my relief, it was all smiles and hellos. Roger went back upstairs to get his coat whilst Mary chatted to the guys. When Roger came back down, he left with the gruesome foursome.

I confided in Mary, explaining that I had felt a bit uneasy when the group arrived and inquired about Roger. She reassured me, revealing that they were all close friends and that they intended to pay a visit to the man Roger had clashed with earlier that day. However, I was pretty sure they were not planning to offer an apology.

I carried on working at the shop with Roger managing the band for about another year before we eventually disbanded; it marked a turning point in my life. The changes that ensued prompted me to recognise that it was time to embark on a new chapter and move forward.

Chapter 2

Then There Was Music

In 1957, at the tender age of five, I recall my preschool companions aspiring to become police officers, firefighters, or nurses.
For me the turning point occurred when my mother took me to see the movie, *The Tommy Steele Story* and from that moment onwards, I wanted to be Tommy Steele, then the year 1960 found me yearning to be Elvis Presley. That was until 1963 and with the advent of the Beatles, my ambition then shifted to buying a guitar, learning to play and forming my very own band.

Every day, both before and after school, I would visit my local music shop. There, I would stand, my nose pressed up to the shop window, captivated by the sight of a magnificent acoustic guitar on display. My mother diligently set aside funds over the course of several months until the much-anticipated day finally came. Now I was armed with not only enthusiasm but I had the means to pursue my musical dreams.

As 1964 unfolded and the Fab Four's meteoric rise swept the world, an ever-increasing number of youngsters harboured the desire to wield an instrument and join a band.

Mastering the art of playing the guitar proved challenging enough, but finding fellow kids my age who shared the same aspirations proved even more difficult.

Among my schoolmates was Demetrius, fondly known as Dimmy. He divulged that he possessed a drum set and that his father owned a café where we could rehearse in a secluded backroom after closing hours.

With Dimmy's revelation, he immediately earned his rightful place as a member of my evolving band. With a team of two now in place, word spread that we were piecing together a group and it wasn't long before I achieved my objective.

Locating a 12-year-old vocalist proved to be a fruitless search, so our only option would be focusing on instrumental tracks. Consequently, our modest repertoire of songs consisted of approximately six or seven hits by the Shadows and "Wipe Out" *by* the Surfaris.

The Somerset Café in Kennington was situated just a couple of minutes from the Granada Cinema, it served as my weekly refuge and I would spend hours on end immersing myself in films transporting me to the uncharted depths of my own imagination.

During the day, when there were no film goers, celebrated bands and artistes would use this cinema to rehearse in. Inevitably at some point, hungry and in need of a break, they would make their way to the Somerset Café for lunch.
When luck would have it and a famous artiste arrived at the café whilst we were

there, Dimmy's father would invariably seize the chance to introduce us. The exhilaration of encountering the likes of the Tornados, Millie and Jess Conrad was beyond measure. These artistes generously signed photographs and gave us a few words of encouragement, they were all monumental stars in the eyes of this 12-year-old.

The Tornados were especially encouraging when they discovered we were also in an instrumental band. Several years down the road, my journey led me to collaborate with and establish a lasting friendship with the drummer Clem Cattini, the founding member of the Tornados. This was a bond that would continue to endure to this very day.

Jess Conrad

Born in Brixton, South London, Jess Conrad embarked on his career as a repertory actor and film extra. His path took a turn when he was selected to play the role of a pop singer in the television play '*Bye, Bye Barney,*' marking his entry into the world of music. He was noticed by the producer Jack Good, who included him in his TV series *Oh Boy*. Conrad then signed to Decca Records and had a number of chart hits. He also recorded for the labels Columbia, Pye, President and EMI.

When I met Jess in The Somerset Café, he gave me one of his publicity photographs and he kindly autographed for me. But when I looked at the picture, I asked myself "Could this really be the same person?" It was obvious the guy in the photo was Jess Conrad, young, good looking and smoothed faced, unquestionably a star. But the guy that was sitting in front of me only slightly resembled the photo, he had the addition of an awful pitted face, riddled with acne, not evident in the photo. Furthermore, he spoke with a remarkably posh voice in contrast to the accent he employed in films and on his TV shows. I found myself pondering over the disparity in his pronunciation, wondering why it diverged so notably from the way I had previously heard him speak.

This marked my initial encounter with the illusion of an image within the entertainment industry.

Just after my 12th birthday, my mother had managed to save up sufficient funds to treat us to a recording session at a professional recording studio. We booked a three-hour session to record our tracks at Gerrard Sound Studios, which was located at 19 Gerrard Street W1. We decided to go with two well-known hits by The Shadows: "Atlantis" and "Apache." These selections were what we believed that showcased our finest performances.

Dimmy's father owned a stunning American Cadillac, quite unusual for the times and, moreover, the area in which we lived. On the day of our much-anticipated session we arrived at the studio, pulling up in the Cadillac. I can still vividly recall the engineer's expression of surprise as he witnessed four of us, not yet in our teenage years, stepping out of this amazing vehicle and bringing our instruments into his studio. This grand entrance had really made us feel very special and totally unique, so when the engineer inquired about the band's name for his studio worksheet, I proudly declared we were called "The Uniques."

Having set up our equipment with the engineer positioning the microphones we were ready to go. With our nerves running riot, we sounded like an explosion in a metal factory. After about an hour, the initial nervousness began to fade and we were able to deliver a decent performance.

The excitement and anticipation for the rest of the session was still quite remarkable, filling the air with a sense of positivity and enthusiasm.

Once we were finished recording each of us received an acetate. An acetate or lacquer is a heavy, black 45 rpm test pressing not meant for general release.

I still proudly possess my copy of that acetate to this very day.

Interestingly, the term "acetate" in this context doesn't actually refer to the material used in their production. Instead, it harks back to the kind of acetate needle that was suggested during the early days of manufacturing.

Over the following years, the band's line-up went through more changes than a jazz bass line. Being teenagers, our voices were altering at an alarming rate, this did however finally provide us the opportunity to find a vocalist.

Alan Carney, a fellow classmate, was the first to step up. While his singing abilities might not have been remarkable, he possessed the courage to take on the role of the band's frontman. His renditions of the latest chart-toppers, vocally speaking, were devoid of any emotion or melody. Yet, paradoxically, this bestowed upon the band the incredible advantage of sounding quite spectacular.

As with many young bands there was an ebb and flow of band members, but one consistent presence was Brian Eden, a schoolmate and close companion. Brian, a year or two my senior, possessed remarkable talents as a musician and songwriter. Recognising my own ambition could compensate for any shortcomings in skill, we jointly embarked on the path of crafting our very own original compositions.

In pursuit of our goal, we transformed my bedroom into a modest recording studio. Using a traditional and pretty ineffective method, we tried soundproofing the space using empty egg cartons, stuffing them with cotton wool and concealing them under polystyrene tiles. We needed recording equipment so we managed to purchase two high-quality stereo tape recorders, nurturing the aspiration to emulate songwriters like Lennon and McCartney, or Simon and Garfunkel.

In late 1968, I found myself employed as a relief manager for a prominent chain of newsagents, travelling between and working at their various central London shops. I would often have to serve, usually with trembling hands, some famous faces at the time, such as Simon Dee and Sean Connery. When Cynthia Lennon, wife of John Lennon, visited the shop one day to request additional magazines for her newspaper delivery, I seized the chance to engage in a lengthy conversation with her. I think she may well have been looking for an escape route at some point.

At six every night I would set off on my Honda motorbike and head over to Marylebone Road to pick up Brian from work, we would rendezvous with our drummer Freddie Pacitti and the lead guitarist Tony Colleti at a different newsagent located on Abbey Road.

The shop in question was both the home and business of Johnny Jones, our manager during that period. It was through Johnny's efforts that I secured a job at the newsagents. Having him as the band's manager enabled us to capitalise on the vast basement situated beneath his shop, where we would conduct our nightly rehearsals.

There were countless occasions when we'd ride past Abbey Road Studios and catch glimpses of the Beatles coming in and out - talk about a thrilling spectacle for us, considering they were our absolute idols.
During one late evening after our rehearsal session, I was stopped at a red traffic light on Grove End Road, just beyond Abbey Road Studios. As I waited for the light to turn to green, my attention was drawn to a Mercedes situated to my right. Ringo Starr occupied the driver's seat, accompanied by his wife, while John Lennon and Yoko Ono occupied the back seats.

Being a huge Beatle fan, I knew John and Yoko had just moved into Ringo's ground floor apartment and surmised that the car was headed there. In haste, I proceeded to what I knew was Ringo's apartment in Montagu Square and waited for a brief period. As the Mercedes arrived and came to a halt, I quickly retrieved my camera, darted across the road managed to capture a photograph of John and Yoko as they made their way towards the apartment.

My heart was racing and unfortunately my nerves got the better of me, resulting in me only capturing John in the snapshot. In the midst of this photographic frenzy, I suddenly heard a loud sound resembling a cow's moo. It was then that I realised the source of the noise was actually Ringo honking the car horn at me in apparent frustration.

Feeling rather foolish, I promptly retreated. Although the term *"paparazzi"* wasn't familiar to me at the time, it was clear that this particular career path was not for me.

On another occasion, as I was passing the Abbey Road studios, I spotted George Harrison descending the stairs on his way to his white Long Wheelbase Mercedes-Benz.
On reaching the car park, I noticed that George was already in the driver's seat and John Lennon was heading towards the passenger door.
Coincidentally, I happened to have a copy of *The Magical Mystery Tour* EP with me. Just as John was about to open the door, I mustered the courage to ask him for his autograph.
Just, as the car door swung open, it collided with my hand, causing the EP to go flying and hitting the floor. Simultaneously, Lennon uttered, "Why don't you fuck off?" Bending down to retrieve my EP from the ground, I couldn't help but say

"I helped pay for that bloody car you're getting in!"

The Day That Would Change My Life

This happened one afternoon whilst I was working at the Seymour Place newsagent a chauffeur, resplendent in his uniform, came into the shop. We had a chat and he shared the exciting details of his profession, driving the rich and famous around. He told me he had just dropped off the actor Tony Curtis at the Dorchester hotel and had to collect him again in a couple of hours. He had several days assigned as his chauffeur whilst he was in London.
As he spoke, he nonchalantly dropped so many names I thought I'd need a broom to sweep them up when he left. Enthusiastically, I began to boast about the band I was in, emphasising our aspirations to become the next Beatles.
I saw him as the potential manager we needed, someone with an eloquent demeanour and told him so.

The next customer that entered the shop caught the chauffeur's eye. Without missing a beat, he turned to the customer, stating, "Take this guy, he's probably part of the music industry." To my astonishment, the somewhat portly customer responded, "Indeed, I am, why do you ask?" Taking advantage of the moment, the chauffeur embarked on an impressive spiel, asserting that he was the manager of our band. He described us as talented young songwriters, emphasising that we crafted all our own material and nothing could hinder our ambition to become the next Beatles. This clever opportunism skillfully painted a picture of us as remarkable performers.

To my utter surprise, the customer pulled out a card from his wallet and handed it to the chauffeur and introduced himself as George Schmitt, asking the chauffeur to get him a demo tape as soon as he could.
After this brief exchange, George bought a newspaper and left the shop.

The chauffeur turned to me, handing over George's card casually remarked, "See, it's easy." He wished me the best of luck and departed, never to be seen again.
This chance encounter would go on to transform my life in ways I could never have anticipated.

I was straight on the phone to Brian to share our stroke of good fortune. I suggested that we should quickly put together a demo tape for George and over the next few days that's exactly what we did.
Within the week, we handed the tape to George and he swiftly secured an audition for us with Young Blood Records. A company which boasted a modest recording studio within their own premises, a notable upgrade from our cramped bedroom setup.
Miki Dallon, the MD, selected "Someday Soon" from our demo tapes as the most appropriate song and under the supervision of Tony Ritchie, the company's A&R man, we recorded the chosen track. The exact fate of the recording eludes me, but the memories of that session remain vivid - it was an indication that my musical journey had begun.

My tenure at the Seymour Place shop continued for a few weeks, which led to regular encounters with George as he often stopped by to buy newspapers.

During one of these visits, George suggested that I sit in as a guest on a Young Blood recording session at Pye Recording Studios. This weekend session would centre on vocal overdubs only, the band's instrumental parts having already been recorded. I was brimming with excitement, after all, this was Pye Recording Studios, a label that graced half of my record collection.

On the following Sunday, I arrived at Pye Studios in Bryanston Street just off the Edgware Road and entered through the large brown double doors. There was a security guard stationed in a small room to the right, I gave him my name and explained my purpose. He phoned down to the studio for verification then directed me to wait at the bottom of the stairs.

Descending the staircase, I entered an unfamiliar world that would soon become my second home. George was waiting for me by the entrance of Studio One, extending a welcoming smile.

Stepping into the control room, a surge of exhilaration almost left me numb. As I looked through the expansive glass window of the control room into the studio beyond, I saw for the first time, the very essence of a bona-fide recording studio.

A majestic grand piano, an array of microphones, headsets and numerous music stands stood aligned like an army battalion, poised for action. The control room boasted enormous speakers and an awe-inspiring Neve recording console. Surprisingly, the control room's decor exuded an unassuming aura, far from flashy or ostentatious, it's dimly lit, slightly dishevelled and well-lived-in atmosphere blended seamlessly with the electric ambiance that pervaded the entire studio.

George quickly introduced me to everyone and found a seat for me in a corner of the room. Occupying the recording desk was Miki Dallon, a figure I had briefly encountered at the Young Blood offices. Miki sported a black mohair suit, complementing his stylish shoulder-length black hair. His white satin shirt showcased an exceptionally large collar and his shoes boasted wooden Cuban heels adorned with coloured suede on the upper portion.

This image of Miki seemed to epitomise the appearance of a record producer in my mind, a perception that lingered for years to come. In fact, I procured a similar pair of shoes within weeks, despite buying the shoes it would take some years before I would learn any real production techniques.

Adjacent to him sat Dave Hunt, the engineer who would eventually become a lifelong friend.

Mesmerised, I observed Miki's meticulous guidance of the vocalist through successive takes, investing hours in perfecting every nuance of the three-minute song. Although each take sounded impeccable to my ears, I recognised that Miki's role as the producer was rooted in this pursuit of perfection. Sadly, for me that afternoon flashed by faster than an English summer.

In the subsequent weeks, George told me that a position as a tea boy at Pye Studios had become available. He offered to set up an interview if I was interested. This was a golden opportunity and I seized it with both hands, believing that even if nothing else remarkable occurred in my life, the chance to spend even a few more minutes at Pye Studios would make me happy beyond belief.

In the week prior to my interview, I found myself working in a small shop located in Montrose Place, just adjacent to Belgrave Square. This shop was small and operated without any staff other than me, resulting in prolonged hours without breaks.

One morning, I received a call from the area supervisor, Mr. McAndrews. Our relationship had never been particularly positive. He informed me that he needed to meet me after closing time to discuss a matter of great significance. Anticipating trouble, I sensed that this was more serious than any previous reprimands. Despite my uncertainty about securing the job at Pye, over the past few weeks I had had a taste of what it might be like to work in the music industry. Consequently, I wasn't overly concerned about the outcome of the impending meeting.

As the day progressed, I convinced myself that McAndrews was going to terminate my employment. This led me to give away much of the shop's stock to random customers.

I concocted various stories to justify the free items, claiming that the shop was closing down or that they were special recipients of the day, ultimately finding any excuse to give most of the stock away.

At 6 p.m. McAndrews arrived. Fortunately, he didn't seem to notice the near-empty shelves. After closing the shop, we retreated to the back office where he conveyed surprising news.

He revealed that Head Office was highly pleased with my management of the various shops and intended to promote me to a permanent position on Kensington Church Street, a shop with a history of problematic management and was rumoured to be a place where the company assigned employees they wanted to get rid of. He explained that since I was unmarried, I wouldn't receive accommodation above the premises but my wages would significantly increase.

My heart sank as I reflected on my actions earlier that day. Regardless, I had no choice but to accept the offer, expressing gratitude for the opportunity. This, however, placed me in a predicament as I had committed to starting at Kensington Church Street on the same day as my interview at Pye Studios.

D-Day arrived on Monday. I arrived at Kensington Church Street around four a.m. to prepare the newspapers, but by six, three out of the four paperboys failed to appear due to the heavy rain.

Under normal circumstances, I would have waited until the regular staff arrived at nine and personally delivered the papers to irate customers, making up various excuses for the earlier non-delivery. Unfortunately, on this particular day, preoccupied with my upcoming interview, my motivation was sadly lacking.

As morning staff began to arrive, I delegated responsibility for handling phone calls and explanations for the delays with the morning paper delivery, planning to address the situation when I returned that afternoon. Hurriedly, I left for Pye Studios.

Once there I introduced myself to the security guard, who notified the personnel downstairs of my arrival. As I descended the stairs, my nerves were starting to take over. My legs were turning to jelly and my mouth was drier than Gandhi's flip-flop.

I entered the compact outer office to find it bustling with individuals. My voice seemed to have taken on the deep timbre of Johnny Cash as I addressed the youthful secretary, stating, "I'm Kenny Denton, I've come to meet with Mr. Godwin."
In a raised voice she called out, "Pat, your appointment has arrived."
A gravelly tone from behind the inner office door said, "Send him in."

The office was notably plain, devoid of gold records or lavish posters, the most distinctive features being two fridges positioned in each corner of the room like stereo speakers. I had only witnessed multiple refrigerators on display in one room in a department store, the truth was we didn't even have one at home.

Inside his office, Pat was sitting at his desk, his large black-rimmed glasses perched on his nose, he appeared to be engrossed in a newspaper. He didn't bother to glance up, seeing that it was this morning's paper he obviously wasn't one of my Kensington Church Street customers.

He told me to sit down and I duly obliged; Mr. Godwin started the conversation. He asked about my connection with George and my job search, inquiring about my current employment and income. He quickly laid out the demanding nature of the job; long hours, irregular start and finish times, obligatory overtime and ever-changing session arrangements.
At this point he finally looked up at me waiting for a reply. I disclosed my current situation and salary, which was £22 per week, this prompted him to outline the job's terms, £7/10s a week with time-and-a-half after six and double-time after midnight. He also mentioned I could claim a cab home after ten.
Overwhelmed with nervousness, I expressed my eagerness to accept the job. Truth be known, I would have gladly paid £7/10s a week to work at Pye Studios.

He then suggested a month-long trial and asked when I could start. In astonishment, I responded that I needed to give a week's notice at my current job, to my absolute joy and surprise, he readily agreed.

Walking out of the interview, I felt a mix of disbelief and exhilaration. Despite the unconventional interview experience, I was now set to start my new career at the one and only Pye Studios.

Hurriedly returning to the shop, I attempted to rectify the chaos I had left earlier in the day. As I arrived, I encountered McAndrews, who asked me for the shop keys, then took the opportunity to abruptly terminate my employment, without any prospect of a reference.

Whether it was due to my behaviour that morning or my carefree actions the week before, I hardly cared, my mind was consumed with the newly acquired Pye Studios opportunity.

Keen to start my new role as soon as possible, I contacted Mr. Godwin's secretary, offering to begin the very next day. To my dismay I was instructed to start work on the following Monday morning at nine a.m. Despite my disappointment, I managed to endure what felt like an interminable week.

In the subsequent years, I crossed paths with McAndrews once more, at De Lane Lea Studios where at that time he acted as the chauffeur for the band Cockney Rebel. This gave me the opportunity to thank him for firing me that day.

Chapter 3

Pye Studios

The much-anticipated Monday finally dawned and at 8:45 a.m. I entered Pye feeling both proud and anxious. I greeted the security guard with a proclamation of my new employment. Making my way downstairs to the main office, I was taken aback to find it deserted. The expansive studio bookings diary lay open on a desk, prompting me to look through its pages to discern the day's studio clients. Studio One's schedule was on the left page, while Studio Two occupied the right. A sense of relief washed over me when I discovered that Young Blood Records had booked Studio Two. As I continued reading, I learned that the session engineer, Dave Hunt and assistant engineer Peanut, were set to start at ten.

A few minutes later, a plump, ginger-haired kid with a freckled face entered the office. He greeted me with, "Hi, I'm Peanut. Can I help you?" After introducing myself and explaining that it was my first day working at Pye, his face lit up with a grin as he said, "Are you mad?"

Mr Godwin's secretary entered the room and Peanut said to her, "This is the new kid, I'll show him around."
She replied reassuringly "Alright, I'll inform Pat that you are looking after him and showing him the ropes."

Wandering off Peanut said "Follow me. First, I'll give you the tour." I followed him as we navigated through a complex network of corridors until we arrived at a spacious room enclosed by a large cage. This expansive area served as the studio library, filled with tapes bearing the names of many renowned artistes. Continuing on, we entered what was known as the remix room.

This really matched my idea of what a studio room might look like; a thick red carpet, a striking mixing desk taking centre stage, flanked by two impressive Tanoy speakers, the main tape machine and a couple of stereo master machines. The ceiling was decorated with an array of coloured lights all controlled by dimmer switches on the wall. Peanut clarified that this room was solely intended for remixing tracks; overdubbing was not conducted here.

As we continued down the corridor, more and more people were appearing. I found myself being introduced to each person as the "new arrival".
Our journey led us through the technical workshop, then through the copying rooms and the disk cutting room, before finally arriving at Studio Two.

My initial reaction was slight disappointment - it struck me as a bit run-down. It was hard to think that numerous chart-topping records had been produced within this, frankly, dilapidated room; the equipment seemed so old and disorganised.
We made our way down into the live room, despite being dark and dreary in appearance, the thought of the incredible music created in this very space made it easy to ignore the decor.

Peanut began arranging the chairs for the upcoming string session, explaining about the setup as he worked. The session had to accommodate six violins, two violas and one cello, each musician requiring music stands, headphones and, of course, microphones.

The engineer's responsibility included documenting all necessary details, such as the microphone to be used for each instrument. This information would be noted down and left in the office for the tape operator's reference. It was essential to ensure everything was meticulously confirmed, with a spare microphone always prepared in case of any breakdowns during the recording. All this needed to be set up before the engineer's arrival.

Subsequently, we started to "scratch around". This procedure involved verifying the functionality of each microphone and ensuring their positions were properly assigned on the mixing console. This way, if the engineer adjusted the cello microphone, it wouldn't inadvertently affect the violin sound.
Having finished this task, Peanut led me through a side entrance to introduce me to Studio One. He was most surprised when I mentioned having already visited the studio during a session a few weeks prior.
Returning to the office, we bumped into Pat Godwin. He seemed to struggle to recall who I was, but he extended an offer to come to him if I encountered any difficulties. He then instructed Peanut to continue guiding me through the processes.

We returned to Studio Two where the engineer Dave Hunt had now arrived. Peanut loaded the master tape on the machine ready for the musicians to overdub their parts, at the same time introducing me to Dave who gave me a quick courteous "Hi" as he was setting up the recording console. Peanut whispered to me one vital instruction, "While on the session say nothing unless spoken to."

By now, the string players and the conductor had arrived and were taking their positions, down in the live room.
A few minutes later, Miki Dallon entered the control room, exuding an aura of total success. With a smile, he greeted everyone with a friendly "Hi."
Having already spent some time at Miki's office it made me feel like an old friend had arrived and was enhanced by Miki's simple but polite, "Hi Kenny, so you're working here now, it's good to see you again."

The remainder of the day was devoted to absorbing Peanut's tasks and closely observing the ongoing proceedings. These activities were only interrupted when I brought in teas, coffees sandwiches as needed.
As the session drew to a close, I found myself totally enthralled by my inaugural day. On the bus ride home, I couldn't believe my good fortune; a job within a professional recording studio and getting paid for it. I did wonder how much time it might take to reach the level of expertise displayed by engineer Dave Hunt and with Peanut's amiability and assistance I was left with a strong sense that we would become great friends.

Throughout my tenure at Pye, I would work on numerous sessions with Miki, with his meticulous attention to detail at every phase of the recording process he aimed for nothing short of perfection.

Even in instances where an artiste's performance was falling short, I never witnessed Miki losing his composure. He remained patient and persistent, offering encouragement to the artiste until the desired performance was captured. In contrast, later in my career I witnessed other producers resorting to screaming and berating artistes, often driving them to tears. Such behaviour was self-defeating, only succeeded in cultivating a negative atmosphere in the studio.

Miki's sincere devotion to his work was unmistakable. I remember him sharing, "I create records to sustain my ability to create records any chart-toppers are a bonus." He also imparted a memorable insight, stating, "In this industry, it's not about what you earn, but what you get."

His track record included major hits like "Indian Reservation" by Don Fardon and "In A Broken Dream" by Python Lee Jackson as well as hits with the duo, Matt and Katie Kassoon.

Within a few weeks, I found myself promoted to the position of tape operator. Peanut's constant presence proved invaluable, always available to address any queries or help me tackle challenges that arose. Essentially, the tasks mirrored what I had observed on my initial day. I was also charged with setting up a quarter-inch machine as an echo device. Before the days of digital reverbs and delays we made our own, sending a sound signal to an EMT reverb plate and back via the quarter inch machine which created a small delay on the reverb sound.

If this sounds a bit archaic by today's standards, consider the approach to recording a drum kit, we used just two microphones; a Sennheiser on the bass drum and a Neumann 67 positioned three or four feet above the kit.

In times of troubles there were other tape assistants, aside from Peanut, whom I could seek help from but I often found them somewhat distant. Curious about this, I questioned Peanut about why I felt a bit of an outsider.

He confided, "There's a rumour circulating that you're Pat Godwin's favourite." Evidently, someone had wrongly said that I was related to Louis Benjamin, the chairman of Pye Records and a founding member of ATV Music and that Louis Benjamin had played a pivotal role in securing my job.

I reassured Peanut that I was oblivious to any special treatment from Pat and that I had never even met or heard of Louis Benjamin. In fact, I went out of my way to avoid Pat, fearing that any mistakes might jeopardise my employment.

"Just steer clear of upsetting any of the engineers or clients and you'll be just fine," Peanut advised, referring to the other tape operators or "tape apes," as he called them, suggesting that I should allow the rumour of being Pat Godwin's favourite to persist. This way, I would likely avoid the usual initiation pranks that were customary for newcomers like being tied up with masking tape, placed in the elevator sent up to the ATV offices above. Another classic prank was handing a new person a typewriter ribbon on a reel instead of quarter-inch splicing tape for practising tape editing.

Great fun usually but who would dare to play such tricks on someone related to

Louis Benjamin.

During my time at Pye, the engineering team included Ray Prickett, Howard Barrow, Alan Florence, Dave Hunt, Terry Evennett, Larry Bartlett and Vic Maile. Ray Prickett held the most senior position among the engineers. Starting his career in 1952, he predominantly collaborated with well-established Pye artistes such as Petula Clark and Jackie Trent.
Working with Ray left me with the impression of him being quite stern and not easily approachable. On the other hand, Howard Barrow and Terry Evennett exhibited a much more understanding attitude towards newcomers. Dave Hunt and Alan Florence seemed to strike a balance between these two extremes. Vic Maile served as the Pye Mobile studio engineer, while Larry Bartlett possessed a smooth-talking, witty persona that made him quite popular with the female crowd.
Each of these engineers boasted incredible technical skills, which I was eager to learn and absorb, particularly Larry's expertise.

Life at Pye had settled into a predictable routine. I had grown comfortable enough to even attend the Friday afternoon gathering in Pat's office when I wasn't on a session. This event was an extension of the lunchtime drinks at the local drinking hole the Masons Arms. The reason for Pat having two fridges had become clear to me now.
The Friday afternoon event was an open invitation to a select group of regular clients, artistes and close friends. It resembled a lively New Year's Eve party and had gained quite a reputation within the industry.

During that period, Pye Records used the studios mostly for their own artistes. Prominent producers like John McCloud were actively involved in writing for and producing acts like Pickettywitch. John Schroeder was producing Status Quo and Barry Murray had recently joined Pye to oversee their new progressive label, Dawn Records. Barry Murray had also signed the band Mungo Jerry to this label.

Mungo Jerry

Mungo's greatest triumph was with the track "In the Summertime" which dominated the UK charts for seven weeks during the early 1970s. Additionally, this song clinched the number one position in 26 countries globally. Their subsequent release, "Baby Jump" also claimed the top spot in the UK and maintained its position for two weeks. Initially known as The Good Earth, the band underwent a name transformation to Mungo Jerry on the insistence of Pye's new label - Dawn Records.

Terry Evennett served as the recording engineer for the project and Barry Murray as both the band's producer and label manager. Barry played a pivotal role in the band's success. While he was initially working on new album tracks, he made the decision to mix a single for an immediate release, with Terry already committed to another recording session, Howard Barrow stepped in to handle the mixing.

Barry was unwavering in his insistence, much to the band's displeasure, that the single should be "In the Summertime." The only challenge was that the recording itself was a mere two minutes long.

Howard came up with an innovative idea to solve the problem. He extended a microphone cable from the studio all the way to his Triumph TR6 Roadster parked on the ramp outside the building, placing a microphone near the exhaust. Around ten seconds of the car's revving engine noise were recorded and seamlessly added to the end of the two-minute track. He then edited the entire song back in from the beginning after the engine sound. The edited track could now be faded out at three minutes and 30 seconds, creating the final version. This unconventional approach marked the debut release on the newly established Dawn label.

Barry had devised a clever strategy when launching the record, releasing it on a maxi-single. Essentially, this format was akin to an EP, containing three to four tracks played at 33 1/3 rpm. It would be packaged in a picture sleeve and priced slightly higher than a standard 45 rpm single.

On release the record skyrocketed to the number one spot, reigning for a remarkable seven weeks and ushering in the era of Mungo Mania. What struck me as curious was that, apart from the lead singer Ray Dorset, the remaining band members still maintained their day jobs. When I queried guitar player Paul King about his continued employment, he offered the response, "Who knows how long this will all last?" I never established whether he referred to the chart success or the dynamics within the band.

With each subsequent recording session, the growing tension between Ray and the rest of the group became increasingly evident. Ray basked in the praise from the press and fans, seemingly starting to believe that "Mungo Mania" was solely attributable to his efforts. During one session, Ray rushed into the studio, brandishing a children's music songbook that featured "In the Summertime" among its contents. His excitement inadvertently or perhaps deliberately irritated the rest of the band as he raved about it nonstop.
A calmly composed Barry Murray, leisurely enjoying his peanut butter and banana sandwich, astutely pointed out the oddity of a children's songbook incorporating the lyrics "*When the sun goes down, you can make it, make it good in a lay-by.*" That shut Ray up for a bit, much to the band's delight.
By the time their second single "Baby Jump" ascended to the number one spot, John Godfrey had replaced bass player Mike Cole, but the internal disputes persisted throughout every session.

Embracing their previously successful formula, they employed the same repetition technique for the follow-up "Baby Jump," albeit without the car sound. In a reversal of roles, due to Howard Barrow's work commitments, he recorded "Baby Jump," while Terry handled the mixing duties.

The track, at two minutes and 47 seconds, was duplicated from the start and

replayed in its entirety, fading out at four minutes and ten seconds.
I must note that, despite the tensions that simmered within the studio, the entire band and Barry were unfailingly amiable towards me, I was, after all, just the tape op and tea boy.

With everything in my life going so smoothly, I believed things couldn't possibly improve any further. But they did.
Shortly after the triumph of Mungo Jerry's chart-topping hit "In the Summertime," I met Sue, my lifelong soulmate. At just 15 years old, she radiated all the traditional values and virtues of the day.
Eager to impress her, I invited her to the studio one evening to listen to their follow-up single, "Baby Jump."
I had major doubts about its ability to capture the same success; I was certain it would never reach number one. Sue listened to it and immediately declared it a sure-fire number one hit. I laughed sceptically, saying "I don't think so, it probably will have some chart success but no way will it be number one and remember, I'm the one in the music business."
The following day, casting aside my own doubts about the single's potential, I relayed Sue's prediction to the producer, Barry Murray, who simply nodded and remarked, "Well, she knows a hit when she hears one."
True to Sue's instincts, the record soared to the top of the charts, a fact that she has never failed to remind me of whenever we hear it on the radio.

To this very day, Sue remains my better half. Back in those days, I carried a certain arrogance within me, wandering through life cloaked in ignorance, guided solely by my self-assuredness. Fortunately, fate blessed me undeniably by granting me the incredible fortune of meeting the one person who would never question the paths we would tread, who would offer unwavering support and guidance whenever needed. Throughout the unpredictable ups and downs of life's journey, she would always stand by my side without hesitation, regardless of the outcome. For the last 54 years we have lived all of the marriage vows several times over except the last one, of course.

Status Quo

For more than five decades, Status Quo, now affectionately referred to as Quo, have amassed a remarkable record of success. They have notched up over 60 chart hits in the UK, with an impressive 22 of those tracks ascending to the top ten.
Regrettably, the passing of two original band members has left Francis Rossi and John Coghlan as the sole torchbearers, continuing to rock stages around the globe albeit in separate bands.
During my early days at Pye my time was consumed by wonderful collaborations with exceptional artistes. It was almost surreal, as I still couldn't quite believe that I was being paid to pursue my passion. I had assumed the role of tape operator and one of my memorable assignments involved recording an album with Status Quo. These weeks turned into a period of unadulterated delight.

Working with Quo proved to be an absolute joy. The band members were an incredible set of individuals to collaborate with. Unlike some of the other groups, there were no disputes; instead, they radiated a real sense of enjoyment which was completely contagious. These down-to-earth, affable guys genuinely relished the process of creating their music.

During those times, bands like Quo led a nomadic existence, constantly touring to build a fan base and scrape together just enough to sustain their chosen path. Securing a record deal and gaining access to a studio was a monumental achievement in itself. Should you be lucky enough to have a hit record it would be the icing on the cake, a real moment of triumph.

The sessions were scheduled from 4 p.m. until midnight. As the days progressed, the work settled into a routine, each session would commence with a playback of the previous night's recordings followed by a round of hilarious anecdotes from their experiences on tour. Even now, half a century later, some of these stories are best left untold.

John Schroeder had the role of producer with Status Quo at that time. He was a recognised British composer, arranger, songwriter and record producer, known particularly for his work in pop and easy listening music.

John began his career as an A&R assistant to Norrie Paramor at Columbia Records. Notably, he co-wrote the song "Walking Back to Happiness." Sung by Helen Shapiro, it was a UK number one in 1961. During the mid-1960s, Schroeder transitioned to Pye Records and, alongside Johnny Pearson, formed the instrumental ensemble Sounds Orchestral.
Their rendition of "Cast Your Fate to the Wind" secured international acclaim, peaking at No. 5 on the UK charts.
Interestingly, although in 1968 he orchestrated Quo's inaugural hit with "Pictures of Matchstick Men," Schroeder might have appeared an unconventional choice for a rock band such as Quo, however, given his position as an in-house producer at Pye, he undertook the projects that came his way.

John came across as a softly spoken, polite and unassuming individual, sporting a hairstyle that resembled an explosion in a bird's nest. His demeanour was very much in line with Pye's in-house producers during that era. When not occupied with their personal projects, they seemed to display minimal interest, if any, in the bands they were overseeing, their focus appeared solely directed at fulfilling contractual obligations.

John would typically arrive around 6 pm, greeting everyone and expressing a desire to listen to the recordings from the previous night. Following this, he would settle down behind the desk and immerse himself in his newspaper. The session would then begin, Quo would descend into the studio and start playing live, not necessarily the material chosen for recording, but just jamming together and enjoying every second of it.
One of my roles as a tape operator was to venture into the studio and fine-tune

microphone placements. On entering, the volume in the room was so deafening that it seemed as if one's very body might implode. Around 10 p.m. The band would be primed and ready to record, marked by the illumination of the record light.

This was Quo's cue to do what they do best, turn up the talent and deliver their signature hard rock boogie. Between takes Schroeder would, without looking up from his newspaper, make quiet comments to the band via the talkback mic. Phrases such as "Mmmm - try another one" or "That one was OK, want to have a listen?" His approach to producing was markedly distinct from most other producers I had encountered.

Around midnight, John would close his newspaper and depart for the day, setting the stage for the process to recommence the following day.

One evening, as the session drew to a close, the band inquired where I lived.

I told them I lived in Kennington, South London. Francis Rossi then kindly said, "We're headed that way, we'll give you a lift."

It was an exhilarating prospect and I eagerly hopped into the back seat of their beautiful maroon Bentley, with Bob Young at the wheel.

At that point, Bob assumed the roles of roadie, tour manager, co-writer, harmonica player and all-round nice guy. While we were en route, I couldn't help but remark on the tremendous volume at which the band played at in the studio.

Bob started recounting a tale about his youth and his mother cautioning him about the potential dangers of listening to loud music, adding that her words might have been concerning my demise due to excessive exposure. "But I couldn't hear her."

As we cruised down Park Lane, the 8-track stereo system reverberated with music, I felt like an honorary band member. As we neared Kennington, Bob asked me where I lived exactly. I really didn't want them to witness the modest place I lived in, it was a structure that seemed more fitting for slums than anything else. So not to expose my less than lavish living situation, I suggested they drop me off by the Oval tube station.

As we reached The Oval station Bob asked for further directions. I said to turn left, pull over and I would get out there. With a hint of frustration in his voice, Bob once again questioned me for my address but more pointedly. I gave him more directions, but after about five minutes of driving, we found ourselves almost back at the starting point. I suggested he let me out here, but Bob, his patience wearing thin, stopped the car abruptly, turned to face me in the backseat and shouted, "WHERE THE FUCK DO YOU LIVE?"

With no other option, I directed him on the shortest route to my block of flats. It was around 1 a.m. by the time we arrived and the entire neighbourhood was eerily quiet. Although the band seemed unbothered by the state of my dwelling, I couldn't help but wish my neighbours could witness the sight of me getting out of a Bentley and not just any Bentley, but one that contained members of Status Quo.

This routine of them dropping me off continued every night after the sessions. I had no inkling at the time that, unbeknown to me, their living situations were pretty similar to mine. It was only, after meeting my girlfriend Sue and learning more about her, that I discovered a fascinating connection. She actually lived in a little prefab, right next door to Francis, also just a prefab house and she was a babysitter for Simon, his son.

I crossed paths with Bob on multiple occasions after my time at Pye. By 1979 he had teamed up with Whitesnake guitarist Micky Moody, operating under the rather ingenious name Young and Moody.
I introduced them to a track called "The Devil Went Down to Georgia" by the Charlie Daniels Band, a discovery from my recent trip to the USA. Although it was a country song that had yet to make waves in the American charts, there were no plans at that time for a European release. The song's hero was a fiddle player so swiftly we transformed the character into a guitarist, propelling us into the studio in just a matter of days.

Given our modest budget, I was delighted when Bob called his close buddies from Quo to lay down the rhythm track and lend their voices for backing vocals. Due to Quo's contractual obligations to the Vertigo label, we couldn't openly credit their involvement. This rekindled my earlier experiences with these wonderfully quirky and endearing individuals. I was pleased to see they retained the same relaxed and humorous demeanour that had left a lasting impression on me during my Pye days and despite their numerous successes since those early days, they remained unchanged, retaining their ardently passionate approach to their music.
As fate would have it, both our version and the Charlie Daniels Band's original rendition were released simultaneously. Sadly, while their version swiftly ascended to the top of the charts worldwide, ours didn't quite follow suit. As they say, "C'est la vie."

Dave Hunt

Dave was the perfect mentor, I collaborated with him more extensively than any other engineer during my time at Pye, he appeared to have a closer rapport with his clients than most, clients such as Miki Dallon, a regular who reserved a substantial amount of time in Studio Two. He also collaborated closely with the in-house producer, John McCloud, who was achieving remarkable success with Pickettywitch at the time. Another regular client of his was Dave Miller, owner of the budget label Damil which churned out albums at an alarming rate.
It wasn't until later that I learned that Miller had been the initial producer for the renowned rock 'n' roll legend Bill Haley. As time passed, Dave Miller and I developed a strong friendship and, in a curious twist of fate, I found myself becoming Bill Haley's last ever producer in 1979.
Undoubtedly, I gleaned a wealth of knowledge whilst working with Dave Hunt. He consistently made an effort to break down concepts at a pace that I could readily grasp.
His expertise in tape editing was exceptional and he generously shared numerous insights into the intricacies of cutting and splicing these quarter-inch tapes.
Dave Hunt's prolific portfolio included the recording of numerous hit records and

the production of several movie soundtracks. His expertise led him in later years to become the lead engineer for Sir Cameron Anthony Mackintosh, the distinguished British theatrical producer and venue owner renowned for his involvement with a multitude of commercially successful musicals.

Having recognised that becoming proficient at operating a sound mixing desk would require time in the control room, I realised that mastering tape editing was a skill I could quickly acquire in the more readily available tape copy rooms.

At Pye, each individual was provided with a personalised tape editing block bearing the engraving "Pye Records." This implement was used daily for tasks such as trimming the beginnings and endings of quarter-inch tapes (referred to as "topping and tailing") and of course, for intricate editing work.
Should one misplace their editing block, the onus fell on them to cover the costs of replacement, the wait to receive a new one could be considerable and would pose a significant setback, as borrowing someone else's block wasn't that easy. Remarkably, I have held onto my original block to this day.

Eventually I perfected my skills as a tape editor and through hard work and practise my abilities exceeded mere competence, it turned out that I was exceptionally good at it. Fuelled by this confidence, I approached Pat, the studio manager and declared my readiness to tackle any forthcoming editing tasks that might come our way.

Tim Rice

In a matter of days, I found myself faced with my first client, none other than Tim Rice. Mr. Rice stands out as a remarkably versatile and highly prolific lyricist in contemporary times. His creative output extends across both musical theatre and the enchanting world of Disney animated films.

He had reserved a tape copying room for a two-hour session, intending to undertake edits on quarter-inch tape. Strangely, just before his scheduled arrival, an unexplained surge of nerves got an iron grip on me.
As I stood in the office, awaiting his arrival, he walked in, a tall, well-spoken young man carrying a briefcase. I introduced myself and invited him to accompany me to the designated copying room.
We entered the room and he took out a pair of quarter-inch tape reels from his briefcase, explaining the tapes were of a musical he had just recorded called, *Jesus Christ Superstar.*

Making a duplicate of the tape before editing was a standard procedure, aimed at safeguarding the master tape. We replicated the titles that required editing and I began executing seemingly very straightforward cuts.

Being my first client and with my nerves out of control, my hands were shaking like a recovering alcoholic. I proceeded to cut the tape in all the wrong places and slice my fingers to ribbons in the process.

It was tricky to hide the blood dripping from my fingers as it was now drenching the tape and turning my white marking pencil scarlet.

Observing my evident nervousness, he compassionately proposed creating an additional copy, offering to leave the tapes in my care, along with notes indicating where the edits should be made. He said that he would call back in a couple of hours to retrieve them.

After his departure, I cleaned up the blood mess and proceeded to edit the tape once more. Interestingly, every edit now went smoothly on the first try. With the client not present, I also took advantage of the opportunity to create a personal copy of this incredible musical.

Although I never crossed paths with him again, I carried a persistent desire throughout my career to express my gratitude for his patience and tolerance on that day. So, in 2003 I contacted him for advice regarding a musical I was working on. In my letter, I referenced our initial encounter in the editing room.

Mr Rice personally responded, offering valuable suggestions for my project. He also expressed in his letter that it was an honour for him to have been my first client. He truly was an incredibly generous individual.

Jack Fishman

My next client happened to be Jack Fishman, a multi-talented individual who was a songwriter, journalist and real-life spy catcher. Among his accomplishments, he co-wrote a string of hits including "If Paradise is Half as Nice," "If I Only Had Time," "Something is Happening," and "Help Yourself," amassing sales of over ten million records.

A dedicated workaholic, Fishman tirelessly pursued his passions throughout his life due to his genuine love for his craft. Despite achieving significant success, he chose to maintain a simple and unassuming lifestyle.

In addition to his musical pursuits, Fishman took on the management of composer Roy Budd, collaborating with him on the theme songs for the films *Soldier Blue* and *Get Carter*. Despite major budget constraints for the movie *Get Carter*, Fishman convinced a hesitant Roy Budd to compose and perform the music with his trio for minimal expenses. This decision resulted in a soundtrack performed by The Roy Budd Trio that achieved cult classic status, sending Roy Budd's movie career stratospheric.

During the 70s, Fishman was music supervisor for more than 100 feature films. Notably, he is also credited with exposing Kim Philby, the most infamous spy Britain had ever known, showcasing his skills as a spy catcher.

Jack had reserved time to perform some edits on a quarter-inch tape of the soundtrack album for the film *Get Carter*, which he was actively involved with. My awareness of Jack stemmed from his numerous achievements as a songwriter. On arriving I saw he was in his late forties, moderately built with receding hair and his speech was characterised by an intense delivery.

Around mid-morning, I proposed to Jack that we take a break, suggesting I could fetch tea and sandwiches from a nearby café. He liked the idea and insisted on covering the costs for both of us. Given my modest weekly income of £7/10s, it was clear I was no match for the income of a highly successful songwriter and author, so naturally, I agreed.

From his jacket pocket, he produced a small amount of change and handed me a shilling. Although a cup of tea and a round of cheese sandwiches cost well over two shillings, I was too embarrassed to point out that he hadn't given me enough. In a somewhat awkward situation, I accepted his shilling, all the while wondering when he last visited a café and bought a round of sarnies. Returning to the studio, feeling uneasy, I thanked Jack for buying the tea and sandwiches and even gave him a tuppence in change.

Several years down the line, I ended up collaborating with Jack on numerous recording sessions and our relationship developed into a strong friendship.

We even co-wrote a few songs together. Remarkably, Jack's frugal habits remained consistent. He consistently brought homemade sandwiches to the sessions and opted to remain in the control room while everyone else ventured to the restaurant for lunch.

During one of our interactions, Jack shared a quite remarkable childhood memory with me. When he was around ten years old whilst visiting Berlin with his parents, they found themselves inadvertently present at a Nazi rally. As fate would have it, Adolph Hitler was descending the steps, as he passed by Jack, he lightly patted Jack's full crop of blond hair. He often mused that this encounter might have been the trigger for his early hair loss.

Dorothy Squires

I was tasked with assisting Howard Barrow on a session featuring Dorothy Squires, the Welsh diva who had a string of hits between 1953 and 1970 and was also partly responsible for Roger Moore becoming James Bond after she married him.

The session, held in Studio One, entailed a full live orchestra with accompanying live vocals.

It was thought by the bosses at Pye that Howard was the only engineer capable of establishing a comfortable recording environment for Miss Squires; she was known to be quite demanding.

In Studio One there was a row of seats provided for guests positioned in front of the mixing desk in the control room providing a wonderful view of the live room. These seats were occupied by some of Dorothy's relatives and friends who had come to witness their virtuoso perform.

Once the initial recording was completed, Dorothy made her way from the vocal booth back to the control room to listen to the playback. As the song concluded, a remarkable wave of applause erupted from her guests, creating a truly strange and unprecedented scene in my recording session experience.

As the applause gradually subsided, a stunned silence filled the room as she erupted into a barrage of self-praise.
"Jackie Trent? Fuck Jackie Trent! She could never sing like that, listen to that voice, I'm the best fucking damn singer around, no one's got a voice like mine. Vicky Carr eat your fucking heart out."

Following this outburst of self-adulation, Dorothy refocused and returned to the live room to tackle the next song, the timeless classic "My Way."

Once the initial rehearsals were done, the red recording light illuminated and the tape began to roll. Towards the culmination of the song, where the lyrics emphasise, *"The record shows, I took the blows and did it..."* a dramatic musical pause was to be executed. According to the arrangement, the entire orchestra was to halt at this juncture, which they did, all except for one violinist who inadvertently held the final note for a fraction too long.

Noticing this tiny musical error, Dorothy's instantaneous response boomed down the microphone, resonating with a swirl of reverb into the control room. In a burst of frustration, she exclaimed, "What fucking cunt did that?"

While it was widely recognised that Dorothy's choice of language could be quite colourful, the mood in the studio, particularly among her guests, was one of sheer astonishment.

The song managed to reach number 25 in the UK charts but this particular take, swearing included, was a bigger hit within studio circles as a well-liked outtake for many years to come.

Vic Maile

Vic started life as a sound engineer in 1965 at Pye Studios. His rise in the industry was rapid, by 1968, he had reached the position of Head of the Pye Mobile, aided by Neville Crozier. The Pye Mobile was, just as it sounds, a mobile recording studio housed in a truck sent anywhere somebody needed a studio.
Vic's portfolio as both an engineer and producer boasts collaborations with some of the most prominent figures in the music industry including such luminaries as Led Zeppelin, Jimi Hendrix, The Kinks, The Small Faces, Dr Feelgood, Motorhead, and The Who. This illustrious list comprises merely a fraction of the artistes who were fortunate to have their work captured and shaped by Vic's talent.

I was assigned to a session in the remix room collaborating with Vic Maile, this would be our first meeting. Vic's primary responsibility was overseeing the Pye Mobile unit. He was less involved in traditional studio sessions, focusing more on remixing his live recordings made in the mobile.

As I was waiting in the remix room, a little wary of the prospect of collaborating with an unfamiliar engineer Vic walked in.

We made our introductions, Vic greeting me in a soft-spoken manner, exuding a calm and relaxed personality. He briefed me on our objective: remixing a track from the recently recorded album *The Who Live at Leeds*.

The excitement was overwhelming when Pete Townshend himself made an appearance, I couldn't help but be starstruck. Despite the notable presence of Pete, the details of the session remain a bit vague in my memory.

Before long, Vic extended an invitation for me to join the crew on the mobile truck, a step that would prove significant in my journey.

Chapter 4

Isle of Wight Festival 1970

In 1970 the Pye Mobile was enlisted to record the complete proceedings of that year's Isle of Wight Festival. Taking place on East Afton Farm on Wednesday, August 26th until the early hours of the Monday, 31st, this was a huge event. While exact figures differ, it is widely recognised that around 600,000 people attended.

The Pye Mobile crew during my tenure consisted of Vic Maile, Neville Crozier, Alan Perkins, Tony Carey and me. We all travelled down to Southampton in the mobile and took a subsequent ferry ride to the Island.

We arrived on Tuesday the 25th and although we initially explored the festival site, the full setup process wouldn't commence until the next day.

The following morning Neville and Alan immediately began setting up microphones, while Vic and I worked in the truck, ensuring that microphone feeds were correctly reaching the control desk. There was a headset complete with a microphone for the engineer on the stage, this was wired to a large orange coloured box that contained the Neumann U67 microphone power packs. This setup was to facilitate communication between the truck and the stage.
Due to the occasional unreliability of this communication method, one of my responsibilities involved dashing between the two locations, effectively relaying messages to ensure smooth coordination.
The opening act Judas Jump was performing on stage, whilst Vic was still setting up.

Teo Macero

As Judas Jump neared the end of their set, an individual suddenly appeared at the front entrance of the truck where I was sitting next to the eight-track machines. Speaking in a stern New York accent, he inquired, "Is the tape running?"
Assuming he was the band's manager, I responded politely, "Sorry, not at the moment." Immediately, his mood swiftly changed and in a more aggressive tone, he demanded, "Run the fucking tape." Looking to Vic for confirmation and receiving a nod, I proceeded to start the tape recording.
Vic continued his efforts to ensure the smooth running of the recordings, diligently examining and marking the soundboard to pre-empt any issues which may appear in the forthcoming days. When the next performer, Kathy Smith, took the stage, Vic instructed me to halt the tape, as recording during her setup and sound check at this point seemed pointless.

Unexpectedly, the assertive American reappeared, this time entering the back of the truck where Vic was situated. He glanced at me and sharply questioned, "Is that tape running?" I replied in the negative, prompting an explosive reaction from him. He shouted, "RUN THE FUCKING TAPE AND LEAVE IT FUCKING RUNNING."

In response, I said, "He's my boss," indicating Vic, "not you. I do what he tells me."

Vic, looking somewhat sheepish, directed me to put the tape machine in record. The American then turned to Vic, issuing a warning that any further defiance from the kid would result in my removal from the truck for the remainder of the event.

Once he left the truck Vic explained that the man was Teo Macero, representing Columbia Records, USA, the client funding the mobile service. Teo was overseeing the recording and this encounter highlighted his authority.

This terse exchange ensured a noticeable silence between Mr. Macero and myself until the subsequent Sunday.

Kris Kristofferson

Kris was relatively unfamiliar to the UK audience, so he took to the stage for his first of two performances on Wednesday. His set was infused with his trademark dry humour and a collection of songs that would ultimately become timeless classics. Unfortunately, the live sound crew did little justice to Kris and his band, resulting in a subpar sound for the audience through the PA system.

The audience, because of the poor sound, responded with undue hostility, unwilling to show him any form of real appreciation. Undeterred by the unfavourable atmosphere, Kris displayed his unwavering professionalism and persevered through his set. During his performance, some members of the audience shouted requests for songs they wanted to hear, songs penned by more established artistes.

Kris's response was gracious but firm: "We only play the songs that I wrote, so maybe someone else will be along later and play that for you."

After finishing one particular song, as he tuned his guitar, the sound of a ringing telephone emanated from the side of the stage.

Kris seized the moment to inject some of his wonderful sense of humour into the situation, saying into the microphone, "Will someone get that, or do I have to do everything around here?"

As his set neared its conclusion and during an introduction to one of his songs, he remarked, "I can't believe I've been singing now for 20 minutes," then with the perfect length of pause continued "…but I bet you can."

Thankfully, when he returned on the following Sunday, the audience's reception was somewhat more favourable, offering a more welcoming atmosphere for his performance.

Chicago

On Friday, approximately an hour prior to Chicago's scheduled stage appearance, the tranquillity of the truck was abruptly interrupted by the influx of several members from Chicago's entourage. To Vic's delight, Columbia Records had dispatched their own engineer to record the band's performance. Despite needing to be present to guide the engineer with the soundboard, this marked one of the few instances, alongside Miles Davis, when Vic didn't oversee the recording of a performance throughout the festival.

This ensemble of characters resembled the Marx Brothers on LSD. Each of them held their distinct notions about the optimal recording approach for Chicago's show, or perhaps they were attempting to justify the expense of their presence. The ensuing chaos was a spectacle to behold; disagreements, heated arguments and clashing egos combined in a truly captivating manner.

Vic and I did our best to assist in any way we could, but the challenge was discerning whose directives we should follow. Vic worked diligently to configure the soundboard in alignment with their engineer's instructions, while I relayed microphone requirements to our crew on the stage.

Finally, the recording was underway as Chicago commenced their performance. All appeared to be progressing smoothly when, out of the blue, the 8-track machine stopped recording and the entire truck plunged into complete darkness. The potent and tightly-woven sound of Chicago, resounding powerfully through our speakers, abruptly ceased, leaving only the distant sound of their performance coming from the stage. This unforeseen event marked the singular instance of a power failure within the mobile recording setup during the festival.

The band continued playing but the tape remained inactive so pandemonium erupted in the truck. It was difficult to discern who among the entourage would have a heart attack first, but it certainly wasn't Vic or myself. Leaving them shouting, screaming obscenities and generally being useless, we focused on identifying the cause of the power outage.

After around ten minutes of investigating outside, tracing various leads and cables, we discovered a surprisingly simple explanation: someone had inadvertently dislodged the main plug connecting our truck's extension boards to the power socket. Once rectified, power was swiftly and restored recording resumed.

Despite the evening outside being quite warm, inside the truck, the atmosphere remained distinctly frosty for the duration of Chicago's set. In this particular scenario, all the preparation and expertise in the world paled in comparison to a skirmish between a large boot and a standard 13-amp plug.

By Saturday, August 29th, the festival was in full swing, but backstage, tensions were escalating between the organisers and artistes concerning payment matters, generating significant unpredictability in the event's schedule and running order for the day. Nobody knew for certain which bands would ultimately take the stage.

John Sebastian

With no other bands available to perform, John Sebastian took to the stage armed with what he humorously referred to as his "cheapo cheapo guitar." The prospect of a lone individual with a guitar performing for such a massive audience might have been readily dismissed as a makeshift stand-in act. Nonetheless, Sebastian's innate charm cast a spell over the entire crowd before the first song had even finished.

His enchanting charisma effortlessly led the audience on a journey through a collection of 21 songs, most of which he had composed for his band, The Lovin Spoonful, which many have achieved classic status.
This extraordinary performance lasted nearly three hours, delivering a mesmerising experience that can only be characterised as sheer enchantment.

By mid-afternoon, resolutions had been achieved and the festival gradually regained its momentum. Despite this, the earlier disruptions had wreaked havoc on what could have been a well-structured timeline for all the participating artistes.

The Doors

As the Saturday evening progressed, reports started pouring into the truck about The Doors' reluctance to take the stage. While not uncommon given the numerous bands engaged in negotiations and discussions with the organisers, mainly revolving around financial matters, this situation was certainly not unique.

The Doors were in the midst of a dispute, primarily stemming from their aversion to being filmed. Eventually, they consented to perform, albeit under a specific condition: the stage lights had to be turned off. Their reasoning was that this would render any filmed footage unusable, aligning with their desire to minimise the impact of their appearance being captured on camera.
They launched their set opening with the song "Back Door Man."

Shortly after their performance commenced, Vic alerted me to a major issue - the bass microphone was failing to capture the bass guitar sound, a serious problem that required prompt attention. Vic instructed me to get up on the stage as quickly as possible and let Neville know so he could fix the problem.
The challenge of tracing the problem was compounded by the fact that the stage lights were turned off and the entire stage area was in darkness. Consequently, it took me some time to locate Neville amidst the obscurity. Eventually, I managed to find him and promptly relayed Vic's instruction. To my astonishment, Neville responded, "Go back and tell Vic they don't HAVE a bass player."
Returning to Vic, I conveyed Neville's response verbatim. In response, Vic's frustration was more than excitable as he exclaimed, "Get back up there and tell Neville not to be so fucking stupid and fix the bloody mic." Back on the stage, in the darkness, I approached Neville once again, relaying Vic's stern message. Nevertheless, Neville stood his ground and insisted that they genuinely did not have a bass player for that performance.
Once more, I dashed back to the truck, recounting the interaction to Vic. By this point, I felt like a referee in a tennis match, volleying between Vic and Neville with a series of messages.

It seems that Vic's unyielding determination to convey the message about the missing bass player reached a breaking point. In an abrupt move, he left the truck, marched onto the stage, and joined Neville.
Ready to express his frustration, Vic's gaze shifted towards the band and suddenly the realisation dawned on him. He saw that the keyboard player was in fact covering all the bass lines using his left hand.
It was evident that the bass guitar microphone was as superfluous as an actual bass player for The Doors' performance.

Throughout the festival, Vic was under immense pressure to ensure meticulous recordings, a task with only one opportunity for success.
Despite this considerable pressure Vic's unswerving professionalism remained evident. With the exception of one or two acts he managed to make recordings of every artiste's performance at the festival, a responsibility he carried with unwavering dedication.

The Who

It was around 2 am, when The Who finally took to the stage but within three or four minutes of the opening song there was a problem. Vic shouted out to me that Keith Moon had hit the large tom-tom mic with his drum stick and busted it. He told me to get up on stage and put another mic on the drum pronto.
I ran to the backstage entrance to find it guarded by several large and rather frightening looking Hells Angels.
One of them, a six-foot longhaired ape of a man covered in leather and tattoos said to me,
"No one goes on stage while the band's playing."
I explained the problem we had on stage but unfortunately it appeared that this was not negotiable.

I rushed back to tell Vic that I couldn't get onto the stage due to the primate situation, he yelled, "I don't give a shit! Get on the stage and get a mic on that tom."
I rushed to the back of the stage again to be greeted by the same mandrill who gave me the same grunts as before, enhanced with a "Now fuck off."
I ran back to explain to Vic there was no way I could get on the stage.
I was to become close friends with Vic over the next 19 years and this would be one of the few times I would ever see him really angry or hear him raise his voice. He screamed, "Go back and tell that fucking ape the recording is going to be fucked, he will be personally responsible and the band will be furious with him."

Returning to the stage once again, this time equipped with Vic's precise instructions, I repeated them word for word. I tactfully omitted the reference to the guy's heritage. Thankfully, this approach proved effective and I was promptly granted access.
As I reached the stage, The band was in the midst of an energetic performance, unleashing such a powerful surge of noise that made it impossible to discern the actual song they were playing, the stage reverberated as though a minor

earthquake were underway.
The band's outlines were all I could see as they were illuminated from the front by intensely brilliant white lights, while the audience remained obscured in the darkness beyond. I was fully aware there was the looming presence of over 600,000 individuals that lay beyond this blinding radiance.

At this moment, a paralysis overcame my entire body, it suddenly dawned on me that there was no way I could just casually stroll on to the stage, in front of such an enormous audience, locate a spare microphone and replace the broken one - especially while Moon was in the midst of his somewhat dynamic performance. Given Moon's well-known reputation, there was a real chance that he might stop playing midway through a song and tell me to fuck off.

Recognising the potential scenario, I was left with only one viable choice: to delegate this task to someone else. Looking around for a likely victim I spotted Neville nearby. I approached the prime candidate and bellowed into his ear that Vic had dispatched me to instruct him to replace the microphone. Nev's expression instantly changed, his face registering a mixture of astonishment and trepidation, likely fuelled by his awareness of Moon's unpredictable behaviour.

It was apparent that he was undergoing the same rush of terror that had engulfed me - it seemed that Neville may have required a change of underpants.

Nev began to conjure up various excuses, but I was resolute in conveying Vic's insistence that the task needed immediate attention. We looked over and sure enough, the Neumann U67 microphone head had been shattered and lay on the ground.

As I stood by, Nev, with evident nervousness, navigated around the drum kit on his hands and knees.
Displaying remarkable courage, he picked up the fractured microphone head and proceeded to attach a replacement head to the remaining body.
With the mission accomplished, I swiftly returned to Vic, carefully omitting the specifics of Nev's involvement. Many years later, I did share the genuine story with Nev, who reacted exactly as I had anticipated - with pure laughter.

The Warning

Around midday on Sunday 30th, I observed Teo Macero bidding farewell to various individuals, which struck me as odd given that several significant acts were still scheduled to perform. I hadn't anticipated any interaction with him, so I was taken aback when he approached me. What he said next left me utterly astounded. His words, roughly recalled, were along these lines:

"Young man, I'm going this morning and although our initial interaction wasn't the best, I want to say thank you for your hard work and the long hours you've dedicated. Also, please refrain from going on stage when Hendrix performs tonight."

"Why?" I asked.
Teo responded, "There's a possibility that someone might attempt to kill him tonight."
"Really?" I replied totally bewildered.
"Exercise caution," he advised, we shook hands with an air of uneasiness hanging between us.

As he walked away, a tremendous sense of relief washed over me at the thought of his departure. In hindsight, I recognise that he wasn't the arrogant figure I initially believed him to be; his warning was out of genuine concern for my safety and he was merely a person fulfilling his duties, well at least some of them.

Macero has been acknowledged for supervising the live recording of Leonard Cohen's performance at the festival. However, the reality is that he had already left hours before Cohen took the stage.

Jimi Hendrix

Later that night, after keeping the crowd waiting for a considerable time, Hendrix finally stepped onto the stage, confronting an audience that was both edgy and fatigued. It became apparent within minutes that he had lost the natural charisma and sense of purpose that had once been his hallmark.
As his performance progressed it was evident that his attempts at mostly out-of-tune progressive improvisations were not resonating with the crowd, who grew increasingly impatient and disgruntled.
They were eager for the familiar hits, not the experimental deviations he was offering.
Sensing the tension in the air, Hendrix leaned into the microphone and began to speak: "You wanna hear all those old songs, damn!" Hendrix reluctantly uttered, sensing the crowd's yearning for familiarity. With a hesitant start, he tried again to win over the audience. While there were instances of brilliance, it was apparent that the once-great performer was more immersed in his legendary persona than truly connecting with his audience.
As his performance drew to a close, wisps of smoke began to envelop the stage, triggering alarm among the spectators who believed a fire had erupted. The reverberations of Macero's warning from earlier in the day resounded in my mind. Ultimately, it was revealed that the smoke had resulted from a lit flare that had been thrown onto the stage by a member of the crowd. After the initial confusion subsided, the evening pressed on. It would appear that the sole noteworthy aspect of Hendrix's presence on stage that night was its documentation on film for future historical records.
On September 18th, a mere 19 days later, I awoke to the shocking news of Jimi Hendrix's passing. Macero's prescient caution resurfaced in my thoughts, causing me to wonder if he had possessed some foreknowledge on that fateful day.

I've come to believe that had Hendrix lived, he might have gradually receded from the spotlight, fading into relative obscurity, perhaps performing for modest audiences in small-town bars across the USA. His eventual demise might have garnered only a fleeting mention within the pages of newspapers worldwide.

All this aside, one undeniable truth remains: Hendrix has since become one of the most extraordinarily successful posthumous artistes, a status that endures to this day.

A Beautiful Dream Ends

On the Monday morning as the festival was over the promoter Ron Foulk said, "This is my last festival, enough was enough, it began as a beautiful dream but it got out of control and became a monster."

My recollection of the festival, luckily being backstage, side stage and in the front enclosure, was that, if there was one, then the monster had passed me by. I was 18 years old and being paid to work at a festival where rock legends were performing and where I was honoured to see the newcomers of the next decade, Tony Joe White, Kris Kristofferson, Emerson Lake & Palmer and the like. It was a privilege to have witnessed the end of one era and the beginning of the next.

At the end, after five days of glorious weather, the rain started to fall as we were de-rigging the equipment and packing up the trucks. We were all totally exhausted so to find we had a puncture on our truck was a bit of a bummer to say the least. Nev and I set about changing the wheel whilst Vic and the rest of the crew carried on loading the other truck.

Nev and I were getting to it, when we heard a friendly voice say, "Hi, would you like a hand?" Looking up we saw a large man with a beard standing before us, it was none other than Kris Kristofferson. Before we could answer Kris was down, knee deep in mud, helping us change the wheel.
After fixing the puncture on the truck we headed back to our hotel to get some rest before the long drive back to London the next day.
None of us had actually had any proper sleep since the previous Friday.

Neville took the wheel and drove the truck, Tony Carey and I slid into the passenger seats and within a few minutes we were both sound asleep.
Somewhere along the journey, I opened my eyes, taking a moment to survey the scene: Tony appeared to be in a deep sleep but worryingly I saw that Nev was dozing off, his head had lowered towards the floor, eyes shut, but his hands still fixed to the steering wheel. Instead of reacting to the impending danger that this situation posed, I inexplicably shut my eyes and promptly fell back asleep. The next thing I knew, I was jolted awake as the truck veered off the road and onto a grassy embankment.
Miraculously, with Nev, wrestling with the steering wheel, he somehow managed to navigate this alarming change in road surface, keeping us upright and managing to return to the tarmac to continue our journey. How we ever reached our destination remains a mystery to me considering our level of fatigue.
In a recent conversation I asked Neville to inquire about his recollection of what transpired, his account provides some insight:

"The drive back to the hotel is a vivid memory. I recall suddenly waking up, having dozed off, the van had drifted to the left and left the road, travelling along a raised grassy bank. The sound and vibrations of the truck rumbling along the grass brought me back to awareness I fully woke up just as we were leaving the bank and returning to the road.

When I looked over, both of you were still asleep, so I carried on driving. Just another day's work on the truck!"

As we arrived at our hotel, breakfast was being served. Despite our hunger, everyone bypassed the meal and headed straight to our rooms, seeking much-needed rest. We slept the sleep of the dead until Tuesday morning, when we set off back to London to return the 108 reels of tape to Pye.

Chapter 5

Back To the Studio

Dave Miller

I first met Dave Miller at Pye in 1969 when he was deeply engrossed in recording for his Damil label. He was a robustly built man with silver hair, possessing a voice that resonated like that of a seasoned American voiceover artist. When engaged in conversation, he exuded humour, wit, entertainment and a deep well of worldly wisdom. Among the individuals I've had the privilege of encountering, Dave was one of the three exceptional minds I've come across, the other two being Jack Fishman and Dr Shyam Singha. Despite their remarkable qualities, all three of these modest individuals would likely have disagreed with my assessment.

Miller has been the subject of numerous articles and stories over the years, often depicted as a smooth operator and occasionally compared to Colonel Tom Parker, the infamous manager of Elvis Presley. Born as David Leonart Kleiber in 1925 in Germany, both he and the Colonel emigrated to the USA during the 1930s and, on their arrival, adopted new names.
They both shared a talent for shrewd business dealings, making the most of every financial opportunity that came their way.

In 1949, Dave Miller established the Palda Record Company in Philadelphia. a label featuring various acts, including The Navy Shipmates, The Four Aces and The Blind Boys of Alabama, all experiencing modest sales locally. Dave, with an unrelenting passion for promoting records, seized every opportunity to produce and distribute a diverse range of content, from children's audio stories to recordings of local wedding ceremonies.

In an interesting twist, he even ventured into producing spoken pornographic records which, although not selling in large volumes, found a small but consistent market. After a while, one of these ventures encountered a significant setback when, due to an unfortunate mix-up during manufacture, the labels on the pornographic records were mistakenly applied to the wedding ceremonies records and sent to some deeply distressed newlyweds.

In 1951, Philadelphia, PA became the home of Holiday & Essex Records, a company founded by Dave Miller. This record label gained significant recognition by the local music scene, largely thanks to its early releases featuring Bill Haley and The Comets. Dave initially transformed the band's name from the Four Aces of Western Swing to Bill Haley and the Saddlemen. Later on, he suggested changing the name to the Comets, drawing inspiration from Halley's Comet.

The same year Miller inked a deal with Bill Haley for his Holiday Records label marking the inception of a new musical genre with Haley recording the first-ever

track in this emerging style.
The song was a rendition of Jackie Brenston's "Rocket 88."
Notably, this event occurred around three years prior to Sam Phillips being recognised for producing the pioneering rock 'n' roll crossover record, where a white artiste covered a track originally recorded by a black artist.

Dave has often been associated with the decision to turn down "Rock Around the Clock," but he consistently denied this accusation. An interview with the Comet's bass player, Marshall Lytle supports this so my belief in his denial is justifiable.
In the interview, when asked about song selection whilst recording with Miller, Lytle clarified that Bill Haley was primarily responsible for choosing most of the material. Whilst Dave Miller occasionally made suggestions, they were just that - suggestions. Lytle mentioned that "Rocket 88" was one of the songs that Dave Miller suggested, but when it came to choosing songs like "Rock the Joint" and others, it was Bill that had the final say.
Given this insight, I'm sure that if Bill Haley had wanted to record "Rock Around the Clock" with Dave Miller, he would have done so.
The fact that song choices were largely determined by Bill Haley himself underscores the idea that Miller's involvement in song selection was not as controlling as some accounts might suggest.

Throughout the years, Dave frequently recounted tales from his early days, which I often suspected were embellished and exaggerated. Surprisingly, in 1979, after listening to Bill Haley's perspective on the same events, it became evident that if anything, Dave had downplayed the stories.
Bill remarked, "Miller was an absolute wild man. Do you know he's the one who essentially invented Payola? When he put out a record, there was no stopping him. He'd go to extreme lengths to ensure the record got airplay and made its way into stores." Payola, within the music industry, refers to the illicit practice of providing compensation or gifts to commercial radio stations in exchange for playing a song, all without the station openly disclosing the financial arrangement.

Dave consistently maintained that his entry into the industry was facilitated by a US Government loan. Surprisingly, Bill confided in me that the financial support had, in fact, originated from the Mafia, with the purpose of funding non-union bands during a musicians' strike. This strike had left radio stations and jukeboxes along the Eastern Seaboard hungry for new material and Dave's operation had stepped in to meet that demand.

In the late 60s Dave Miller founded the Damil label in the UK with the aim of creating budget albums. These cost-effective recordings featured economical packaging and affordable pressings, supplying record labels such as Pickwick and Golden Award.

Dave had already set a precedent in the USA with his budget label Somerset Records. He further refined this business model with his Europa budget label by setting up his own pressing plant which was headquartered in Hamburg,

Germany. It's fair to say that Dave's influence to this day is responsible for populating charity shops and car boot markets with more records than any other individual.

During this period, the notion of budget albums was relatively new in Europe. Dave would rapidly book studio time to record a variety of albums. We would conduct direct-to-stereo recordings, capturing classics like *Banjo Spectacular* and *All Time Great Film Themes,* featuring a small orchestra led by a piano.
Each album was swiftly recorded, edited duplicated within a single day. These albums were then promptly dispatched to Dave's licensees for release around the globe, making them available in stores within a week or so.

Dave once shared with me that his most successful and profitable release in Europe was *The Hammond Organ's Greatest Hits,* spanning volumes 1 to 3.
A single musician would perform all the chart-topping songs on a Hammond organ, recorded directly onto a stereo master. His expenses consisted of just session fees for the player, arrangement costs, studio time and tape.

Dave always ensured that he held the publishing rights to at least one track on each album he produced. This could involve a public domain composition that he could claim the arrangement for or a simple instrumental piece occasionally improvised on the spot within the studio.

Kalamazoo

During one of the sessions for a nondescript instrumental recording, I approached Dave with an unusual request. I told him I wanted to come up with the title for a track, explaining that I wanted to impress my girlfriend, Sue. Without hesitation, Dave agreed.

The next time I saw Sue, I asked her to come up with an unusual song title, something really out of the ordinary. I told her to write it down for me, emphasising that it was going to be a surprise. Sue wrote the word Kalamazoo on a piece of paper and handed it to me.

I gave the piece of paper to Dave, who promptly incorporated Susie's chosen word as the title of an instrumental on his upcoming album. Remarkably, within about a week, the album was released so I took Sue to the record section of a Woolworth's store and reminded her of the word she had suggested just a few weeks prior. As she reached for the latest Damil album from the racks, she was met with the sight of her special word "Kalamazoo" printed on the album sleeve. This album was now available in every Woolworth store across the country.
At that moment, I became her hero, but was relieved that she didn't ask for royalties for her creative contribution.

Dave, unlike some other clients, had a remarkable knack for including everyone in his conversations possessing a fantastic ability to make each person feel valued, even extending this warmth to the tape assistant.

I recall one evening in 1970 when, at the conclusion of a session, Dave extended an invitation to me and several others to join him at Biaggi's, an Italian restaurant located just off the Edgware Road in London.

Despite my lack of experience with upscale dining, I saw the offer as too good to pass up, although I found the prospect a bit daunting. With my limited understanding of fine dining etiquette, I purposely entered the restaurant last, placing me beside Monty Presky, one of the directors of Pye Records.

As the waiter arrived to take our orders, the question of starters arose. Not entirely sure what to choose, I noticed that melon appeared to be the popular option among the group but an unfamiliar choice for me. I decided to go with the flow and ordered melon.

I was somewhat surprised when one half of a large melon arrived on a plate, it was all in one piece and looked rather imposing. Nevertheless, armed with a spoon, I launched into this unfamiliar experience.

As we ate the conversation continued, covering a variety of topics most of which I was ill-equipped to contribute to due to my nervousness. I really did feel somewhat out of my depth.

Monty tried his best to engage me in a discussion about Vienna and asked if I had ever been there. I answered with a simple "No," focusing intently on correctly eating my melon.

As I continued to eat, I realised that everyone else had finished their starters and seemed to be waiting for me. In my eagerness to finish and not keep others waiting, I stabbed at the melon with a little too much vigour, inadvertently sending it flying off the plate. It shot down the table like it had been fired out of a cannon, with wine glasses falling like skittles and cutlery flying in all directions, it finally ended up in the lap of a nearby dinner guest. I was mortified.

Looking around I noticed that those who had eaten their melon had started from the centre and worked outward, unlike me, who had begun from one side, causing the melon to lean heavily in one direction and causing the bloody thing to turn into a weapon of mass destruction.

While no one appeared overly concerned, likely out of empathy for my embarrassment, the waiter shot me a stern look as he cleaned up the mess and reset the table.

Thankfully, my choice for the main course was steak, which I made sure to consume with more caution, ensuring it only travelled from plate to mouth by way of the fork.

Though I had much to learn about upscale restaurants, that evening at Biaggi's marked a turning point and despite the earlier mishap, it became a regular spot for me to dine.

In 1980, following the completion of an album with a new artiste I was backing financially, I asked Dave if he could lend a hand in trying to place the album with a label during his upcoming trip
9080 to the USA. Impressed by the album, Dave agreed to offer his assistance, even though he mentioned that many of his previous business contacts had retired

or moved on to different roles in the industry.

When he returned Dave shared his experiences, explaining that generating interest had proven challenging. It appeared that the A&R staff were primarily young individuals who were hesitant to make decisions that might jeopardise their positions. Dave recounted a particular meeting where a young executive asked him, "Where's it happening in Europe?" Dave answered with characteristic wit, "If this were happening in Europe, you'd be coming to see me."

He also recounted a delightful anecdote involving the renowned director Billy Wilder. Wilder, who had been in the filmmaking industry since 1934 and had received numerous Academy Award nominations for movies like *Sunset Boulevard*, *Some Like* and *It Hot Witness for the Prosecution*, was trying to secure funding for his new film *Buddy Buddy* in 1979. Unfortunately, the decision-makers were mostly young individuals seeking the next blockbuster *Star Wars*. During a meeting, a young executive asked Wilder, "Sorry, Mr. Wilder, I'm not familiar with your work. Can you tell me about your successes?" Wilder's response was simple yet clever: "You first."

Smart Moves

Dave achieved millionaire status on three separate occasions in his career. He experienced the loss of his fortune once, only to reclaim it, followed by another setback, but remarkably, he managed to regain his wealth for a third time.

I recall a story he shared about the initial downturn in the late 1950s. Facing a deluge of bills and lacking the funds to cover any of them, he took a rather unconventional approach. He invested $2.00 in a red ink pad and a rubber stamp inscribed with the word "Deceased." Dave proceeded to stamp this word on each bill and returned them to all his creditors.

When Dave relocated his family permanently from the USA, he acquired a brand-new residence on the prestigious Moor Park Estate in Rickmansworth. His first order of business was to widen all the doorways. When I inquired about this, he replied, "You can't walk through any doorways in the UK with your hands in your pockets."

I paid a visit to the property a few months later and it had been distinctly "Dave Miller-ised." What truly caught my attention was the flooring. Dave explained that when he left America, he had shipped all his furniture and family possessions packed in the finest wood crates. Once they had arrived in the UK and were subsequently unpacked, he repurposed those wooden crates for his flooring.

My relationship with Dave Miller was one of great friendship and collaboration, we worked together until his unfortunate passing in 1985. Even to this day, I find myself missing him dearly.

Pye's Saturday Special

John Smyth, also known as 'Peanut', had an established tenure at Pye, initially serving as a tape operator before advancing to the position of a fledgling first year engineer. As a result of this progression, when relatively straightforward sessions were scheduled such as vocal overdubs or instances where a small number of musicians were adding overdubs to a multitrack, coupled with mixing, these tasks would be entrusted to junior engineers.

This practice served as valuable groundwork for these novice engineers, allowing them to not only apply their technical skills in practical situations but also to acquire an equally crucial skill: adeptly managing the clients.
First-year engineers also had the opportunity to record full sessions, on what was called the *'Saturday Special'*.

The concept of the *'Saturday Special'* was devised by Pat Godwin, the studio manager, with the intention of optimising studio use during weekends. This innovative idea involved offering the studio at a reduced rate to individuals or groups, allowing them to utilise the studio facilities instead of leaving it vacant over the weekend.

This arrangement was only implemented when the studio wasn't booked by Pye's established acts or regular paying clients. It provided an invaluable opportunity for first-year engineers to gather hands-on experience in recording entire bands performing together. During these sessions, bands could secure the studio for a three-hour period at a highly affordable rate.
This time span was allocated for recording and mixing their demos. As part of this package, the bands were also provided with a few acetates of their recorded material.
These acetate discs held the potential to serve as valuable tools, bands could use them to showcase their music to managers or record companies, aiding in the pursuit of a potential record deal. Although it's important to note that the quality of these acetate discs would start to decline after approximately five or six plays.
Peanut generously extended an offer to record our band during what was known as downtime, referring to any unreserved studio hours.
Remarkably, we were not required to make any payment for this opportunity; our task was simply to ensure we sought permission from the studio manager, Pat Godwin. Curiously, in the studio's official diary, these sessions were cryptically labelled as "*Stoner Music*," a detail that remained somewhat enigmatic.

The prospect of recording left us elated and Peanut himself welcomed the chance to take on additional engineering responsibilities.
The band line-up consisted of Brian Eden on vocals and rhythm guitar, Freddie Pacitti manned the drums, whilst George Curry skillfully handled lead guitar duties. George would later become a founding member of the successful 70s band, Darts. I also shared vocals and guitar.
With a lack of any permanent bass player, my friend Cliff Williams, who would eventually join the ranks of the stadium-filling rock band AC/DC, stepped in on bass duties. He went on to play for us on numerous sessions throughout the early 70s.
During these sessions, we successfully recorded two of our finest tracks, "Louise" and "I Will Solve It Drinking" and a sense of pride enveloped us in the

wake of these accomplishments. We held a strong belief that these meticulously crafted pieces had the potential to finally secure the coveted record deal we had been fervently pursuing.

Jack In the Box

I nearly always assumed the role of tape operator on Peanut's own recording sessions, amongst the many sessions we did together, one in particular stood out, a collaboration with emerging songwriters Dave Meyers and John Worsley.
The duo had scheduled a session to add vocal overdubs to a track titled "Nashville Rain," performed by their artist, Les Charles.
Les possessed an astonishing vocal prowess, evoking a blend reminiscent of Brook Benton and Otis Redding, while the song itself showcased undeniable excellence.

Dave Meyers' unwavering enthusiasm and fervour left a strong impression on me. He firmly believed in their prospects for success within the music industry. Meyers recounted that just a year prior, he had been employed as a GPO telephone engineer when he noticed John's advertisement in a newspaper seeking a song writing partner. Following their initial meeting they forged a partnership.

Their collaborative efforts bore fruit sooner than anticipated, resulting in a publishing deal with Southern Music. This arrangement encompassed not only the opportunity to record their compositions but also a budget allocated for discovering new artistes to interpret their songs.
Additionally, Southern Music provided access to their compact in-house studio situated in the basement of their offices, facilitating the creation of a demo.
As the session drew to a close, I took the opportunity to share with Meyers that I was a part of a band actively seeking a record deal. With a repertoire composed entirely of our original compositions, I asked whether he could offer any assistance. Meyers, the unequivocal business-oriented member of the Meyers/Worsley partnership, was clearly distinguished from John, who predominantly contributed musical talent.
In response, Meyers requested a sample of our music to evaluate. Swiftly, I made my way to the tape library to retrieve our master recordings. With a sense of pride, I played our two tracks for him. I had no idea that this encounter would be the inception of an exceptional and unique relationship with Dave, one that would endure for the subsequent five decades.
Armed with a copy of our tape, Dave and John went straight into action.
Within a matter of weeks, they extended an offer to manage our band, eagerly, we seized the opportunity.

Their initial move involved securing a publishing deal with Southern Music for both Brian and me. This arrangement not only provided us with an advance but also granted us access to Southern's modest recording studio when necessary. Brian and I found ourselves spending a significant amount of time at the Southern studio whenever feasible. Additionally, we frequented the Giaconda Café, which offered remarkable networking opportunities.

The Giaconda served as a vibrant hub where writers, musicians and publishers converged, fostering a fertile environment for the exchange of stories and ideas. This unique setting facilitated meaningful connections and collaborations.

The café, located at 9 Denmark Street in London's Tin Pan Alley, was situated practically adjacent to Southern Music.
Just picture the scene: sitting at a table where musicians like David Bowie, Elton John and Marc Bolan would gather, sharing aspirations of one day achieving stardom.
Here, everyone lived and breathed music and for years it functioned as the epicentre and nurturing ground for the very foundation of the British music industry.

One day Brian and I were seated in the Giaconda Café when Meyers burst in, his enthusiasm radiating in that familiar, almost manic manner, of his. He couldn't wait to share an idea he believed would expedite his success in the industry.
With boundless excitement, he declared, "I've got it! It's so simple! We're going to win the Eurovision Song Contest, establish our very own record label then use the proceeds to acquire our own recording studio."
As if to substantiate his claim, he added, "We've already written the winning song, come and have a listen."

We followed him back to the studio and he played his masterpiece. Brian and I were left flabbergasted as the tune "Jack in the Box" resounded through the loudspeakers. When the song concluded, Brian and I exchanged glances; both of us struggled to find words to match our astonishment.
Brian broke the silence, saying, "Yeah, that's great, but who's doing the vocals?" Meyers bellowed at the top of his lungs, "A singer named Elaine Paige." He recounted that Elaine had recently visited the Giaconda for coffee where he had mustered the courage to ask her to contribute vocals to the track for a session fee. In Dave's view, it was clear as day: "Can't you hear it? It's a winner, a sure-fire hit!" Meanwhile, John Worsley, always the slightly more reserved member of the partnership, injected a note of caution, advising, "Calm down Dave, it might just have a chance."

We both held a genuine appreciation for the song writing and production skills of Dave and John. Just prior to this they had played us a fresh track by Les Charles titled "Baby You've Got Something".
This composition resonated as an instant hit to our ears. However, in contrast, "Jack in the Box" seemed more of a comedic song. Despite our reservations, we refrained from voicing our opinions, as we were cautious about not offending our managers.
Nevertheless, Dave and John proceeded to submit their recording of "Jack in the Box" with Elaine Page singing and against the odds, it managed to secure a spot among the final six contenders.
In an astonishing turn of events, to our disbelief, "Jack in the Box" emerged as the winning entry for the UK in the Eurovision Song Contest.
The following stage saw Clodagh Rodgers representing the UK in the

competition held in Dublin, ultimately securing a respectable 4th place finish. This surprising journey from initial scepticism to witnessing their victory undoubtedly left Brian and me dumbfounded

On March 9th, 1971, Dave contacted us, urgently requesting that Brian and I meet with him. Anticipating positive news about the band, we promptly headed over that evening. Sadly, what awaited us was not the good news we had hoped for - rather, it was quite the opposite.

Dave initiated the conversation, saying, "You know Ali has never lost a fight."

"Not until last night," I responded sharply.

Dave's appearance shifted and with an air of sheepishness and nervousness, he continued, "I did it for you guys." An impatient tone from Brian prompted him to continue "tell us already! What did you do for us?"

Meyers cautiously explained, "Well, you know the advance money for the band? I put it all on Ali to win. I thought I could get some extra money for you guys, to improve your equipment."

Despite the fact that our bank account required two signatures (either Brian's or mine, along with a counter-signature from Dave), he had forged one of our signatures to access the funds and place the bet. After the initial shock, considering his intentions at the time were to genuinely assist us, we eventually found it within ourselves to forgive him. In retrospect, perhaps we should have immediately rebranded the band as "*The Simpletons*."

Following this incident, their management commitment to us rapidly declined. While we persisted under the Southern Music contract and maintained friendships with John and Dave, which lasted for many years, we formally parted ways with them on a contractual basis.

Dave and John continued their collaborative aspirations as songwriters and producers for the next 15 years.

They eventually established a thriving recording studio, but despite their ongoing efforts, they were unable to replicate the level of success achieved through their Eurovision triumph.

Despite their earnest efforts, Dave and John faced challenges in securing a significant record deal for Les Charles. Dick Leahy of GTO Records delivered a candid assessment, stating that his vocal style resembled that of a pub singer and was unlikely to change. While their attempts to secure a major deal for Les proved challenging at the time, fate would soon intercede.

I spent many hours with Les hanging out at Giaconda. One on one of these occasions his wallet seemed to be playing hide-and-seek, so he approached me with a "serious face" and pleaded for a life-saving 4 shillings loan to rescue him from the brink of a coffee and sandwich catastrophe. Well, let's just say I saved him from a hangry meltdown by throwing him a proverbial financial lifeline. Who knew being a musical saviour could come on such budget-friendly terms?

A few years down the line, I was on my way out of North London's Tangerine Studios, run by Dave and John, just as Les was preparing to begin a vocal recording session. During our encounter, he shared his deep frustration with the music industry, explaining that his recent efforts to secure a chart position had not yielded the desired results. In a candid conversation, he revealed his plan to undergo a significant transformation by adopting the new stage name "Billy Ocean." He was determined to give it one last shot, putting all his hopes into a song titled "Love Really Hurts Without You".

I wished him the best of luck and chose not to mention that he still owed me four shillings.

Apparently, his contract with Meyers and Worsley had concluded but Leahy and GTO Records decided to revisit the prospect. This time, they signed Les under his new moniker - Billy Ocean.

From this point onward, Billy Ocean's career took an extraordinary turn and the rest, as they say, is history. His sales have reached over 30 million records and he has not only enjoyed a successful solo career but has also contributed songs to numerous renowned artistes.

This tale exemplifies the twists and turns that often define the music industry, with opportunities sometimes unfolding in unexpected ways, leading to remarkable outcomes for those involved.

It would be almost 40 years later before I would meet Les again. Coincidentally, just like the last time we met, I was leaving a studio when he was arriving. He didn't immediately recognise me but I said "Hi Les, you owe me four bob." As he was looking a little bewildered, I introduced myself and we spent the next three hours reminiscing about those early days.

During the conversation he kept laughing, on asking why he said "You keep calling me Les and no-one else does." I explained I can only remember you as Les.

Having heard a hilarious story about him I felt I had to ask if it were true, it turned out that it was. The story in question revolved around an incident whilst Les was at home in Surrey tending to his garden, an elderly woman from his neighbourhood walking by, stopped and called out to Les, "Excuse me young man, do you take care of all the gardens around here?"

Our paths crossed once more about a week later and this time he was in the company of his two children. It was truly heart-warming to witness his evident happiness and contentment with his life during that encounter.

Les was undeniably a kind and gifted individual who absolutely earned every moment of his well-deserved success.

Disaster Strikes

I had spent a little more than a year at Pye when a disaster hit. An official statement declared that a number of job positions would be eliminated. As individuals we were summoned into Pat's office, I braced myself for what was to come. It appeared that nobody was exempt from the job cuts.

I was in the tape copying room when Peanut came in, his expression a mix of shock and dismay; he had been instructed to depart immediately, joining a

considerable list of colleagues in the same situation.
Even Neville, who operated the Mobile truck with Vic, was not spared from redundancy, though he was eventually rehired after several months. His skills and experience made him invaluable.

With a profound sense of relief, I discovered that I had retained my job. Dave Hunt later told me that I likely escaped the staff reduction due to my position as one of the studio's lowest-paid employees, making my removal financially insignificant.

I stayed in contact with Peanut, who quickly secured a position at Chalk Farms Studios, where he eventually gained a reputation as a highly talented reggae-recording engineer. From that point on, I took nothing for granted, this experience served as a pivotal lesson in understanding the unpredictable nature of the industry.

Due to the unfortunate circumstances that befell the other tape operators, I unexpectedly found myself being promoted, accompanied by a modest salary increase. In a matter of weeks, I was guiding the newly hired recruits through their roles. I had grown entirely at ease in the Pye environment.
I had developed a strong rapport with both the engineers and the clients and felt a genuine sense of mastery over my contributions to the recording sessions. Everything appeared to be progressing smoothly.

One Hell of a Surprise

When Dave Hunt informed me that he, along with several other colleagues, had decided to depart from Pye, I was quite taken aback. They were ready for a new venture at a recently established studio complex in Wembley.

The new studio in question bore the name De Lane Lea, a homage to Jacque De Lane Lea, the proprietor of the similarly named Kingsway Studio and had been conceived and constructed under the expertise of Dave Siddle. Siddle's reputation as a studio engineer was illustrious, having recorded a plethora of amazing artists including Jimi Hendrix, The Beatles, Deep Purple and The Animals.

With plans for a visit to the studio within the upcoming days, Dave Hunt extended an invitation for me to explore this new complex with him. Naturally, I was enthusiastic about discovering what was attracting so many members of the Pye staff to the studio.

Unfortunately, on the afternoon of our intended visit, Dave couldn't make it, but he proposed that I proceed independently and he would arrange for Dave Siddle to give me the tour. Eager for a look I jumped on a train journey to Wembley. As I walked down Empire Way, the towering structures of Wembley Stadium came into view, an imposing sight for the first time. Drawing nearer, I turned right onto Engineers Way, where an immense new brick edifice stood before me. At the pinnacle of this remarkable building, distinctive half-pyramid glass windows jutted out.

Stepping through the expansive double glass doors, I found myself within a sprawling, contemporary reception area. To my left, a staircase beckoned, leading to the upper floor of the facility. Directly ahead, a commodious seating area furnished with black chairs. The mammoth circular mirrors adorning the walls reflected my presence, while a collection of LED clocks showcased the time across several global locations.

On the right side, a semi-circular desk hosted two youthful and pleasant receptionists, one stationed at the back operating a telephone switchboard with the other positioned at the front to greet visitors

I informed the receptionist that I had an appointment with Dave Siddle and the young woman manning the switchboard promptly called Mr. Siddle to inform him of my arrival. She told me he would be down shortly and suggested I took a seat. Despite their contemporary appearance, the modern chairs provided little comfort and made it challenging to relax while seated.

After waiting for about five minutes a towering but slender man descended the stairs. He sported tinted eyeglasses and moved with a slight limp; his shoulder-length blonde hair somewhat reminiscent of a scarecrow.

He came over to me and he introduced himself as Dave Siddle, extending a gracious welcome, offering a few introductory words about the building.

Subsequently, I was treated to a comprehensive tour of this extraordinary facility. Our journey commenced with Studio 3, at the far end of a long corridor, the smallest of the three studios. We then retraced our steps down the corridor to Studio 2, which boasted a notably larger footprint. Our next destination was Studio 1, an awe-inspiring space. The control room loomed grandly and as I approached the glass window, I peered down into the expansive live room. Dave explained that it could comfortably accommodate around 130 musicians.

A massive movie screen adorned the rear wall and he went on to reveal that the projection rooms were situated on the floor above the control room. Moreover, all the studios were interconnected by tie-lines and could be seamlessly linked.

Dave had personally devised the consoles and multi-tracks. Each console featured an integrated remote control, allowing the engineer to control the multi-track functions from the heart of the desk. Additionally, the desks included built-in error indicators to promptly alert the engineer to any issues.

On the opposite side of the building, an extended corridor led to several copying rooms and disc cutting suites.

Moving to the upper-level revealed offices, projection and film sound rooms and an expansive restaurant with ample seating.

Beyond, a large car park stood ready to accommodate everyone in the event of the complex operating at full capacity.

These final two amenities were unprecedented in other studios during that era. Truly, this was an extraordinary facility, though from my perspective, it was somewhat marred by a rather unusual colour scheme, there were distinctive red, white and purple hues adorning the walls of each live room. I later learned that

Dave Siddle was colour-blind which shed a little light on this strange combination of colours.

During my conversation with Dave, he exhibited straightforward communication, devoid of any confusing jargon or nonsense. I immediately felt a strong connection with him. As our tour concluded, we found ourselves in the reception area, where Dave inquired about my impressions of the building. Despite choosing not to mention my reservations about the Stevie Wonder colour scheme, my enthusiasm shone through.

To my astonishment, Dave dropped a bombshell, stating, "If you're interested in joining us next month, I can offer you a weekly salary of £27.50, four weeks holiday pay and standard overtime rates." It dawned on me that I had just experienced the second most unconventional job interview of my career. Without any hesitation, I enthusiastically accepted his offer.

My main predicament now centred around facing Pat Godwin back at Pye. The very next morning, I mustered the courage to request a meeting with Pat.

As I entered his office, I politely inquired if we could have some privacy by closing the door. Taking a seat, I felt a wave of nervousness wash over me, reminiscent of the day I had first interviewed with him - a distant memory now.

Pat greeted me with a smile but wasted no time in addressing the elephant in the room.

"If you're here to tell me you're leaving to join that fucking studio in Wembley," he said "I'll cancel the reference for the bank loan you're eyeing to buy that car." With a sense of humility, I replied, "Pat, you'll have to cancel it; I need to give a month's notice."

To my dismay, his expression shifted to one of genuine shock. This was the man who had given me my start and I couldn't help but feel awful about my decision. It seemed like everyone was leaving.

Pat, in a bid to retain me, made an enticing counteroffer with more money and a promotion, but deep down, I believed that this move was the right path for me. He didn't end up cancelling my bank reference; in fact, he gave me his blessing and reassured me that if things didn't work out, there would always be a place for me back at Pye.

Nearly three decades later, I received an invitation to join a reunion event at the Pye Studios, which was in the process of closing its doors for good, having undergone a name change to PRT. Pat was also in attendance at this gathering, providing me with the perfect opportunity to convey my heartfelt appreciation for everything he did for me and how much Pye Studios had meant to me as we bade farewell to an era. I will forever hold deep gratitude towards Pat Godwin.

Over the next few weeks, I spent countless hours reminiscing about my time at Pye - the joyful moments, the camaraderie, the recording sessions and the numerous parties.

One story sprung to mind, that of a young tape assistant who was burdened with the monotonous task that we all despised: converting old mono Pye albums into what was dubbed "*Mock Stereo.*"

This process involved taking the original mono tape and splitting it into two channels on the mixing desk, adding bass frequencies to the left channel and high frequencies to the right channel. The result was a less-than-impressive imitation of stereo sound. It was essential that when played back on a mono system, it sounded identical to the original record. For one particular album, *Donovan's Greatest Hits,* on one of Pye's budget labels, the young tape assistant decided to take matters into his own hands.

Finding the mock stereo process rather dull, he took the mono track and panned it from left to right. This unconventional move made it seem as though Donovan and his band were playing first from the left then the right speakers, showcasing a remarkable stereo effect. However, this was far from what mock stereo was intended to achieve. The mistake was only discovered after a few thousand records had been pressed, all of which had to be discarded. The young tape operator was promptly asked how long he had been working for Pye, not including the next day.

I couldn't deny feeling apprehensive and having reservations about leaving Pye. I was intimately familiar with the studio and its operations, but on the other hand, I would be reuniting with many of the friends and colleagues I had worked alongside for a considerable time.

Chapter 6

De Lane Lea,

A Brief History

In 1969, an expanse of land adjacent to Wembley Stadium was acquired, marking the beginning of a new chapter for De Lane Lea. A purpose-built studio complex emerged from this undertaking, officially opening its doors in 1971. This distinctive establishment found its home on Engineers Way and consisted of three progressively sized studios.

At the helm of technical ingenuity and studio direction was Dave Siddle. With visionary foresight, he conceived a workspace that harnessed cutting-edge technology and the latest design paradigms. Notably ahead of its time, Dave envisioned a control room devoid of complex patching using jack plugs, a concept that would only materialise decades later. The heart of the complex was adorned with a computerised mixing console, meticulously crafted by Sound Techniques. Complementing this setup were Scully tape machines and the sonic precision of Lockwood-Tannoy speakers for monitoring.

In 1972, the reins of leadership were passed to Louis Elman, who assumed the role of Managing Director. This pivotal moment coincided with Louis enticing CTS to relocate from Bayswater to the vibrant hub of Wembley, operating under the name The Music Centre.
Louis decided to leave in the late 70s and Peter Harris took over the role of MD, then in 1987 the studio found a new steward in Adrian Kerridge.
Despite all efforts, progress often dictates change and the June 24th, 2000 saw the closure of the complex. This step was taken to pave the way for the ambitious redevelopment of Wembley Stadium and the area around it. The year 2002 brought a temporary renaissance as Peter Fielder rekindled the studio's spirit under the banner of Phoenix Sound. Sadly, the passage of time marked another sombre juncture; the complex met its demise in June 2004, replaced by a thoroughfare leading towards the new stadium. In the annals of audio history, the tale of De Lane Lea stands as a testament to innovation, adaptation and the inexorable march of progress.

The Staff Assembles

My initial weeks at De Lane Lea brimmed with a real sense of anticipation. Upstairs, the offices gradually populated with an eager staff dedicated to managing bookings and accounts. Among the core audio team were seasoned engineers Martin Birch and Louie Austin, previously of the Kingsway Studio. Alongside them were Alan Florence, Dave Hunt, Dick Plant and myself, all hailing from Pye. Together, we formed a united front under Dave Siddle's guidance, poised to propel the studio into a triumphant venture.

This resplendent studio boasted an array of novel equipment and amenities, yet its location on the outskirts of the city posed a question: How would we lure clients to Wembley? In hindsight, such queries now appear quaint, but at the time, the epicentre of the music industry was firmly rooted in Central London. We resembled a grand ocean liner, fully furnished and prepared to set sail, yet lacking the passengers to embark on its journey.

Terry Yeadon, a prominent technical assistant working closely with Dave Siddle, extended a generous offer of free studio time to a fledgling band named Smile who sometime later changed their name to something more familiar - Queen.
This gesture served a dual purpose: testing the capabilities of the equipment and gauging the extent of sound leakage between studios. While the issue of leakage was evident, it was merely the tip of the iceberg in uncovering a host of substantial challenges. The subsequent months were rife with hiccups as both the staff and the equipment grappled with teething problems.

The consoles and machines seemed to have a penchant for breaking down, a frustrating pattern that persisted. The sessions that did manage to take place, mostly clients of Martin Birch and Dave Hunt, descended into chaos due to these technical glitches. Amidst these trials, a collective sentiment emerged among the staff – a whisper of doubt about the hastiness in aligning with Dave Siddle's visionary pursuit.

Chapter 7

Fate Calls Time Out

As I pondered the uncertainties that lay ahead, fate entered the scene with its customary indifference. Returning home from work one Friday evening in February, I discovered an unwelcome change - my wrists and ankles had swollen without me really noticing until now, accompanied by a general sense of malaise. As Saturday dawned, the discomfort in my joints intensified, prompting me to contact a doctor. Following a thorough examination, the physician deemed it prudent to subject me to several hospital tests. While I held reservations about the idea, the doctor assured me that my stay would be brief, expecting my return home by the following Thursday. With a tentative nod, I consented. I never expected to step into a dimension reminiscent of *The Twilight Zone*, embarking on a journey that would consume almost a year of my life.

Transported by ambulance, I found myself at Guy's Hospital, eventually landing in the William Gull Ward - an attic ward tucked away up on the fourth floor. My first impression was that this felt like a haven for those on the final leg of their journey. The ward exuded an antiquated air, its space inhabited predominantly by elderly individuals; some sleeping, while others emitted a chorus of groans and pain-filled screams. The atmosphere evoked a sensation of time travel, as if I had been abruptly transported to a WW1 hospital ward.

The only portals to the outside world were a couple of skylights, offering a glimpse of the sombre grey sky and the skeletal branches of leafless trees. The sleeping quarters comprised of approximately 40 beds, tightly aligned and separated by only enough space between to navigate a medical or food trolley through.
The ward had two small areas partitioned off, one providing a compact kitchen, the other a storage area for medical supplies. They also led to the adjacent female ward, situated a mere six feet away.

Over the next few days, a series of examinations and X-rays were taken, culminating in a sobering diagnosis of rheumatic fever. The prescribed course of action was equally sobering, I was instructed to remain immobile for the next three months, avoiding any unnecessary movements.
The rationale behind this directive was the potential risk of triggering severe cardiac issues should I defy the mandate to stay still. Duly, I embarked on a long-enforced period of inertia, my gaze fixated on the skylight overhead.

The next 12 weeks unfurled and my mind drifted into the realm of daydreams. The thought of sleeping for the entire three months and reawakening anew would be the perfect solution. Yet, the brief respite of even a few hours of continuous sleep proved elusive during this period of confinement.

The adjacent bed was occupied by a man around 50 years of age. During visiting hours, he engaged in lively conversations and laughter with his family. But this atmosphere shifted one fateful night with the nurses drawing curtains around both his bed and mine. By the time the curtains were drawn back sometime later, he had vanished. Inquiring about his abrupt departure, I was met with the stark reality: he had passed away. I fixated on that now-empty bed for hours, a silent witness to the transience of life until a new occupant took his place.

As the weeks unfolded a disheartening rhythm took hold. Day by day, I bore witness to individuals succumbing to the grasp of death. I couldn't shake the thought that perhaps I might never depart from the ward alive.

With the arrival of spring, a renewed vitality emerged outside the skylight – leaves sprouted on the once-bare trees, growing fuller with each passing day. Seeking a diversion from the morbid surroundings, I began to count those leaves, despite my attempts to distract myself, my mental state had begun to erode.

Frequent visits from my girlfriend, Sue and my mother served as small respites amidst the gloom. Nonetheless, my deteriorating condition instilled a sense of unease.

I repeatedly implored Sue to cease her visits and seek companionship elsewhere, but her unwavering commitment prevailed. This led to mounting tensions with her parents, who understandably were concerned about their young daughter devoting her nights to a hospital bedside, the future uncertain. These disagreements escalated, ultimately prompting Sue to make a drastic decision - she left her own home and moved in with my mother.

Three months had elapsed, during which time I had witnessed my body relinquish half its weight, my mind wane, bedsores mar my skin and a grim cocktail of medications saturated my system. In the midst of this grim ordeal, a revelation shattered the previous diagnosis - the doctors acknowledged a major error.

The ailment was not rheumatic fever, but rather juvenile arthritis. The prescription for healing? Contrary to my protracted period of stillness, I was now instructed to move, to rise from my bedridden state, a complete reversal of prior directives.

Guided by this new mandate, I embarked on a new course of treatment, one based on mobility. As I was assisted into a wheelchair for the first time, a frightening transformation took place. Once in an upright position, I completely lost my vision and was left in total darkness, my screams reverberated through the air, for what seemed an eternity. The onset of blindness was due to the recalibration of my blood circulation as it adapted to the shift to my upright position.

Over the next few weeks, the days consisted of physiotherapy sessions and long stretches of time spent idle in a wheelchair, engrossed in my own melancholic thoughts. In the adjacent ward there was a young woman named Marianne, graced with a pretty visage she would assist the nurses in serving, distributing tea and coffee to the patients from a trolley. She weighed 32 stone and was admitted to the hospital for medically supervised weight loss. Her immense size was something I had never encountered before. Whilst nowadays individuals tipping the scales at over 20 stone are much more common, back then it was a rarity.

As the days passed, Marianne and I struck up a wonderful friendship. I became oblivious to her size. Her size ceased to be the focal point for me, thanks to our regular and warm interactions.

With spring's arrival, she extended a kind offer - to push me in the wheelchair for a jaunt outdoors, affording me a dose of revitalising fresh air.

Upon our return, she proposed a repeat outing for the next day. I met the suggestion with an emphatic "No!" prompting her to inquire further. My response was straightforward: the upset of being observed in a wheelchair by onlookers proved too much for me.

Marianne responded with a hearty laugh then posed a question that would really shift my perspective: "Do you really think they were all looking at you?" We formed a deep friendship, realising that it offered us the added benefit of mutual support.

A Giant of a Man

Amidst the chaos of my recovery, a new acquaintance came into my life. After returning from a physiotherapy session one afternoon, I found a new patient in the neighbouring bed. His name was Reg and initially, I mistook him for a young boy due to his small stature. Although, it became clear that he was an adult of shorter height when he got up to introduce himself.

Despite my initial lack of social interaction during that period, Reg didn't give up on trying to befriend me and would attempt his inane chatter at every available opportunity. This continued for a few days until a child, much younger than me and the typical patients in the ward, entered one late night.

Intrigued by this new arrival, Reg was soon at his bedside.

When Reg returned to his bed next to mine, I sought to learn more about the boy's reason for being there.

This gave me the chance for a genuine conversation with him. I asked about the young boy and Reg shared the heart-breaking story of the lad who had attempted suicide at just 16 years old, suffering from incessant bullying due to his appearance.

Reg's words of encouragement and his own life story of being picked on nearly all of his life, had truly inspired the young boy.

Afterward, I mustered the courage to ask Reg about his own condition. He explained that he had stopped growing at the age of nine, despite various attempts to find a cure.

When Reg was discharged, he occasionally visited the outpatient department at the hospital, always making the effort to come see me. I appreciated his visits though often he would appear at my bedside completely out of breath and sweating. I asked why this was and the answer was simple: if he was alone in the lift, he was unable to reach the buttons above the third floor so had to get out and take the stairs the rest of the way.

This served as a poignant reminder of how some people must adapt their lives for the simplest tasks that many of us take for granted.

Freedom

I spent several more months in hospital before being transferred to a rehabilitation

centre in New Cross.
At the centre I would swim every day and slowly I began to walk again. I never saw Reg after leaving the hospital. I did keep in contact with Marianne and in 1974 when Sue and I got married, Marianne attended our wedding looking wonderful. She had managed to lose 14 stone, but also gained 12 by way of a new boyfriend.

During my hospitalisation, apart from the comforting presence of Sue and my devoted mother, my visitors were rather scarce. Jack, my friend from school who would later serve as the best man at our wedding, came to see me during those days. Martin Birch, associated with De Lane Lea studios, made a visit as well.
My school friend, Brian, with whom I had collaborated on song writing for an extended period, also came by. He shared his disillusionment with the music industry. Despite having a couple of our records released and a few sporadic radio plays before my hospitalisation, our aspirations hadn't truly materialised.
The chapter of our Southern music publishing venture had ended, motivating him to marry his girlfriend Stella and relocate to Wales - an arrangement that persists to this very day. It seemed his optimism in my recovery had diminished.

I hated my time in hospital, it was one of the darkest periods in my life. Yet, amid the difficulties, it provided some invaluable lessons: to never underestimate the gift of life, or the individuals who grace it and don't judge by appearances or you may miss something wonderful within.

Chapter 8

A Welcome Return

Though my direct contact with Dave Siddle was limited during my hospital stay, I did receive well-wishing cards from the staff, along with an assurance that my position at De Lane Lea remained open. Once I was discharged from hospital, one of my first tasks was to contact Dave. He kindly proposed a return to work on a part-time basis, gradually building up to full-time as my strength and well-being permitted.

When I returned to the studio, I was met with warmth and consideration from everyone. Although the workload had slightly increased, the studios were far from what one might call bustling. Persistent issues with equipment breakdowns being the major reason.

In anticipation of the official inauguration by Princess Margaret, a crucial event, it was imperative that sessions were scheduled for that particular day in order to create the illusion of a fully operational establishment. We decided to provide free studio time to fill the diary but this proved to be no easy task.

One notable session was arranged with Ken Dodd and a full orchestra in Studio One, under the expertise of Terry Johnson, a new addition to our team. Terry brought with him years of experience from Decca studios, particularly in recording large orchestras.

Along with Ken Dodd, the one prominent artiste we managed to secure for that significant day, the other studios were inhabited with fictitious clients conjured up and played by our staff and friends.

Princess Margaret arrived with her entourage and was shown into Studio One by Dave Siddle and Jacque De Lane Lea, an accompanying pair of photographers were journaling the visit. Not even royalty could fail to be impressed by the grandeur of Studio One and Ken Dodd performing in front of a large orchestra. The day transpired smoothly we stood officially open.
Although Martin Birch was contributing a few albums with bands such as Thin Lizzy and Deep Purple, the facility remained relatively unoccupied. It was apparent to all that something needed to change, given the surplus of staff, the dearth of work and the persistently unreliable equipment. Change did come, as events would soon unfold.

One fateful Monday morning, I walked into the studio to discover an influx of suited executives swarming the premises. They approached each of us, inquiring about our roles at the studio - questions that left a real tension in the air. A wave of uncertainty rippled through the studio, as the names of Dave Siddle and his secretary were being stripped from their office doors.

The prevailing sentiment among us was that the studio might be shutting its doors that very day. These new figures were dispatched from De Lane Lea's headquarters in Dean Street in London, with a clear mission: to, as one of them put it, "sort this out."

We were summoned into a meeting, where a Mr. Louis Elman introduced himself as the newly-appointed managing director. With a tone of reprimand, he underscored what we were already aware of; the prevailing chaos within the studio and its mismanagement. He declared that from this point onward, everything was to change. Acknowledging the severity of the situation, he emphasised that his reputation was at stake and he was not willing to tolerate any mistakes.

He was resolute in his commitment to overhaul the establishment and make it functional. During this meeting, we learned that Dave Siddle had been dismissed. Those who felt they couldn't align with the new direction were given the option to leave on the spot. It was my first experience of the phrase, "a new broom sweeps clean."

Within the initial week under this new management, a pivotal incident transpired. Martin Birch, a highly respected engineer with a significant clientele, arrived half an hour late for his session. To everyone's astonishment, Mr. Elman promptly terminated Martin's employment right there at the reception. The abruptness and severity of this decision reverberated throughout the studio, leaving us all profoundly unsettled. The atmosphere had been thrust into a state of constant unease and tensions were high.

CTS Studios

Originally established as Cine-Tele Sound Studios, CTS Studios came into existence through a partnership including renowned jingle writer Johnny Johnston, Peter Kay in the role of managing director with John Elliot as technical director. The company was incorporated in 1956 and commenced operations in London's Bayswater district. Their primary objective was to make inroads into television advertising and film scoring, offering state-of-the-art facilities and techniques. The CTS team consisted of around 12 staff members, with notable figures such as Chief Technical Engineer Peter Harris, Senior Recording Engineer John Richards and Recording Engineer Dick Lewzey.

Louis Elman instigated the integration with CTS in late 1972. It marked the beginning of a renaissance, with the studios being promptly renovated to accommodate Neve mixing consoles and new Studer multi-tracks featuring interchangeable heads for both 16 and 24 track recording.

The notorious equipment malfunctions that had plagued the studio soon became a thing of the past. Undoubtedly, this amalgamation under the direction of Louis Elman proved pivotal in rescuing the studio. CTS now had a well-established reputation in film and TV work and their clients were prepared to follow them anywhere.

There was a notable divide between the De Lane Lea and CTS personnel, with differences in approach and work style. CTS were accustomed to using two microphones to record a drum kit and were cautious about recording levels going into the red. On the other hand, the De Lane Lea engineers, rooted in the world of rock 'n' roll, embraced higher recording levels on tape, including the "red" zone and the use of only two microphones on the drums by this time was unthinkable.

For the first six months, a sense of separation persisted. CTS took control of Studio One and the projection rooms, while De Lane Lea mainly operated in Studio Two, Studio Three and the remix room. Even in the studio's restaurant the two groups congregated at different ends.

Chapter 9

The Music Centre and Clients

As time progressed, the bustling workload caused the differences to dissolve. The studio was renamed "The Music Centre," and it began to attract a great deal of film work which brought welcomed prestige but it was the rock bands that generated substantial revenue, booking studio time for weeks or even months at a time.

The work involved to record an orchestra for a few hours was disproportionate to the income generated. Prior to the session it would require assembling as many staff as possible, including the office workers, to set up microphones, music stands and headphones for up to 130 musicians. A typical film session would run from 10 a.m. till 1 p.m. then a break, from 2 p.m. till 5 p.m. Then another break and perhaps 7 p.m. till 10 p.m. This would continue for just a few days.
Compare this to a band booking several months at a time with a lot less setup involved and it is easy to see where the real income came from.

It's worth noting that the merger with CTS not only breathed new life into the studio but also united disparate realms, cultivating a fusion of talents and methodologies that ultimately played a pivotal role in the studio's remarkable achievements.

I recently requested Louis Elman to review and provide feedback on the content above, here is his response:

I'm truly appreciative, Kenny. You're the first person who's spoken candidly about the situation. Whenever I've had the chance, I've mentioned that while it was an honour to have the credit of recording a Bond film and alike, it didn't bring us any financial gains. Our real success came from our 'pop' work.
And, of course, there was the memorable experience of having Paul McCartney in Studio One overdubbing Wings over America, for ten months. I still vividly recall John Richards complaining to me that he couldn't get into Studio One to record any music for movies! I responded with a resounding - GREAT!!!!

Under the guidance of Louis Elman, the Music Centre thrived, brimming with an abundance of projects. Although he might not have been well-versed in the technical intricacies, he excelled in personal charm and charisma, these qualities allowed him to build strong rapport with clients, ensuring their satisfaction and repeat business. He was also astutely aware of the need to generate significant revenue to satisfy the Board of Directors, after all they had entrusted him with the task of turning the complex into a profitable venture.

He was a shrewd negotiator with a balanced approach, forging deals wherever possible, ensuring fairness whilst also securing excellent terms for CTS.

One notable arrangement was struck with Don Arden, the owner of Jet Records.

Louis and Arden agreed on a fixed price for a block booking in Studio Three over the course of a year. Louis recognised that receiving the full payment from Arden might be a challenge, so he built a cushion into the deal. The price he gave Arden was 30% higher than Louis would have normally quoted and he still managed to persuade Arden, a somewhat tricky customer, to accept it.

Another innovative agreement struck was with Kevin Metcalf who managed the disc cutting room. Louis outlined a weekly revenue target for Kevin to achieve, allowing Kevin to retain any earnings surpassing that benchmark. This arrangement motivated Kevin, who often hit his target within just a few days, frequently working six days a week.

Louis didn't stop at internal dealings; he also utilised the vacant office space on the upper floors of the building by renting it out to small record companies.

This symbiotic relationship encouraged these companies to book studio time while also providing additional income for the Music Centre.

The Sting

In 1973 Jack Fishman returned from his time working in America, he was bubbling with excitement about a new movie he had watched called *The Sting*.

This film prominently featured the tune "The Entertainer" by Scott Joplin and Jack was overflowing with enthusiasm for both the music and the movie.

He embarked on a mission to secure the music rights for Europe, but regrettably, his efforts ended in failure.

Undeterred, he hatched a new plan. He reserved studio time at the Music Centre and extended an invitation to composer Roy Budd, whom he was managing at the time, to join him. The task: to perform and record their own version of Marvin Hamlisch's rendition of "The Entertainer."

For reasons of his own Roy opted not to have his name credited on the single so Jack being ever resourceful, devised an alternative pseudonym: The Ragtimers. With this clever workaround, Jack moved forward and arranged the sale of the track with a swift release on Pye Records.

Scott Joplin, the original composer, had passed away for more than half a century, rendering the title free from copyright restrictions, thus accessible for anyone to utilise.

For Jack's rendition of the recording, the writing credits displayed the names Joplin and Fishman, diverging from the original Joplin and Hamlisch credits found on the American version. Interestingly, he chose to publish the work through Leeds Music, this seemed a bit peculiar at the time, given that Jack had his own publishing company.

His version of the record was unleashed to the public and swiftly ascended the charts.

The American company, poised to release their version of "The Entertainer" with Marvin Hamlisch in conjunction with the movie, were taken aback to witness Jack's entry into the charts with his own version. What startled them further was that Jack's rendition had claimed a share of the writing credits without any reference to Hamlisch whatsoever.

This discovery left them seething with anger, prompting them to initiate legal proceedings against him only there was a major problem. They found themselves suing Leeds Music, a publishing company, ironically, that they themselves owned.
This was an outcome clearly not in their favour. Faced with limited alternatives, they ultimately had no choice but to pay Jack his full royalties.

Buoyed by the outcome of this, Jack proceeded to create an entire album of Joplin instrumentals. This album, released by Pye Records, enjoyed resounding success. Several months later, Jack made an ingenious decision. He penned lyrics for the instrumental album he had already produced and ingeniously added singers onto the existing recordings he had previously sold to Pye. Subsequently, he resold the same album to Pye once again, effectively executing a clever manoeuvre that can indeed be likened to a "sting."

The Electric Light Orchestra

ELO is a renowned rock band hailing from Birmingham, England. By the mid 1970s, they had achieved substantial commercial success, solidifying their position as one of the most prominent acts in the music industry.
Throughout their initial 13-year span of producing music and touring, they achieved remarkable success, selling in excess of 50 million records across the globe. Their accomplishments include receiving 19 CRIA awards, 21 RIAA awards and 38 BPI awards. Between 1972 and 1986, they managed to secure an impressive 27 Top 40 UK singles and an outstanding 15 Top 20 hits on the US Billboard Hot 100.

At the helm of the band's creative efforts is the accomplished musician and songwriter, Jeff Lynne. His contributions as the frontman and leader have been instrumental in shaping their distinctive sound and no doubt contributing to their enduring popularity.

In early February 1974, Louis Elman, informed me that Jet Records had reserved studio time for The Electric Light Orchestra to work on their new album. Dick Plant, who had previously engineered for them was unavailable due to another commitment, consequently Louis asked me to begin the recording process.
I had to remind Louis that I was getting married and going on honeymoon on February 16th.
To my surprise, Louis assured me that everything would work out. He explained that Dick would complete his ongoing session and then take over. So, in February, I commenced the recording sessions for an album that would eventually be titled *Eldorado;* I started by capturing the fundamental elements of the songs, including drums, bass, guitars, piano and guide vocals.

The band members consisted of Bev Bevan on drums, Michael de Albuquerque on bass, Richard Tandy on keyboards with Jeff Lynne on guitar, piano, vocals a fair share of ego. I think Jeff Lynne would probably be the first to say he was difficult to work with and I would certainly be the second.

The group was a talented and easy-going bunch, except for Jeff, who I found challenging to connect with during the sessions. Building a rapport between an engineer and an artiste takes time and Jeff had already developed this dynamic with Dick Plant on their previous album so his initial reservations were understandable.

The first day of recording was dedicated to perfecting the drum sounds, a meticulous process that required patience and experimentation. We employed various techniques, such as taping cigarette packets and small pieces of sponge to different areas of the snare drum, along with masking tape and clothing around the toms. After rigorous testing, we achieved a drum sound that everyone agreed sounded great, particularly Bev Bevan.

Jeff, always keen to experiment, suggested a technique that involved placing the overhead microphones around four feet away from the kit, then recording a stereo track doubling up the drum track, which created a distant ambient drum sound.

While Jeff was thrilled with the outcome, the rest of us were less enthusiastic about the altered drum sound. Despite our reservations, this technique was implemented on every track we recorded.

During the recording process, Jeff would lay down guide vocals, often singing melodies with slurred nonsensical phrases interspersed with the occasional sporadic lyric.

As an example, the original guide lyric for the chorus of "Laredo Tornado" was simply "I'm dying."

These initial stages of working with Jeff's non-lyrical vocalisations over ambient sounds left the tracks sounding rough and unpolished.

The absence of the exquisite string arrangements and captivating choral contributions from Lou Clark made the album sound like a collection of crude demos. Even Don Arden, who visited the studio during playback, expressed his displeasure after hearing a few tracks and left in disgust.

Simultaneously, a feud was brewing in the music press between Jeff Lynne and Roy Wood of the band Wizzard and ex-member of ELO. Jeff's negative comments about Roy, which I read in those articles, did little to endear him to me.

Bassist Michael de Albuquerque's retrospective interview with ELO fan and writer Martin Kinch summed up the situation well. He noted that the *Eldorado* album felt like Jeff's earnest attempt to find a new direction amid intense pressure. The album struggled to find its footing due to several factors, including high expectations and various external pressures.

Listening to the finished album playback, I noticed that there was no reverb used at all but there was plenty of echo on the vocals. The mixing technique was quite dry which showcased the instruments' textures. Despite the efforts of Lou Clark and John Richards in adding orchestral and choral elements, to me the album still felt like a bunch of unfinished demos.

Interestingly, once the album was released in the USA, it achieved platinum status, with Don Arden proclaiming it a masterpiece.

Revisiting the album, I had a newfound appreciation for its remarkable drum sound and the innovative recording techniques applied to all the instruments. I had to admit that, in this case, Don Arden and Jeff were right - it was a masterpiece.

Over the years, my personal feelings about Jeff Lynne have been overshadowed by his incredible talents as a record producer and songwriter. His ability to create and produce some of the most acclaimed pop recordings in history is undeniable.

As with many artistes, personal dynamics during recording sessions can be complex, but the end result often stands as a testament to their craft.

The Weird and Wonderful

David Carradine, briefly explored a music career, but his true claim to fame was his remarkable acting prowess. His most respected portrayal was that of Kwai Caine in the popular 1970s television series, "Kung Fu."

Despite his extensive work in television and cinema, nothing could rival the unparalleled success he achieved as Kwai Caine.

Carradine was no stranger to troubles, frequently finding himself entangled in various legal matters, often connected to substance abuse.

In 2003 a new generation of viewers discovered Carradine's talents through Quentin Tarantino's *Kill Bill* films, reinvigorating his career.

Tragically, in 2009, while in Bangkok working on the movie *Stretch,* Carradine was discovered lifeless in his hotel room, hanging from a rope in the closet. Initial speculation pointed towards suicide, but subsequent investigations, including two autopsies, determined his cause of death to be accidental asphyxiation.

When asked about the most captivating artiste I've ever collaborated with, the challenge lies in selecting just one from a multitude of intriguing personalities.

Although I would say that, David Carradine unquestionably stood out as a formidable contender and my experience with him in the studio ranks among the most peculiar I had ever encountered.

Back in 1974 my knowledge of Carradine was primarily confined to his immensely popular television series, "*Kung Fu.*" I had no inkling of his capabilities as a singer-songwriter; thus, it was quite the revelation when Jet Records scheduled a recording session with him at the studio.

As an ardent admirer of the TV show, I initially perceived Carradine as possessing an undeniable star quality even before our first meeting.

Although I only worked on a couple of the sessions for this album, as each one unfolded, that initial impression gradually dwindled.

Typically, during the initial days of a recording session, a certain rapport with the artiste begins to take shape. Unfortunately, with David, this usual process did not unfold, even his producer struggled to engage in meaningful conversation with him.

Occasionally, one would pose a question to him, only to receive no response at

all or, occasionally, a completely unrelated assortment of words delivered in an uninterested, monotone voice. I distinctly recall him responding to a perfectly ordinary question with the enigmatic statement, "Everyone's three degrees."
I had no idea what he was talking about and to this day it still remains a mystery, But I did feel sure it wasn't a reference to Sheila Ferguson and the Three Degrees.

Although the sessions were most peculiar throughout, the zenith of eccentricity was reached when David requested the services of five session musicians - a flautist, a violinist, an oboist, a trumpeter and a saxophonist.
On their arrival, David assumed his place at the piano and informed everyone that there would be no customary run-through or rehearsal for the song. There would be just one take and that was it.

Before we commenced recording, each instrument was assessed individually to ascertain the correct recording level. No sheet music was provided for the session musicians, just to compound matters, David refused to divulge the song's key.
The concept he proposed was simple: once the multi-track recording was underway, he would begin to perform and the musicians were instructed to play whatever they felt in the moment. The expressions of trepidation on the faces of those musicians were truly a sight to behold.

As the red recording light illuminated, the producer made the announcement, "Take one - tape's running." As Carradine began to play and sing, it swiftly became apparent that he was the sole individual in the studio privy to both the song and the key. The resulting cacophony of these unguided instruments was beyond imagination.

The ensuing four minutes felt like an eternity, marked by moments of complete harmonic disarray. At one point, the producer turned to a colleague and remarked, "He's completely lost it."
After this interminable ordeal and with the last notes reverberating from the piano David turned to the producer and asked, "How was it?"
With all the politeness he could muster and completely dodging the question, the producer responded, "Come in and have a listen." David and the bewildered musicians then made their way into the control room. Listening to the playback of the song proved to be even more agonising than the recording process itself. As the track finally concluded, a sense of mortification enveloped everyone in the room, except for Carradine.
The room fell into an eerie silence, with David sitting motionless, fixated on the floor, not uttering a word. Breaking the uncomfortable stillness, the producer, in a composed tone, declared, "Well, David, that's it for the ensemble, we should release them and move on to something else."
A collective sigh of relief surged through the room as the musicians returned to the live room to stow their instruments away.

In a somewhat surreal moment, one of the musicians re-entered the control room, clutching a piece of paper and a pen. With due reverence, he approached Carradine and politely asked if he might be willing to sign an autograph for his son but David seemed to gaze right through him, as though he were invisible. Without a word, he abruptly stood up and exited the room, leaving the man standing there, holding his piece of paper.

It remained uncertain whether David's indifference stemmed from his disappointment with how the track had turned out, falling short of his expectations, or if it was an expression of his profound weariness with the fame brought about by his portrayal of Kwai Chang Caine.

Thankfully the ill-fated track never found a place on the album, as it was considered totally unusable.

On the final night of the recording sessions, a few guests arrived to partake in a playback of the completed album. To everyone's delight, the playback was well-received and for the first time since the outset of these sessions, there was a genuinely euphoric atmosphere in the control room.

Considering that this might very well be my last encounter with Mr. Carradine and bolstered by a touch of Dutch courage from a couple of glasses of wine, I summoned the audacity to embark on the seemingly impossible mission of coaxing a smile from him.

I asked David whether he was aware of the origins of the name for his TV show *Kung Fu,* he said nothing and fixed me with a bemused expression but I pressed on.

"You see, at the start of each episode, there's that dramatic sequence where several spears are hurled at you, but you skillfully deflect them," I began, leaning into the story. "Now, rumour has it that during rehearsals, one of those spears actually struck you in the chest and you said, - what Kung Fu that?"

Everyone in the room roared with laughter, except for David Carradine.

A few weeks later, I was taken aback when I read the news that he had been arrested in Los Angeles for attempted burglary and malicious mischief. The peculiar twist to the story was that he was found in a state of undress and under the influence of drugs.

Bing Crosby

In the summer of 1975, within the walls of the Music Centre in Wembley, a remarkable event unfolded, Bing Crosby and Fred Astaire were collaborating as a duet on an album.

There was an air of uncertainty surrounding Bing's reputation for being challenging to work with in the studio, but this was swiftly dispelled during their time at the Music Centre. Here is a glimpse of the Bing Crosby I had the privilege to encounter.

During a break in recording, Bing embarked on the short journey from the studio to our in-house restaurant for a well-deserved lunch. Just outside the studio, Peter Wilson, a member of the studio staff, was engaged in a phone conversation with his mother. It was her birthday and he was partaking in the time-honoured tradition of sharing birthday wishes with his dear old mum.

As the studio was playing back the recording it could be heard clearly from where Peter was telephoning. He held the phone aloft so that his mother could hear Bing's glorious voice resonating from the studio's speakers, evidently, she was an ardent fan. Unbeknownst to Peter, Bing was approaching, with a gentle curiosity, Bing inquired, "Who's that on the phone?" Peter, perhaps a touch nervously, replied, "It's my mother, it's her birthday today."

Responding with a wink and a warm smile, Bing took the phone from Peter and with such grace and kindness, he proceeded to sing the remainder of the song directly into the phone, serenading Peter's mother from afar.

As the final notes of the song trailed off, Bing simply offered, "God bless," and handed the phone back to a bewildered Peter.

Overwhelmed and nearly rendered speechless by the surreal encounter, Peter managed to find his voice and exclaimed, "Mum, THAT was Bing Crosby!"

This extraordinary and impromptu gesture by Bing showcased his genuine and kind-hearted nature, leaving an indelible memory for Peter, his mother and anyone who has the privilege of hearing this heart-warming tale.

Fred Astaire

After completing the duet album with Bing Crosby, Fred Astaire decided to extend his stay at the studio by an additional week to work on his own solo album.

Amid this productive period, Fred received heart-wrenching news - his mother had just passed away back at home in the USA. Despite this profound loss, Fred remained steadfastly committed to his work and obligations, including completing his solo album and fulfilling various scheduled TV interviews.

A tribute to his professionalism and dedication during this challenging time.

During a quiet moment over lunch in the studio restaurant, Fred shared a poignant memory of his mother, illustrating his enduring bond with her. He recounted a tale from 1957 when he had written a song titled "Life is Beautiful" The song had been recorded and sung by Tony Bennett and was poised for release as a single. As the songwriter, Fred received a copy of the finished recording from the record company.

Filled with pride and anticipation, Fred sent the record to his mother in Philadelphia, eager to hear her reaction. After a few days, he made a call to inquire, "Mum, what do you think?" Her response was uniquely motherly and laced with affection. She exclaimed, "Fred, it's marvellous! How on earth did they get your voice to sound like that?" Mums can be so wonderful.

Tommy Boyce

Tommy was an American musician who gained widespread recognition primarily for his association with the Monkees and his creative collaboration with Bobby Hart. His initial claim to fame as a songwriter came with the track *"Be My Guest"* for Fats Domino.

In 1961, he ventured into song writing alongside Curtis Lee, co-authoring hits

like "Under The Moon Of Love" and "Pretty Little Angel Eyes," both produced by the one and only Phil Spector.
The year 1964 marked a pivotal moment in Tommy's career as he joined forces with Bobby Hart, yielding their first joint success with Chubby Checker's "Lazy Elsie Molly," followed swiftly by Jay and the Americans "Come A Little Bit Closer," a top ten hit later the same year.

In 1966, Boyce and Hart took on a unique project, recording demos for the pilot episode of a ground-breaking TV series called *The Monkees*. This innovative concept, envisioned by TV producers Bert Schneider and Bob Rafelson, aimed to cast a rock 'n' roll band that would star in their own weekly television show. To fulfil this vision, Schneider and Rafelson placed an advertisement in Variety magazine, seeking four talented young men who would become the band's members.

Ultimately, the auditions led to the selection of Michael Nesmith, Peter Tork, Davy Jones and Micky Dolenz, all of whom played pivotal roles in the band's success. Contrary to a rumour, Charles Manson was not among the auditionees who were rejected during this process. Manson, notorious for dabbling in song writing, did gain some notoriety when The Beach Boys and Guns 'n' Roses recorded songs he had penned.

Boyce and Hart were subsequently hired to compose songs, record backing tracks and sing the guide vocals for the Monkees' first album, imaginatively titled *The Monkees*. Then the vocals of Davy, Micky, Peter Michael replaced Boyce and Hart's original guide performances and the backing vocals were all performed by Boyce and Hart. Boyce and Hart's partnership thrived, resulting in the creation of over 300 songs and the sale of more than 42 million records.

I was introduced to Tommy Boyce in 1975 at one of those typical, euphoric gatherings in the music industry where everyone mingles, hoping for that ultimate accolade - recognition.

Tommy, a handsome silver-haired gentleman with a youthful countenance, had the unmistakable aura of success and I was well aware of his remarkable accomplishments as both a producer and songwriter. Our initial meeting was pleasant and we quickly found ourselves engrossed in conversation about his three favourite topics; music, songs and girls.
Before long, during this introductory encounter, Tommy asked if I would be interested in engineering his next project. I readily shared my studio's contact information, always open to the prospect of collaborating with new and accomplished clients, especially someone of Tommy's stature.
Little did I know that over the next few years, I would embark on a journey of learning, laughter and occasional exasperation with this remarkable individual The insanity I encountered in my career, working with other artistes, paled in comparison to the wild, mercurial genius of Tommy Boyce.
A few weeks later, Tommy arrived at the studio with his new partner, Richard Hartley, a highly talented musician who possessed the polar opposite

characteristics of Tommy himself. Richard was quiet, unassuming and seemed almost motionless in comparison to Tommy's vibrant and dynamic persona.

Tommy, in his role as the producer, had a distinctive approach to our recording sessions. As we delved into the work, it quickly became evident that Tommy relished the privilege of his position, often guiding me to employ unconventional microphone placements, sometimes straying from the norm. He paid meticulous attention to certain sounds while remaining relatively unconcerned about others. Once he was content with the setup, Tommy transformed the session into a lively spectacle. He would spend the remainder of our time in the control room, frequently indulging in air-guitar performances, briefly interrupted to convey instructions to the musicians or myself. It seemed as though he couldn't sit in a chair for more than a few moments during any of our recording sessions; he was perpetually in motion.

I made a critical blunder during our initial run-through when I adjusted the master volume midway through the recording. Tommy's reaction was swift and forceful. He exclaimed, "Kenny what the fuck are you doing?
Never alter the volume once the track has started. How am I supposed to tell if the feel of the take is right?" His dedication to capturing the perfect take was unwavering.

Tommy carried a small bag with him, which he would leave in a corner of the studio. Every hour or two, he would retrieve a different shirt or top and swap it for the one he was wearing. When I asked him about this peculiar habit, he simply replied, "Kenny, I'm just changing my mood, man, just changing my mood." It left me pondering what I had got into with this unique and enigmatic producer.

Tommy employed a meticulous process when recording lead vocals. He took on the role of a coach and director, scrutinising every single syllable delivered by the artist. Afterward, he typically joined the backing vocalists to add what he fondly referred to as his "magic touch."

On occasion, he preferred to handle all the backing vocals himself and I was sworn to absolute secrecy regarding the secret behind achieving the distinctive Boyce block vocal sound.
Now, after 45 years, I am confident that he wouldn't object to me revealing his secret.

With each vocal overdub, Tommy had a unique ritual. He would squeeze his nose, producing a peculiar nasal sound, before shifting his position around the microphone for each harmony take.
When finished, he would proudly declare, "See, Kenny, it sounds amazing, even better than the Beach Boys." His enthusiasm was infectious.

Tommy also had a penchant for playing percussion on the tracks but recording his percussion sessions proved to be quite a challenge, particularly when it came to the tambourine. When I asked Tommy to strike the instrument to set the correct recording level, he would stand still and hit it in a conventional manner. But, as soon as the red light came on and the music started, he transformed into a whirlwind, dancing around like John Travolta on acid, tossing the tambourine into the air and executing spins while catching it.

Once he returned to the control room to listen to the playback, Tommy would question why the tambourine's volume seems to fluctuate. Explaining to him that his stage techniques didn't translate seamlessly in the studio was a bit tricky.
Over the next few takes, I learned to closely monitor his every movement while recording, adjusting the microphone fader accordingly when he moved away from the microphone. Coupled with some heavy compression across the track, I managed to satisfy Tommy and myself with the end result, even if it required a bit of studio wizardry.

Mixing a track with Tommy was unlike any other mixing session I had encountered before. We meticulously scrutinised each line of the song individually, playing it repeatedly until Tommy was satisfied it sounded precisely as he envisioned. Afterward, we painstakingly edited each line together. On average, mixing a three- or four-minute song consumed a staggering 18 hours of our time.

With the mix completed around five or six in the morning, I would then proceed to "top and tail" the stereo quarter-inch tape. This involved adding red leader tape after the fade-out at the end and green leader at the front, after removing any extraneous noise, including the drummer's count-in.
This was a trivial task and only necessary to prepare the tape for delivery to the disc cutter.
The first time I performed this task for Tommy, he inquired, "What are you doing?" I explained that I was cleaning up the beginning of the tape. Tommy's response was succinct: "Kenny, please don't fuck with success!"

About three weeks later, Tommy contacted me to express reservations about the mix. He explained, "I'm not satisfied with the third line in the last verse, I want to redo it." This was a time before mixing desks had any form of total recall or digital memory, which would have allowed us to revert to a previous session effortlessly. No one had ever made such a bizarre request before but I thought it seemed like a reasonable proposition until we returned to the studio.
For hours and hours, I struggled to recreate the previous mix, but eventually, I had to admit to Tommy that it was an insurmountable task. Achieving the exact same balance, echoes and compression on this one line and seamlessly inserting it back into the song to make-a perfect match, was virtually impossible.
"Kenny, what are you telling me? Same tape, same desk, same studio, same engineer." He seemed to have a point so I persevered working on through the night.

During the early hours, Tommy had drifted off to sleep. I woke him up to listen to the line I had just inserted. As his eyes opened, he stared at me with an expression that would have made even the Devil pray. "Kenny," he uttered,

"Don't ever do that again. Jane Fonda was just going for my zipper."

It was moments like these that made it impossible not to love this guy.

Remixing that one line took nearly as long as it had taken to complete the original mix.

One Friday afternoon, our recording session had concluded and we were waiting for a taxi to transport Tommy back to London. We discussed the remix we were set to begin on Monday morning. As Tommy's cab arrived, I jumped into my car and we both left the studio.

While I was navigating my way through the near-standstill Friday evening traffic relieved to be on my way home, I glanced into my wing mirror only to spot Tommy exit his cab and sprint down the middle of the road toward me. Fearing something dreadful had occurred, I quickly lowered the car window.

As Tommy approached, slightly out of breath, he exclaimed, "Kenny, on Monday, when we reach the end of the song just before the fade, I want to lower the acoustic guitars and boost the percussion. Have a great weekend, see you on Monday." He then casually strolled back through the traffic to re-join his waiting taxi. Naturally, by the time Monday rolled around, Tommy had changed his mind once more.

On a late Saturday evening, Tommy phoned me at home, he said it was urgent and was filled with panic about a track we had completed several weeks earlier. He insisted that we absolutely had to redo a single line in the second verse before he cut the master on Monday morning at De Lane Lea.

With all the vigour I could muster I attempted to dissuade him, but with his customary charm, Tommy persuaded me to meet him at the studio on Sunday afternoon to re-record that particular line.

We began the painstaking process at 2 pm. I made every effort to match and insert the new ten-second piece of music, a task that would consume the next 13 gruelling hours before Tommy was ultimately satisfied. Afterward, we played the track from start to finish over and over for about an hour, while Tommy danced exuberantly around the room. But just when it seemed we had reached a resolution, he uttered those dreaded words, "Kenny, I don't like it. Put it back as it was."

I looked down and realised that the small piece of tape I'd removed from the original mix had fallen from the side of the tape machine and onto the floor. It was hidden amidst a chaotic jumble of discarded tape fragments from our numerous attempts throughout the night. Worse still, the tape had been stepped on, rendering it unusable.

Breaking the news to Tommy was far from pleasant, I tried to explain that only one of us had been dancing around the control room that night and it certainly wasn't me. After he calmed down, I managed to locate the original piece of tape, but only one half of it was salvageable so I couldn't use it. I asked him if he still had the copy tape I had given him when we first mixed the track a few weeks prior. He responded, "Yeah, it's at my flat in London."

We decided on a new plan: Tommy would take a taxi back home, retrieve the tape and bring it back to the studio. I would then copy the one line from it and insert it back into the original master tape.

After Tommy left in the cab, I reset the desk and tidied up the control room, preparing it for the next session scheduled for 10 a.m. Tommy returned to the studio around 6 a.m. with the copy tape and by 7 a.m. I had replaced the original line, completing the task.

For the next hour, we played the track repeatedly. To my astonishment, Tommy said, "No, I don't like it I've changed my mind. Put the new line back." My heart sank when I realised that the new line, we had spent 14 hours remixing, was crumpled on the floor, but this time, it was my own inadvertent misstep that had damaged it.

Given that I had reset the desk during Tommy's absence, there was no way to redo the line without investing another 14 hours. Tommy's reaction went beyond ballistic. People were now arriving for the next session and we would have to vacate the studio soon.

We reluctantly agreed that the only solution was to use half of the line from the tape he had danced on and the other half of the line from my accidental mishap. It was now 9:30 p.m. and the track was pieced together with these compromised edits. Tommy took the master tape down the corridor to the disc cutting room. Exhausted and disheartened, I went home to bed, silently vowing to myself - never, never again.

I had been asleep for about an hour when my wife entered the room to wake me, informing me that Tommy was on the phone and needed to speak with me urgently. I picked up the phone, ready for anything.

To my surprise, Tommy was shouting excitedly down the phone, his words were filled with praise for the track. He described it as a masterpiece and expressed his eagerness to return to the studio with me to complete the album. We indeed went on to have many more sessions, each one as extraordinary as the last, which was the essence of working with Tommy Boyce.

The last time I saw Tommy was in a bustling part of Mayfair. We were walking toward each other and as we drew near, he casually asked, "Kenny, how are you, man? Wanna try my jacket on?" It was a black windcheater with "White Rock" printed on the back, the title of a documentary for which Rick Wakeman had composed the music. I put it on and asked Tommy how he was, "Fine, fine! The jacket looks great man" and without another word he just walked away. I never saw or spoke to him again.

Sometime later, I learned that Tommy had left the UK and moved to Memphis then on to Nashville where he met and married Caroline. I cherished many wonderful moments with Tommy. Socially he was the same as he was in the studio, always hiding behind the mask of Tommy Boyce, making sure he was the centre of attention, forever performing. As far as I am aware, no one was ever offended by this trait.

Tommy was one of a kind, a wonderful fascinating character and a great talent. Although at times he could drive me to the edge of insanity, I miss him to this day; I loved him dearly.

I wanted to capture the time I spent with Tommy, without understating or exaggerating who he was. So on completing my story, I contacted Caroline Boyce and asked her if she would be kind enough to read through my text and said if she wanted anything changed, to let me know. I told her I would not publish if she was unhappy in any way.

I was so overwhelmed when I received Caroline's endorsement, which confirmed I had captured the essence of Tommy.

Caroline's reply:

Hi Kenny "OH MY GOD ... You had me laughing out loud as it wasn't hard to visualise this at all; he was exactly like that in real life too and would give you the shirt "literally" off his back ... life was magical, exciting and a performance and it was wonderful to experience the world through his eyes.
This touched me sooooooooooooooooo much; well written really capturing the essence of Tommy ...
Thanks so very much for sharing this with me. I absolutely loved reading it and it brought back some funny and super fond memories of Tommy; he truly was one of a kind with a giving heart that surpassed anyone's I've ever known.
He is so sadly missed so thanks for helping to keep his memory and legacy alive.

Jim Webb

With a host of platinum selling songs, Jim Webb's compositions have been performed by legendary artistes such as Frank Sinatra, Elvis Presley and Barbra Streisand. Among his notable hits are timeless classics such as "Galveston", "By the Time I Get to Phoenix" and "MacArthur Park".
A testament to his exceptional talent, he holds a unique distinction in the music industry as the only artiste to have received Grammy Awards in three distinct categories: music, lyrics and orchestration.

Webb had reserved Studio One for an ambitious recording session, set to feature a grand orchestra comprising approximately 130 musicians. While such an arrangement would typically proceed smoothly, a minor complication arose when a new Neve mixing console was still in the process of being installed in the control room just hours before the session was due to commence.
Webb had a specific vision for the session: he requested that no sound separation screens be positioned between the instruments, aiming to capture a Phil Spector-style sound that relied on the close interaction of all musicians.
For the morning session, the instrumentation line-up included two drummers, four bass players, six guitarists, three pianists and five percussionists. Their objective was to rehearse diligently in preparation for the arrival of the full orchestra, accompanied by a choir of 30 members, scheduled for the afternoon session. The entire rhythm section had been brought in from the USA and were

being compensated at the American musician rates. The sole exception to this arrangement was Englishman Nigel Olson, who also served as Elton John's drummer.

The engineer initially booked for the session fell ill unexpectedly the night before, leading to Dave Hunt being called in as the replacement.
Dave felt slightly uneasy about his late calling to the session so, given our extensive collaborative history, I asked if I could assist him. He readily agreed seeing as I had substantial engineering experience.

Jim Webb had requested Robin Cable, an engineer he had previously worked with at another studio, to oversee the recording. When Dave inquired if Robin would like to take charge of the session, Cable declined, citing his unfamiliarity with both the mixing console and the studio although he still wanted to be seen as actively involved despite his obvious shortcomings in orchestral recording.

During his inspection of the setup to ensure that we had adequately mic'd the instruments, Cable experienced a moment of panic when he stood in front of the brass section. While examining the trumpets, trombones and other brass instruments, he exclaimed, "Why haven't you mic'd the French horns?" I responded, "Robin, if you look closely, you'll see that they are indeed mic'd." It dawned on me that he wasn't aware that French horns are mic'd from the rear, confirming my belief in his orchestral inadequacies.

The rehearsals commenced at 10 a.m. with the rhythm section. It appeared that Jim Webb had extended invitations to witness the recordings to everyone from his extensive network. As the hours passed, the control room was steadily filling up with people, notably his sister, tirelessly trailing him, capturing every moment with a large video camera perched on her shoulders.
At 1:30 p.m. the full orchestra and choir arrived but, due to the absence of any sound separation between the instruments, the situation quickly became chaotic.

With two drummers providing a thunderous rhythm, it was, with all due respect to Dave, a less than ideal sonic experience.
Dave attempted to communicate with Webb about the issues, but the lively party atmosphere had completely taken over and he got no response, it seemed that Dave was on his own.
Occasionally, when we did attempt to record something, Robin Cable would quickly chime in over the talkback microphone, announcing "take one" or "take two," seemingly to ensure that Webb would perceive him as actively involved.
Ironically, the control room seemed even more populated than the studio housing the 130 musicians plus the choir members.
The scene in the control room was far from what one would normally expect.
People were everywhere, sitting cross-legged on the floor, laughing and joking, smoking joints, sipping champagne and relishing the lavish spread of food that had been provided. It was increasingly difficult to believe that we were actually supposed to be working a serious recording session.

Each time Webb made his way up to the control room for a playback, more and more friends arrived in the room, this would spark yet another break as everyone engaged in a meet-and-greet session. Looking down at the studio during these breaks, you could see that the musicians had abandoned their positions to chat with acquaintances on the opposite side of the room.

When Webb eventually returned to the studio, it would take at least ten minutes to coax everyone back to their seats and resume the recording process.

Around 6 p.m. the esteemed Derek Taylor, the head of WEA Records, arrived accompanied by Harry Nilsson, but we still hadn't managed to record anything worth keeping.

Derek Taylor, a colleague I had collaborated with on a couple of occasions before, was one of the most pleasant individuals you could ever wish to encounter. He had solidified his reputation in the 1960s as the Beatles' press officer and had subsequently become a prominent figure in the music industry.

Regrettably, even with Derek's arrival, the session showed no signs of improving. The crowd of onlookers and revellers were far too much of a distraction, so once Derek joined in, Dave and I decided we may as well join in the festivities as well.

Since there was an open bar in the lounge, rather than taking advantage of the free drinks, we approached the bar manager Ted and I asked him to transfer our existing tab over to Mr. Webb's account, which he kindly did.

As the scheduled session was booked until 10 p.m. and with still nothing of value recorded on tape by 9:30 p.m. Derek and Webb engaged in a friendly argument about who would foot the bill for an additional three-hour session, I believe Derek emerged as the victor in that debate.

When the session finally concluded at 1 a.m. we had managed to capture only two pieces of music on tape.

Robin Cable took these recordings away to mix at another studio but for me and the staff the ordeal was far from over. As each musician departed the building, they were required to complete a blank cheque at the reception desk, a process that consumed an additional two hours.

Several months later, we received the disheartening news that both recordings from that session had been discarded. During the 1970s, such wastage and extravagant spending were not uncommon in the music industry. Many engineers bore witness to the creation of albums that incurred substantial expenses but were never released.

In this particular instance, it appeared that the session had been driven by pure ego and indulgence on the part of Mr. Webb.

Delben Music

In the mid 1970s, Louis Elman continued his ambitious plans for the studio's future and came up with the idea of launching a new production division called Delben Music. To help with this venture, he had enlisted Ben Nesbit, who had recently retired from his role as the managing director of Feldman & Co Music Publishers.

Although I found myself incredibly busy working as an engineer at De Lane Lea Studios, in whatever spare time I could find, I dedicated myself to song writing and collaborated with anyone willing to join in. My perseverance led to a few single releases under various pseudonyms and my work caught the attention of Louis Elman, the managing director.

I was thrilled to be offered the role of a talent scout by Louis. I would be responsible for discovering promising new acts for Delben Music alongside my primary commitment as an engineer for the studio.

Delben Music launched an extensive advertising campaign in Melody Maker, which was the best-selling music weekly paper at the time. The headline boldly proclaimed; *Do you think you have got what it takes to be a star?* This was followed by an invitation to; *contact Kenny Denton*, along with a dedicated studio switchboard phone number and the postal address of the studio.
The response was overwhelming. As soon as the ad hit the paper, the phone lines were flooded with inquiries and in the days following, we received a deluge of mail. There were hundreds of letters that arrived each week and I would diligently sift through them, occasionally discovering an act that I believed had the potential for a successful audition.

Sham 69

One of the first phone calls I received was from a young man named Jimmy Purcey. I informed him that he needed to provide a demo tape before we could consider scheduling an audition. He told me that they didn't have a demo tape.
Jimmy's enthusiasm was so infectious and the name of his band, Sham 69, held a strangely appealing quality. His confidence left such a strong impression on me that despite the lack of demos, I decided to allocate him the three-hour studio time for an audition.
These auditions also presented a valuable opportunity for our young tape operators to gain experience in recording artistes in a less pressured environment. I would oversee the setup and offer guidance on microphone placement, compression and general recording techniques.
For this particular session, I opted to have Rafe McKenna serve as the engineer. Rafe had worked with me on numerous sessions as my tape assistant and I trusted his capabilities for this audition.

The band arrived on time, which was arguably the most professional aspect of their entire visit. Once they were set up, we began to run through the only song in their repertoire. Unfortunately, it quickly became apparent that the whole performance was, in a way, a "sham," and I could see where they had drawn inspiration for their band name.

The biggest problem was that it seemed impossible for all the band members to start playing together right after the drummer's count of four. Time after time I would hear the drummer shout "One, two..." and the guitar would come in, or "One, two..." and the bass player would jump in early. After about 15 minutes of this disarray, I decided to intervene.

I made it clear that I didn't care what happened after the song began, but I insisted that the whole band should, at the very least, come in at the same time.

I instructed Rafe to rehearse the intro repeatedly until they managed to synchronise their start. I told them that I would come back in about an hour or so to check on their progress.

When I got back to the studio, I was genuinely amazed to find that the band had successfully learned to begin the song all together. Unfortunately, that seemed to be the extent of their progress. As I listened to a complete run-through of their song, I was left utterly speechless by what I heard. It was painfully evident that even a six-foot cannon placed three feet in front of the band, couldn't have hit anything worth saving.

I called the singer, Jimmy, into the control room and pointed out, "The bass player, he can't play a thing."

Jimmy responded with a shrug, "I know. He's only got little fingers and can't reach the notes."

I had to be honest with Jimmy. I explained that I believed the band needed several more months of intensive rehearsal and that simply owning and holding instruments didn't magically make them play well.

After an excruciating three hours, we managed to salvage something resembling a recording. Rafe mixed the track and we provided the band with a couple of copies. As they departed, we wished them the best, not expecting to ever hear from them again.

To my surprise, it was less than a year later that Polydor Records signed the band and Sham 69 entered the charts with their first of several hits.

Rafe would go on to have a very successful career as an engineer and producer, recording artistes such as UB 40, Wishbone Ash, Foreigner, Bad Company, 10cc, Wet Wet Wet and Big Country to name just a few.

Koffee n Kreme

Among the numerous letters that would arrive each day, I received an exceptionally professional package from an individual named Christy Lee, who managed a duo known as Koffee n Kreme.

Unbeknownst to me at that time, Christy had been a singer and along with her band The Beat Chics, had the privilege of supporting The Beatles on their 1963 inaugural tour of Spain.

Koffee was Lance Ellington and Kreme, Beth Hannah, both had excellent voices and they both looked really good.

Lance was the son of Ray Ellington, a popular singer, drummer and band leader throughout the 50s and 60s.

I contacted Christy and asked them to come in for an audition.

Being pleased with the results, I invited Ben Nesbit and Louis Elman down to the studio to listen to the tracks and introduced him to the duo and Christy.

Both Louis and Ben saw gold with this clean-cut, good-looking duo with a positive pushy manager and so quickly offered them a recording contract which they all duly signed.
We then set about making a single. We chose a Neil Sedaka song called "My World (Keeps Getting Smaller Every Day)".
I had Lou Clark, the renowned string arranger for ELO, to write the parts for the rhythm section and orchestra track.
At the same time, Louis made a deal with the notorious Don Arden. owner of Jet records to release the single on his label.
Don Arden was an English music manager, agent businessman. He managed the careers of rock acts such as Jerry Lee Lewis, Little Richard, Air Supply, Small Faces, The Move, Black Sabbath and ELO.
Legend has it that in 1966 Arden and a squad of "minders" turned up at impresario Robert Stigwood's office to "teach him a lesson" for daring to discuss a change of management with the Small Faces.
This became one of the most infamous incidents from the 1960s British pop business. Arden reportedly threatened to throw Stigwood out of the window if he ever interfered with his business again.
It's evident that Don Arden was an uncompromising and shrewd entrepreneur. The Small Faces achieved remarkable success with 14 hit singles and five hit albums in the UK, as well as commercial recognition across mainland Europe, Australia and New Zealand. According to Ian MacLagan the band's keyboard player they were only earning £20 a week and never received any compensation from record sales or concert performances.

Christy managed to get an audition for Koffee n Kreme on the primetime Saturday night newcomers TV show, *New Faces*. *New Faces* was a British variety television talent show that first aired in the 1970s with guest panellists Tony Hatch, Danny La Rue, Clifford Davis and George Elrick.
Koffee n Kreme, appearing in their first show, managed to win and went forward to the Gala Final in April 1977.

It was Saturday night and time for the Gala Final, the all-winners show. As each act finished their performances the judges presented their scores. It was an extremely close contest between Koffee n Kreme and one other act.
It was all down to Tony Hatch whose score would be the casting vote, it would be left to him to make the final decision.
I was aware that "the Hatchet", as he was known then, had taken the duo, Lance and Beth, out to lunch earlier that week during rehearsals, in an attempt to lure them away from us to his own production company.

I sat with Louis in the studio audience in anticipation as it came to Tony Hatch and the final score.
I remember thinking that if he didn't score highly for Koffee n Kreme, I would contact the newspapers and make them aware of his failed act of subterfuge

earlier in the week, revealing his low score being due to sour grapes.

I couldn't believe it, I was thrilled as "the Hatchet" gave them a high score and said, "I think they have an enormous future and they will go on to make it BIG." Tony Hatch helped them win by 28 points. I know we were biased but we really thought they deserved to win, not only were Lance and Beth great talents, but they were extremely nice people too.
The excitement of the night followed through to the next day, Koffee n Kreme were on the front pages of all the major newspapers, Lance and Beth were the top story of the day.

Don Arden had arranged a lavish champagne reception in several adjoining suites at the top of the Hilton Hotel in Park Lane, to celebrate the win and to launch their new single. The rooms were packed with press, special invited guests and plenty of hangers on.
During the reception my wife, Sue, turned to me and asked "What does Don Arden look like?" I explained "He hasn't arrived yet, but imagine an English "Don Corleone" from the movie *The Godfather."*
Shortly after arriving, Sue spotted him straight away. He strolled into the room with both hands in his trousers pockets looking every bit as intimidating as his reputation hinted at.

During this really wonderful, over the top, bash I noticed Lance, Beth and Christy Lee disappear with Don Arden into a side room. A short time later they all returned to the main reception.
There was a distinct change in their facial expressions, they appeared so optimistic and happy in the last 24 hours but there was a definite change.
I found out the following day that Don Arden had told Christy Lee that he would be taking over the management of the duo.
Much to Don's surprise, as diminutive as Christy was, she was tough as nails and there was no way she was going to stand down as manager and let Don take over.
I'm not sure she was aware of the Robert Stigwood story but I really don't think that would have made any difference. She had worked so hard with the duo for a very long time and they had become great friends.
She also had a firm contract plus, of course, the full support of Lance and Beth.

Don was furious, he had achieved a huge amount of success in his career and was very used to getting his own way.
As the head of the label he said, "no management contract - no release" and that he would bury the act, lucky enough not literally, despite his notorious reputation.
Koffee n Kreme's career peaked on the Saturday night and was over within 24 hours, they disappeared from the limelight faster than a politician's promise after election night.
Sadly, Beth passed away at a very young age, but happily Lance went on to have a very successful career, something he rightly deserved. He worked with many artistes including Sting, George Michael, Gloria Gaynor, Michael Jackson and Robbie Williams he also made regular performances on the BBC programme *Strictly Come Dancing*.

Strange Letters

I would often receive quite fascinating letters from individuals seeking an opportunity to audition at the studio. These correspondents ranged from genuine hopefuls to those who were clearly barking mad. Among the most eccentric letters I ever received was one penned by an individual that went by the name Deodorovic Smith.
In this letter, every line was meticulously adorned with words written in a kaleidoscope of colours, creating a rather unique visual experience.
It went something like this:

Dear Esteemed Sir or Madam,
Enclosed herewith, you will discover a tape featuring my twosome gruesome horror-themed compositions, namely "Blood is for Vampires" and "Phobia and the Beast" I have chosen to unveil this sinister duo to you before reaching out to the influential figures in London's prestigious W1 district.
I must humbly request your forgiveness for the somewhat tremulous vocal delivery in the final verse of "Phobia and the Beast." Regrettably, my recording session was interrupted by my daughter, who, with impeccable timing, decided to swing open my wardrobe door whilst I was in there recording my vocals, taking me completely by surprise.
I am eagerly anticipating the moment when you recognise my undeniable talent and offer me a well-deserved opportunity.
Sincerely, Deodorovic Smith"

I didn't take this any further.

Dr Feelgood

Hailing from Canvey Island in Essex, Dr Feelgood were a prominent rhythm and blues band renowned for their exhilarating live performances. Throughout the 70s they enjoyed notable success with their much-lauded live album *Stupidity* topping the UK charts in 1976.

On August 26th, 1976, my close friend Vic Maile, a skilled producer and engineer, reserved Studio Two for a week to remix a live album he had recently recorded with Dr Feelgood using the Manor Mobile recording studio.

Vic had previously produced their albums, *Down By The Jetty* and *Malpractice*. It was decided their third album would be recorded live at the Southend Kursaal in Essex, for this the band felt they only required Vic's engineering expertise.
Whilst reviewing the tapes before the band's arrival, Vic discovered a significant mishap that had occurred during the recordings: he had inadvertently selected the hi-hat microphone to record across the entirety of the drum tracks. This was a critical error, as when we listened to the individual drum tracks, all that was audible was the overwhelming sound of the hi-hat. The studio had recently acquired a new device called an ADM noise gate, designed to rectify minor issues like this, but the situation surpassed its capabilities. Consequently, Vic used his

skill in EQ adjustment to slightly mitigate the problem.

During the first few days of the project, we overdubbed and rectified various aspects of the recording such as vocals, harmonica parts and guitar solos. Vic then set about mixing the album in his own distinctive style.

Once the album was finalised and the band had left the studio, Vic and I sat back and began chatting. It was clear that he was deeply disappointed by the outcome of the mixes due to the hi-hat mishap.

Despite my attempts to reassure him, Vic, being the perfectionist he was, remained unconvinced. He believed that the mixes had the potential to be far superior.

Vic was certain that the album would be met with negative reviews in the music press and would fail to sell. He assumed that everyone would hold him accountable for any perceived downfall of Dr Feelgood.

However, when the album was released in September and reached the number one position on the UK album charts just a month later, the outcome was entirely different. The Melody Maker's review of the album praised Vic's remarkable live recording technique and specifically highlighted *"the crisp clarity of the hi-hat within the energetic rock 'n' roll fusion of sound."* This unexpected success provided a gratifying turn of events and Vic's concerns about the hi-hat mishap were ultimately overshadowed by the album's triumph.

Lee Marvin

An American film actor renowned for his distinctive gravelly voice, striking white hair imposing six-foot-two stature, Lee Marvin left an indelible mark in the world of cinema. Over his career, he graced the screen in more than 50 movies and also made notable appearances in various TV shows.

In March 1970, Marvin achieved an unexpected milestone when he soared to the number one spot in the UK charts with "Wand'rin' Star*"* from the movie *Paint Your Wagon*. Remarkably, the single maintained its top position for three weeks, temporarily eclipsing even the Beatles from the coveted number one spot.

His co-star, Jean Seberg, eloquently described Marvin's voice as "like rain gurgling down a rusty pipe," a fitting characterisation for the distinctive and unforgettable sound that set him apart in the world of entertainment.

In 1976, I received a last-minute booking for a session with this renowned actor. It all began when Jack Fishman called me at home the night before, informing me that Marvin was in town for an appearance at the Sun Newspaper Awards. Jack asked if I could be at the studio by 9 a.m. the following morning.

Our task for the day was to overdub a vocal on a song titled "O'Reilly's Daughter*"* which Jack was producing for the movie *Shout at the Devil*. Marvin's availability was limited to just three hours that morning due to his other commitments.

I arrived promptly, ensuring that the microphone was set up and the tape was ready to roll. Jack, known for his punctuality, was at the studio well before Marvin's scheduled arrival.

Around 9:30 a.m. the imposing figure of Lee Marvin entered Studio Two's control room.

He appeared dishevelled and clearly still inebriated, likely from the previous night's revelry or perhaps an early morning tipple. Nevertheless, he retained every ounce of his movie star presence.

Before any formal introductions, his slurred voice reverberated off the control room walls, exclaiming, "Before I can do anything, I need a Goddam coffee!" We did have a standard coffee machine with plastic cups in the studio, but given the circumstances and the fact that we were dealing with a movie legend, albeit a somewhat inebriated one, it was decided to place a call to the bar upstairs and have a pot of coffee brought down on a tray with proper cups and saucers.

After a short while, one of the bar staff arrived with the coffee it happened to be a lovely elderly Scottish woman, somewhat short and stout, affectionately nicknamed Mac by the studio employees.

Mac had recently joined the bar staff and wasn't accustomed to the typical clientele that frequented the studio. Whenever she encountered someone famous, she was completely starstruck. As she walked into the room and laid eyes on Mr. Marvin, she realised who he was and nearly dropped the tray.

In an instant, she transformed into a giggly schoolgirl, making it quite a challenge to get her to leave the room.

Eventually, Marvin stood up and opened the control room door for her, expressing his gratitude for bringing the coffee. Mac was utterly overwhelmed by the experience.

As the door closed behind her, Marvin turned to us with a mischievous smile and remarked, "Well! You've gotta be nice, she's the only thing worth fucking around here." Jack's expression shifted to one of pure disgust, clearly disapproving of Marvin's comment.

We eventually began our work, a painstaking exercise considering the circumstances. Jack was seething with anger over Marvin's arrival at the studio in such an intoxicated state.

During a short break, Jack inquired about the recording of "Wand'rin' Star." Marvin's response shed light on a costly and arduous process. He explained, "That recording cost me a fucking fortune. The director, Joshua Logan, decided that, as I couldn't get it the way he wanted, I had to go into the studio and record the vocals every morning. This went on for months until he was finally happy with my vocal and refused to pay for the studio time himself, so it was taken out of my fee."

Considering the results we were achieving in our session, I had a hunch that Jack might be contemplating a similar approach as Joshua Logan.

The session concluded as scheduled and Marvin departed. Jack and I then embarked on the task of piecing together a composite from the various takes to create an acceptable version of the song. It was apparent that Jack didn't hold Marvin in high regard, but for me, those three hours provided a wonderful opportunity to observe a true-life movie legend in action.

Tony Wilson and Hot Chocolate

Tony, the founding member of Hot Chocolate originally hailing from Trinidad, immersed himself in the world of music starting at the tender age of 16. He embarked on his musical journey as a member of the Soul Brothers, a group that introduced three notable singles to the world. His musical career reached a pivotal moment when he co-founded Hot Chocolate in 1968, although he later departed from the band in 1976.

My first encounter with Tony occurred roughly a year prior to his departure from Hot Chocolate.
I must emphasise that Tony Wilson stands out as one of the most amiable, humble and exceptionally gifted individuals I've had the privilege to collaborate with. Despite any conflicting reports on his age elsewhere, Tony is set to celebrate his 88th birthday this year. He currently resides contentedly in Trinidad alongside his partner, Delia and we maintain a regular and cherished line of communication.

In the late 1960s, Tony took a leap of faith and relocated from Trinidad to London, hoping to try his luck in the music industry. During this time, he resided in Brixton, South London where he, along with a couple of friends, dabbled in song writing and dreamed of forming a band.

I happened to live in Kennington, near the Oval cricket ground, during those days, which makes me wonder if our paths ever crossed back then. Tony later confided in me that he used to frequent the cricket matches at the Oval. Whilst I never ventured into the cricket grounds myself, I was a regular presence, diligently cleaning cars for a shilling each with my trusty bucket and chamois leather.

As Tony ardently pursued his music career, fate led him to the accomplished record producer Derek Lawrence. Meeting Derek presented a golden chance for Tony to break into the music business.
Derek possessed a unique talent for discovering artistes, although many of them managed to slip through his fingers.
His connection to Ritchie Blackmore earned him the opportunity to produce the first three albums of Blackmore's new band, Deep Purple.
During the 1970s, I also had the chance to collaborate with Derek on several occasions. He was more of a character-driven producer rather than a musical one. He had a habit of propping his feet up on the recording desk and regaling us with inflated stories from his time in the industry, rather than providing substantial musical input during sessions.
Derek occasionally embellished his connections in the industry, a fact that became apparent when he promised Tony that he would finance some studio time for Tony and his bandmates, with the intent of playing the recordings for his good friend John Lennon at Apple.

When the band arrived at the studio, Derek was conspicuous by his absence. Undeterred, they decided to record their own rendition of Lennon's hit "Give Peace A Chance." Lawrence, after hearing the recording, was less than thrilled, but the band hoped it might make a lasting impression on Lennon. He continually made excuses, suggesting that Lennon was out of the country and the recording was left to simmer on the back burner.

Tony and his friend Errol, who served at that time as the band's part time roadie embarked on a journey to Apple's office at 3 Savile Row in London, armed with their recording and a dash of hope. They knocked on the door, uncertain if anyone would entertain listening to their tape.
To their astonishment, around 15 minutes later, they found themselves sitting in an office with none other than John Lennon and Yoko Ono. John played their tape and was intrigued but asked, "Why did you change the lyrics?" Tony explained that they couldn't quite decipher the original lyrics from the hit single, so they improvised their own.

John Lennon, with a smile, inquired about the band's name. Errol responded, "We don't have one." Lennon smiled and suggested, "Go and get a coffee and ask one of the girls in reception to come up with a name."
Tony and Errol obliged, went from the office and shared John's request with one of the secretaries.
The young lady took a good look at them both and proposed the name "Hot Chocolate." They returned to Lennon's office shortly thereafter. Lennon and Yoko liked the name but suggested adding the word "Band" to it, thus giving birth to the name The Hot Chocolate Band.
Errol's recollection of the meeting may indeed differ slightly from Tony's, possibly because of any embarrassment he may have felt about their unannounced visit to Apple.
In Errol's version of events the reason they went to Savile Row was to seek Lennon's permission to record a cover of "Give Peace A Chance". But, of course, no permission was ever necessary.
The precise details of this story may vary between accounts, but the essence remains a chance meeting that led to the birth of the band's name and their connection to John Lennon.

In a surprising turn of events, John Lennon extended an invitation to Tony and Errol, proposing that The Hot Chocolate Band perform their rendition of "Give Peace A Chance" at an upcoming gig for The Plastic Ono Band at the Lyceum Ballroom in London. This offer left them both in a state of apprehension, as it was the only song they had to perform.
John reassured them by saying, "There are several other acts on the bill so you'll just have to do the one song." Despite their nervousness, they reluctantly agreed to take the opportunity.
Their rendition of the song was eventually released on Apple Records under Cat No 18.

Sadly, this collaboration would prove to be short-lived, as internal disputes within Apple Records eventually led to the breakup of The Beatles and the closure of Apple itself. Consequently, The Hot Chocolate Band, along with the rest of the Apple artistes, found themselves in search of alternative recording deals as the chapter with Apple came to an end.

Fortuitously for the band, Micky Most was on the lookout for talented artistes and swiftly signed them to his RAK label, but with a notable change, he dropped the word "Band" from their name.

This strategic decision would prove to be immensely successful for the group, as they went on to achieve a remarkable ten hit singles with Tony and Errol gaining recognition as prolific songwriters for other artistes. Their song writing prowess extended well beyond Hot Chocolate, with their compositions being covered by notable artistes such as Mary Hopkin, Herman's Hermits and Julie Felix.

Tony initially took the lead vocals on their first hit single, "Love Is Life" and again in 1974 on the single, "You'll Always Be a Friend" but it soon became clear that Micky Most's aim was to gradually shift the spotlight towards Errol, positioning him as the frontman. This gave the impression that Hot Chocolate was merely the backing band for the primary artist, a dynamic that persisted until Errol's departure from the band in 1985.

The hit "You Sexy Thing" had an interesting journey from its recording to becoming the classic it is today. Surprisingly, Micky Most initially didn't recognise its potential and released it as a B-side to Hot Chocolate's single "Blue Night".

As fate would have it, "You Sexy Thing" eventually gained massive popularity. But even though the band's royalties had now increased, Micky Most made the dubious decision to continue paying them the same lower royalty rate that they had earned when they first recorded the song. This decision likely left the band feeling somewhat short-changed given the song's immense success and enduring popularity.

Tony's frustration within Hot Chocolate stemmed from a disconnect in artistic vision. While Micky Most's focus was primarily on creating and selling straightforward pop records, Tony felt that the band was capable of producing more substantial and serious material.

In Tony's perspective, the early hits he co-wrote with Errol truly came into their own when Harvey Hinsley, although sadly uncredited, contributed those memorable guitar riffs. These riffs added a distinctive and instantly recognizable Hot Chocolate sound to each song, elevating them beyond typical pop music and contributing to the band's unique identity.

Tony likely saw these musical elements as an essential part of Hot Chocolate's artistic expression, which may have clashed with Micky Most's commercial-oriented approach.

Tony made the significant decision to part ways with Hot Chocolate and pursue a solo career. He signed with Albert Grossman's USA Bearsville record label. In this new venture, he extended an invitation to the band's rhythm section to join him, but they opted to stay with their stable situation at RAK Records.

Micky Most's influence continued to be felt throughout the band's history. When Errol left RAK in 1985, the remaining members of Hot Chocolate expressed their desire to find a replacement singer and continue under the Hot Chocolate name. Unfortunately, Most was not interested in carrying on without Errol, recognising that a significant part of the band's appeal had departed.

Nevertheless, Micky did allow the band to part ways amicably and agreed to let them continue using the Hot Chocolate name, albeit at a cost of £10,000. This arrangement left the band with little choice but to agree, ensuring that they could carry on their musical journey under the name that had become synonymous with their music.

Bearsville Records

Albert Grossman is a legendary figure in the music industry, his name is widely recognised, even though he maintained a low profile avoiding the publicity and hype often associated with other record company executives. His impact on the music world was profound.

Grossman had a multifaceted role, ranging from his position as an original director of the Newport Folk Festival to overseeing the careers of major artistes such as Bob Dylan, The Band, Peter, Paul & Mary, Janis Joplin and Gordon Lightfoot.

His contribution to the music scene was further solidified when he established Bearsville Records. While overseeing the record company and related operations, he also played a pivotal role in creating and nurturing an artistic community, attracting talent to the local area. His ability to recognise and cultivate talent made him a respected and influential figure in the music industry and his influence continues to be felt in the world of music.

Recording Tony's debut album, *I Like Your Style* in 1976 at De Lane Lea Studios in Wembley proved to be a complex task.

The project initially involved using the rhythm section from Hot Chocolate, this stirred up some complications due to the band's contractual ties with Micky Most's RAK Records.

Learning that some of the Hot Chocolate members were playing on Tony's new album, Most was understandably displeased and the threat of legal action loomed over the project. To address this a decision, he was made to re-record the entire album posing significant challenges not only in terms of cost but also time.

The initial attempt involved re-recording just the rhythm tracks with different musicians while preserving Tony's vocals, bass and various percussion parts; unfortunately this proved to be virtually impossible. As a result, our only option was to overdub some drum and percussion elements and various instruments in an effort to disguise the original backing tracks.

This complex process was undertaken to hide the original sound of the Hot Chocolate band, including the unmistakable guitar work of Harvey Hinsley. While it was challenging to entirely conceal Hinsley's guitar work, the use of various effects helped to disguise the original sound, ultimately allowing the album to move forward.

The album took a long and arduous 18 months to finish, once completed Tony and his family embarked on a new chapter by relocating to upstate New York, specifically the picturesque town of Bearsville, situated just a mile or so from Woodstock.

Bearsville was a unique place where Albert Grossman held ownership of a substantial portion of the town's properties and amenities. These included assets like a ten-pin bowling alley, the local school and the residences where his artistes and staff lived.

My family and I had the privilege of visiting Tony in this charming and artistically vibrant environment. Bearsville had a relaxed, music-oriented atmosphere making it a truly unique and beautiful place. The close proximity to Woodstock likely added to the allure of this remarkable location for Tony and his family.

Not long after my arrival, Albert extended me a job offer at his studio, with a significantly higher salary than I was earning in the UK. Unfortunately, I had to turn down his generous proposal. I conveyed my gratitude for the opportunity and explained that my wife and I held a significant concern. Given our children were still young, we were hesitant to uproot them from their family, friends and schools in the UK. Albert accepted my explanation without any objections.

During my visits to Bearsville, I had the privilege of meeting some captivating individuals associated with the record company, including Ian Kimmet, the Director of A&R and the talented artiste Randy VanWarmer.

In January 1978, Albert had extended an invitation to Ian to leave his UK employment and join him in the USA. Not long after, Randy, known for his sharp and dark sense of humour, followed suit and signed with Bearsville records.

Another notable individual I had the pleasure of meeting during my stays at Tony's place was Vinnie Fusco, Bearsville Records director of international operations and music publishing.

Vinnie was a larger-than-life character, hailing from the streets of New York. He possessed the demeanour of a bold and assertive salesman, with a voice that could easily have belonged to a member of a New York crime family.

Interestingly, Vinnie developed a strong passion for the music of Bob Dylan, becoming an avid fan. His admiration for Dylan eventually led him to a pivotal decision. After watching Albert Grossman in the documentary *Don't Look Back,* Vinnie penned a letter to Grossman, requesting an opportunity for a job interview.

In July of 1979, Vinnie, along with his new wife, Jacquelyn, arrived in Bearsville, where he enthusiastically accepted the position offered at Bearsville Records.

One Remarkable Evening

I had recently arrived from the UK to spend some time with Tony. I had brought our favourite brandy with me, unaware that Tony had also bought a bottle of the same liquor.

Tony's wife, Margaret, told me that they had invited Vinnie and his wife, along with Randy and Ian for dinner that night, unfortunately Ian couldn't attend as he had a prior commitment. She also said that if Vinnie were to ask whether I'd like to hear his wife sing, it would be wise to politely decline and suggest perhaps another time.

Curious, I asked why and Margaret smiled as she replied, "Well, he did once manage Tiny Tim, which might give you an idea."

Everyone arrived punctually, with Vinnie bringing his wife and a bottle of his preferred libation, brandy. Following a delightful dinner, we all gathered in the living room. Vinnie requested Tony to fetch his guitar so that Randy and Tony could treat us to a few songs.

With Vinnie as the centre of attention and a generous glass of brandy in hand, he urged Randy and Tony to perform a newly finished song titled "Just When I Needed You Most." It turned out to be one of the finest ballads I had ever heard. Whilst Tony and I enjoyed a modest amount of brandy, Vinnie had already moved on to his second bottle. Realising where the evening was headed, Margaret decided it was time to retire to bed.

Shortly after, Vinnie turned to his wife Jacquelyn and said, "Sing something for Kenny." My heart skipped a beat and I found myself utterly defenceless.

Jacquelyn initially declined several times, but Vinnie's persistence eventually wore her down. Reluctantly, she agreed. The room fell into hushed silence as she got down on the floor, crouched and curled up with her hands over her head, resembling a frog, which was about to leap.

Within seconds, she began to emit a series of squeals, akin to the haunting howl of a coyote. I could sense Margaret upstairs, probably laughing and thinking, "I told you to say no." Tony and Randy both had their eyes tightly shut, struggling to stifle their laughter.

This peculiar squealing performance continued for what felt like an eternity, although it was only a matter of minutes. Finally, Vinnie spoke up, saying, "Okay, Jacquelyn, that's enough, that was great."

With a swift motion, Jacquelyn rose from the floor, her arms waving in the air like a tree sprouting from the ground exclaiming, "Are you for real? I was just tuning up." To the disappointment of everyone in the room, she continued this bizarre display, resembling more of a street-art exhibition than a recognisable vocal performance.

Once Jacquelyn had concluded her unique act, an unmistakably tense atmosphere hung between her and Vinnie. She grabbed her coat and, with a venomous tone, said, "I'm going to the car, are you coming?"

Meanwhile, Vinnie was in the process of opening the last bottle of brandy and casually replied, "As soon as I finish this drink." Jacquelyn left, giving Vinnie a look that would kill.

I suddenly became the centre of Vinnie's attention as he asked me to remix a track for him at the studio. I politely declined, explaining, "I'm on vacation, I really don't want to do any studio work."

He persisted, pushing me further, until he somewhat ominously remarked, "If you don't do this, you won't get out of Bearsville alive." I replied with a touch of humour, "Well, it looks like I'm going to be here for longer than I thought."

Vinnie continued to press me, asking, "How do you want to die?" Randy spoke up, saying, "No problem there Vinnie; you're gonna bore him to death."

Recognizing how late it had become, Randy decided to call it a night, leaving Tony and me to endure Vinnie's ramblings as he polished off the last drops from the three bottles of brandy.

By this point, it was approximately six in the morning. Spotting his wife asleep in the car, we assisted Vinnie to his feet and guided him toward the kitchen door, leading to the garden where his car was parked. Vinnie insisted, "I'm fine, I'm fine," but as Tony and I stepped back, he took one step forward and two steps to the side, crashing straight into the kitchen wall, sending everything on the shelves tumbling down.

Eventually, we managed to get him to the car, waking Jacquelyn up in the process and placing Vinnie in the back. Reading between the lines, it was clear that Jacquelyn wasn't particularly pleased with him. All in all, it had been an incredibly eventful night filled with unexpected twists and turns.

The next morning, I regretted not having recorded "Just When I Needed You Most" on a cassette. So, I approached Tony and asked if he would sing the song again for me so I could make a recording and he kindly agreed to do so.

Upon my return to the UK, I took matters into my own hands and recorded two versions of the song: one with a male vocal and another with a female vocalist. Despite all my efforts, I couldn't convince anyone that this was a potential hit song.

Alan Sizer, the head of Polydor A&R, explained to me that to secure radio play with a ballad and a new artiste was notoriously difficult. Despite the setback, Randy's finished record emerged, featuring a beautiful autoharp solo played by John Sebastian from the band Lovin' Spoonful, another local musician living in the Bearsville area.

When Randy's version was eventually released and climbed the American charts, he called me to express his gratitude for believing in the song. Randy's rendition went on to sell millions of records and was covered by numerous major artistes, ultimately turning the song into an all-time classic.

Later I received an invitation to work on Tony's second album in the USA, but unfortunately, I had other commitments at the same time I couldn't accept the offer.

In 1979, I was working on an album with Bill Haley and approached Tony with a request to compose a song for the project. A few days thereafter, Tony handed me a cassette tape containing a marvellous song he had crafted, which he titled "Everyone Can Rock and Roll." Bill was enamoured with the song, leading us to use it as the album's title track.

Tony and I collaborated on various projects together until around 1995 when our paths diverged due to fate.

Approximately ten years later, we reconnected when I discovered that several of our productions were being plagiarised around the world. I am still actively pursuing a couple of record companies that have used our material without any authorisation.

Although we no longer collaborate musically, Tony and I continue to stay in touch to this day, speaking at least once a month. Interestingly, Tony now has no real interest in music or the music business but finds enjoyment in following World affairs, as well as having a passion for cricket and football, which have become integral parts of his everyday life.

For those interested in learning more about Tony Wilson's early years, there is an excellent book titled "Pop Icon: The Tony Wilson Story" written by Shawn Randoo. You can purchase the book by contacting Shawn through his Facebook page.

The Portsmouth Sinfonia

In the 1970s a group of students from the Portsmouth School of Art decided to start a rather unconventional orchestra named the Portsmouth Sinfonia. Their foundational concept was refreshingly inclusive: the Sinfonia welcomed virtually anyone who wished to participate regardless of talent or experience.

Inevitably, it drew individuals with minimal musical background and, intriguingly, musicians that chose to embrace instruments completely foreign to them. As one might imagine, this eclectic blend of members resulted in an ensemble with a distinctly idiosyncratic character.

Initially conceived as a one-time, tongue-in-cheek performance art project, the orchestra remarkably evolved into a cultural sensation over the subsequent decade, including memorable concerts, the release of LPs, the creation of a film and even a chart-topping single.

Eventually their public performances came to an end in 1979, marking the conclusion of an era for this remarkable musical phenomenon.

In 1974, I was introduced to the album titled *The Portsmouth Sinfonia Plays the Popular Classics*.

This particular album held a special place in my music collection, as it was produced by none other than Brian Eno, who also happened to be one of the clarinet players within the ensemble. It remains one of the most comically entertaining albums I've ever had the pleasure of listening to.

Surprisingly, this album proved to be incredibly versatile and valuable in certain social situations. It had the remarkable ability to elicit laughter when shared with friends, serving as a delightful source of amusement. Additionally, it came in handy for discreetly encouraging guests who had overstayed their welcome to make their exit gracefully.

Furthermore, for those times when you felt a need to test the patience of your neighbours or perhaps engage in a bit of playful provocation, *The Portsmouth Sinfonia Plays the Popular Classics* unquestionably emerged as the perfect auditory choice.

In the late 70s I was in the studio booking office at Wembley, when I overheard the secretary Miriam on the phone, she was taking a booking for a jingle on behalf of a maker of a famous box of chocolates.

By now I had a real dislike for working on jingles, I was about to beat a hasty retreat from the office, when I heard Miriam confirm to the client the details of the session.

"… so, Studio One 7 'til 10. Artist, The Portsmouth Sinfonia."

I turned around before she had finished the word Sinfonia and much to Miriam's surprise, who knew how much I disliked these mini-TV nightmares, told her, "I'll do that one please, please."

A few days later, with the studio set and ready, about 50 members of the orchestra arrived.

Once seated, they started to run through the music they intended to record.

I was desperately trying not to laugh too loud as I set about getting a recording level.

The music we were tasked with recording was astonishingly brief, lasting only a minute. Achieving the right balance took a few run-throughs. By the time we reached the third attempt, the director turned to me with a hint of impatience and inquired, "How long is this going to take?"

I explained that, given this is a 50-piece orchestra, a few more run-throughs were necessary for optimal results. He pleaded, "Please, do it as swiftly as possible, because the more they play it, the better they become."

In a matter of moments, the recording light went on and we embarked on what would become one of the most peculiar displays of dissonance I had ever witnessed.

By 7:30 p.m. the orchestra had wrapped up, packing their instruments and leaving the studio. Suppressing my amusement once more, I set to work on mixing the track by 8 p.m. we had, mercifully, finished.

This undoubtedly marked the briefest and funniest orchestral session I had ever been part of. In just a matter of days, the advertisement featuring our recording was broadcasted nationwide. Whether it contributed to the sale of chocolates remained uncertain, but for me, it was undeniably a delightful session to have been a part of.

Studio Security

During the mid to late 70s, if you happened to be working at the studio after 5:30 p.m. in the afternoon or during weekends you would encounter Albert Agras, the security guard, at the front desk. Albert was a larger-than-life, incredibly likeable character, with exaggerated features that could rival those of a cartoon character.

His most distinctive feature was his nose, which shared a similar shape but was twice the size of actor Karl Malden's. Albert had a penchant for gambling and he firmly believed he possessed unparalleled knowledge of the Universe's secrets.

If the last session of the day finished before midnight, you could bet your life that Albert would make a beeline for the Victoria Casino, where, more often than not, he'd end up losing whatever money he had with him. There was one memorable occasion when lady luck smiled on him. Returning home around two in the morning, Albert excitedly woke up his wife to share the news of his windfall, telling her that she could finally order the new kitchen she had long desired.

With the blood pumping through his veins and unable to fall back asleep due to the adrenaline rush of his good fortune he got dressed again and went back to the casino where, predictably, he lost all his earlier winnings. The next morning over breakfast, Albert's wife couldn't contain her excitement about the kitchen. She wanted to place the order right away, but Albert, deep in the abyss of his gambling losses, curiously responded, "Winnings? Kitchen? I have no idea what you're talking about. You must have been dreaming."

Donald Sutherland

Sutherland achieved fame through his roles in hit movies such as *The Dirty Dozen, Animal House, JFK* and *The Hunger Games*.

In 1979, Jerry Goldsmith was entrusted with the task of recording the music for the movie *The First Great Train Robbery* starring Donald Sutherland.

I had been in London all day and even though I didn't have a session to work on I decided to stop by the studio on my way home. I wanted to look at the schedule for the next day and check for any phone messages, as they were typically posted on the message board.

It was there I noticed the towering presence of Donald Sutherland, engaged in a phone conversation while leaning on the reception desk. As he concluded his call, I overheard Albert striking up a conversation with him.

I wasn't privy to the earlier part of their exchange, but I could now hear Albert addressing Sutherland as "Oddball" the character Sutherland portrayed in the movie *Kelly's Heroes*. With his ever-knowing and authoritative voice, Albert remarked, "Oddball, let me share something with you. Did you know there are only two types of people in this world?"

Sutherland appeared genuinely puzzled as Albert continued, saying, "Yep, BIG WANKERS and LITTLE WANKERS!" I was left utterly dumbfounded by this unexpected pronouncement and while it was challenging to gauge Sutherland's reaction, it seemed to be one of sheer bewilderment, which was entirely understandable.

Throughout the studio's history, many famous artistes had the opportunity to experience Albert's worldly-wise utterances, adding a touch of unpredictability and humour to their visits.

Stuart Taylor - Everything in moderation and plenty of it

I initially crossed paths with Stuart Taylor in the early 1970s when he secured office space at De Lane Lea while he was involved with Ralph Siegel's German label, "Jupiter Records." Our connection grew and he eventually became a very close friend and served as my manager for many years.

Stuart had been around the business for a while, first finding fame when he left Screaming Lord Sutch's backing band, The Savages, in January 1964 and joined as the lead guitar player with The Tornados.

After leaving the Tornados he went on the road, backing artistes including Dusty Springfield.

Stuart was the most loveable rascal I ever met. He managed me as a producer from the mid 70s to the early 80s and we ventured on through many projects until the late 90s, when he became too unwell to continue to work. He moved to the USA where we would keep in contact weekly until he sadly passed away on April 18th, 2005.

Stuart would truly light up the room in whatever company he was in. He would find a funny outlook in anything that occurred.

It would be impossible for me to write with the humour Stuart was naturally gifted with, but I couldn't write this book without mentioning my dear close friend for over 30 years.

Back when he was rockin' with The Tornados, Stuart and bass player Ray Randall had a genius plan for their epic road trips. Bearing in mind that this was back in the Dark Ages before motorways had been thought of and the British road network was not a smooth and comfortable ride.

They agreed that they would take it in turns on driving duties, ensuring each could catch at least some sleep and be gig-ready.

Ray would drive for a couple of hours and then wake Stuart up to take the wheel while Ray took his turn to get some shut eye. Stuart would then drive for a short while, but as soon as Ray fell asleep and his nose started composing symphonies, Stuart pulled over and went back to sleep for a bit longer. He would then wake Ray and tell him it was his turn again. Ray would happily jump back into the driver's seat to continue what he thought was his part of the journey - What a pair!

Stuart was an exceptionally good storyteller, always quick-witted with a spontaneous remark for any given situation, I have rarely met anyone who could be so funny and would regularly have me in fits of laughter.

On a coffee break during a recording for Chris Thompson, the control room was filled with great musicians, Don Airey, Gary Moore, Cozy Powell, Colin Blunstone & Mo Foster. Stuart and I were sitting at the desk when Chris went into a very long serious story about his career. The climax of the story came with Chris rather sadly saying how his mother and father never wanted him to be in the music business, never mind being successful.

The room fell completely silent when Stuart chirped up immediately with, "They must be very proud that their wish was granted." Everyone fell about with laughter.

Stuart would often throw the most unforgettable dinner parties. One evening at Stuart's house he delivered six soup starters to the table. Five of the soups were wonderful, but one was spiked with several large spoonsful of salt. Compliments were flying left and right, everyone at the table showering Stuart with praise declaring how marvellous the starter was. Meanwhile, the unsuspecting guest with the salty concoction put on their best poker face, grinning ear to ear and valiantly attempting to conquer the sodium sea. Stuart's mischievousness always left us in stitches.

Stuart possessed an extraordinary knack for unconventional ideas; I remember one Saturday evening when he phoned me with a wild suggestion. Stuart proposed signing a kid called Grant Santino to a record deal, having just spotted the youngster on the *Bruce Forsyth, Big Night TV Show,* where he had clinched the Disco Dance Championship. When I inquired about Grant's singing abilities, Stuart responded nonchalantly, "Who cares if he can sing? He can dance and he's on TV."

Despite Grant's limited vocal skills, Stuart managed to secure both a contract with him and a record deal with Polydor within just a week.

The single *Try Love* written by Hot Chocolate's Tony Wilson was released but disappeared faster than a toupee in a hurricane. Nonetheless Grant's exceptional dancing propelled him to great success.

When our wives were away Stuart Taylor and I would take advantage by having a boy's night in. This would consist of great food, a very large joint and even larger portions of alcohol along with great music, bizarre conversations and plenty of debate.

Under the influence of one of the above he once asked me what I thought a graph would look like between 1935/46 in Germany tracking the popularity of the name Adolph.

We would spend hours brainstorming a range of brilliantly bizarre ideas that seemed like pure genius in the heat of the moment but often ended up being a tad impractical the morning after.

One of these legendary brainwaves was "AWOL."

Picture this: An action-hero-style doll, complete with a cardboard box packaging adorned with a striking image of a rugged U.S. soldier decked out in battle-ready gear. These collector's gems would be selling for a cool $25 a pop.

Now, here's where the twist comes in: When you eagerly tore open the box, anticipating the glory within, you were met with absolutely nothing! Except, for a little piece of paper saying, our little soldier had pulled an epic disappearing act and had officially gone AWOL.

"Posthumous Records" was another winner. We had the idea that as soon as a major celebrity passed away, we would make a tribute record and release it in a black pinewood box cover. Arthur Askey CBE, a prominent English comedian and actor, had passed away that day–which gave us the inspiration for this magnificent idea and would be our first release. His catchphrase was "Hello playmates!" We decided to get in the studio the next day and write and record a tribute to Arthur called, of course, "Bye Bye Playmates."

As you can see, this was really strong old stuff we were toking on.

Stuart was the master of the one-liner and never hesitated to use one wherever he could.
One evening we found ourselves in a quaint backstreet café when the young waitress sweetly asked, "Would you like to see a menu?" Without missing a beat, Stuart quipped, "No need, we'll just look at the tablecloth!"

During a visit to a packed restaurant in Central London, the girl on the reception, looking around at the full tables said, "We're very busy, do you mind waiting?" Stuart replied, I'll serve the wine but I don't do food."

Stuart possessed a real mischievous sense of humour and it would manifest itself in the most unlikely of situations. In group photos, he would discreetly unzip his fly and exhibit what he referred to as his "Bishop."
I only became privy to this peculiar aspect of Stuart's humour when a close friend, who had Stuart as his best man at his wedding, recounted a discovery. Nearly two decades after the wedding, my friend noticed, to his surprise, that a framed photograph displayed prominently on his sideboard, captured a candid moment - Stuart's Bishop on full display for everyone.
Not long after, I found myself at a restaurant with Stuart and about a dozen people, predominantly friends from the music business in the USA. Following the meal, a group photograph was taken outside the restaurant and I happened to be positioned next to Stuart. As I glanced down, I observed that his mischievous Bishop was once again making an appearance.

Stuart's marriage was a loving, but at times a somewhat turbulent, affair mainly due to Stuart being reluctant to allow his wife into his chaotic financial affairs.
Regardless of the time he arrived home, whether late night or early morning, he would always make sure he got up very early to walk the dog. This was to ensure he would meet the postman and grab the bad news before it came through the letterbox.

Stuart and his wife Helen had moved into their dream house in the affluent village of Radlett, in the county of Hertfordshire.
A few days later Stuart and I were working in the studio when he received a phone call from Helen and she was furious.
She had been holding her first coffee morning with the local, slightly snobbish, housewives, when the bailiffs turned up and removed most of the furniture including the coffee table they were using. This was one issue that Stuart had missed taking care of.
Even in his low moments he could make light of the situation. After he explained how pissed off Helen was, he remarked, "Marriage - it's so long. It should be like a record contract, three years with options."

Tubeway Army

Tubeway Army, a London-based punk band, featured the charismatic Gary Numan as its lead singer and guitarist. Formed in 1977 during the heyday of punk rock, the band initially embraced the punk ethos. Nevertheless, their musical evolution led them to explore electronic sounds, eventually resulting in their remarkable achievement in May 1979 when their hit single "Are 'Friends' Electric?" claimed the top spot on the UK charts.

As the mid 70s saw the rise of Punk, an explosive new genre captivating the younger generation, it was imperative for me as a producer to explore this musical phenomenon. Stuart Taylor and I decided we should go to a couple of punk gigs to get a first-hand experience.
Unfortunately, amidst the vibrant and rebellious atmosphere of these events, we couldn't help but feel like a pair of geriatric dinosaurs, out of place among the youthful audience who were determined to challenge the industry we had been a part of for so long.

Stuart was in a business partnership with his friend Andrew Heath, who was a very successful music publisher. Andrew had recently begun collaborating with Martin Mills and Nick Austin, who were in the process of establishing an independent record label called Beggars Banquet. Interestingly, they managed this enterprise right out of their small record shop located on Fulham Road.
Beggars Banquet had just inked a deal with a band known as Tubeway Army, with Andrew overseeing their publishing affairs.
Following the release of Tubeway Army's initial single, the label was on the look out for someone to produce their second single.
Stuart, with his keen eye for talent, suggested that we attend one of Tubeway Army's performances to assess if I might be a suitable fit to work with the band. If that turned out to be the case, Stuart intended to propose to Andrew and Beggars Banquet that I take on the role of producer for their forthcoming recording.

In March 1978, Stuart and I ventured out to Dingwalls in Camden Town to catch a live performance by Tubeway Army. On arrival, we found ourselves supplementing a sparse crowd of approximately eight people.
The band was energetically playing through a set of somewhat forgettable songs. However, the thing that stood out was undoubtedly their frontman, Gary Numan.

Numan possessed an undeniable star quality. With his guitar worn low like a gun slinger, he exuded an air of toughness and confidence. His closely cropped blond hair bore him an uncanny resemblance to Heinz from The Tornados, a heartthrob of many teenage girls in the 60s.
Undeniably Numan had that all-important star quality.

Despite this, it was the drummer who stood out as the star of the band in my estimation. This young musician played with a level of excitement behind the drum kit that harked back to the early days of Keith Moon, the legendary drummer of The Who.
Stuart and I were in alignment regarding the band's potential, even though we couldn't quite put our finger on precisely what it was that set them apart. After the show, we patiently waited before making our way backstage to introduce ourselves.

The band members, as it turned out, were quite amiable and easy-going. Although the frontman, Gary, appeared somewhat reserved, the overall atmosphere was friendly and approachable.

The following day, Stuart had a conversation with Andrew about our impressions of the band.
Andrew, in turn, relayed our feedback to the record company, leading to the finalisation of a deal. I was entrusted with the responsibility of producing the band's upcoming recordings.
Given that Beggars Banquet was a small independent label, the budget allocated for the project was rather modest, akin to the cost of an expensive meal at a cheap restaurant.

I faced a decision: the choice between a small, budget-friendly studio that I was unfamiliar with, promising extended studio time at a lower cost, or the familiar terrain of Wembley. It will come as no surprise that I chose the latter. Opting for Wembley meant committing to fewer hours, aligning with my budgetary constraints. However being well-versed with and holding a certain sway at the studio, I might have creatively "adjusted" a few hours on my time sheet - a handy perk of my position. I ultimately decided to schedule the sessions for the weekend of the 15th and 16th of April. This choice would enable me to extend my time in the studio, with fewer staff members present to witness the hours I actually used.

I attended a couple of the band's rehearsals in Slough on Friday, April 7th and again on Sunday, April 9th. The camaraderie between the band members and me was growing, although Gary remained fairly introverted.

On the band's arrival at the studio, I was taken aback to discover that they had a new drummer. Gary informed me that the previous drummer had left the band due to his father's frustration at constantly having to chauffeur him to gigs.
The departure of the previous drummer was quite a disappointment, given that he was exceptionally talented.

In typical fashion, all engineers and producers begin their work by crafting a stellar drum sound. However, in this case, the drum kit at hand was only a slight improvement over the toy drum sets that delight small children at Christmas.
Despite applying every microphone technique and all the studio wizardry I had acquired over the years to record this dreadful drum kit, he stubbornly persisted in sounding like someone building a shed.
In a last-ditch effort, I asked the drummer to play a simple rhythmic pattern, hoping for a minor miracle.
As he began to play, it became glaringly evident that I was facing a significant challenge. I inquired about his drumming experience, trying not to sound too concerned. With confidence, he responded, "Not too long, but I do a Thursday night gig at a restaurant with a friend who plays the organ." My heart sank; I knew we were in trouble.
His drumming skills redefined the term "average". It was a stark reminder of an old joke:

Q: "What does an underwhelming drummer with a job say?"
A: "Would you like fries with that?"

I should mention, though, that the rest of the band, bass player Paul Gardiner and guitarist Sean Burke, displayed competence and skill that suited the music they were creating.
We eventually recorded the backing tracks for three songs: "Bombers", "Blue Eyes" and "O/D Receiver". Having recorded the backing tracks, next on the agenda was laying down the vocals, we started with "Bombers".
Now, when I was a kid, the term 'bombers' was synonymous with drugs that could fuel an exciting weekend so to gain a better understanding and confirm the song's theme, I decided to take a peek at the lyrics.

Look up I hear the scream of sirens on the wall
I see a policeman crying in the backseat of a dying Ford
Hotel waiters leave the bedrooms of stars who are far too old
And no-one ever told me that I could be so cold.

One might easily interpret these lyrics as hinting at a drug-fuelled, mind-altering experience, but I remained sceptical. To dispel any doubt, I decided to seek clarification and asked Gary about the song's meaning.
His response was simple: "Aeroplanes."
Of course it was aeroplanes, how silly of me.

I proposed to Gary that we introduce a Minimoog analogue synthesiser to our setup. I thought it could be a great tool to incorporate sound effects like sirens and aeroplane sounds into our recording. Significantly, this marked Gary's very first encounter with a synthesiser.
While I had come across accounts of how he initially got acquainted with synthesisers in other stories, this was undeniably the inaugural moment he laid eyes on and interacted with one.

Once we had the essential recordings in place, it became evident that I would require a minimum of four hours to complete the overdubbing for the tracks, bringing them to a state ready for final mixing.
On the afternoon of Friday, April 19th, I arranged for Gary to meet me at the studio. I had secured a one-hour studio slot starting at 5 p.m. booking it under the guise of a playback session. This option came at a considerably lower cost per hour, granting me an opportunity to covertly stay in the studio for the additional three hours I needed without incurring extra expenses.
Gary arrived at 4:30 p.m. and so we began the overdubbing process a little early. Around 5:30 pm. I received the news that Albert, my amiable security guard and the receptionist for the night, had called in sick. Albert was known for his relaxed approach when it came to my studio time sheet, so his absence raised some concerns.
Shortly afterward, I learned that Pat, one of the girls from the office, was filling in for Albert that evening. Given that Pat was a close friend, I decided to pay her a visit and explain what I was working on. Studio Two was conveniently just a

few steps down the corridor from the reception area. Thankfully, Pat had no objections to my plans and was understanding of the situation.

After about an hour, Pat rang the control room and in a panicked voice told me that she had just called the police. She explained that a fight had broken out during the session in Studio Three, I couldn't recall any previous incident in the studio's history where police had to be summoned during a recording session.
This alone would have been easily manageable, but Pat also mentioned that she had to notify one of the studio directors, Peter Harris, about the situation. She added that although he was at home, he might be heading over to ensure everything was under control. I, perhaps naively, assumed that, given it was a Friday night and rush-hour traffic, he wouldn't bother.
We were near the end of our session when Pat suddenly appeared at the studio door stating, "The police have come and gone and the clients in Studio Three have left. Peter arrived and asked me to go home. He'll take over phone and reception duties and lock up after the last session in Studio One, which should finish in about half an hour."
Considering that I had originally booked just an hour for a playback session starting at 5 p.m. it was clear that we had stayed in the studio much longer than planned.

With a growing fear that my improvised plan was rapidly falling apart and we might be caught, I urgently requested Pat to find a reason to remain in the vicinity. I instructed her to come inside and let us know the moment Peter left the reception area, enabling us to exit the studio discreetly without being spotted.
Our escape route was clear: we could leave through the fire exit at the back of the building. We anxiously waited for Pat to return with the crucial information. About ten minutes later, she reappeared, notifying us that Peter had just left reception and gone into Studio One.
As the Studio One session was drawing to a close, Peter would ensure that everyone had departed and would take care of locking the studio doors and other necessary tasks.

Sensing we had only about five minutes before Peter's return, I signalled to Gary that it was time to make a swift exit. I whispered, "Just follow me."
We sprinted down the corridor with all the speed we could muster, just as Mike Batt, who had been working in Studio One, emerged from the men's room. In a shocking and unexpected collision, we all slammed into each other, causing Mike to hit the floor like a plate at a Greek wedding.
We quickly helped him to his feet, apologising profusely for the unintended encounter then quickly headed for the fire exit, leading us into the safety of the car park.
At that moment, I couldn't help but wonder that choosing the cheaper, smaller less-equipped studio might have been the wiser decision.
In the aftermath, I arranged to meet Gary on the following Sunday to remix the tracks and we successfully completed the task.

On Monday, July 3rd, I cut the master recordings at Pye Studios alongside Tony

Bridge.
I must admit, I had a strong dislike for the track "Bombers," a sentiment that still lingers to this day. But I did believe that "Blue Eyes" truly captured the essence and spirit of the band during that period.

During my brief time working with Gary, I found it challenging to break through his introverted personality. It seemed to me that he may have drawn more than just vocal inspiration from Bowie.
I also recognised that he had a reluctance to be directed by anyone, including his record company. Fortunately for Beggars, this independent streak eventually led him to become a commercially successful artist.

This small label marked the inception of what has since evolved into The Beggars Group, now recognised as one of the world's largest and most influential independent label groups. I held a deep appreciation for both Nick and Martin due to their genuine passion for music and unwavering belief in their mission.

I once enquired about their artiste selection process with Nick. He explained that they would play demo cassettes in their record shop and if customers expressed interest in the music, they would proceed to sign the band and record their work. It was a straightforward yet remarkably effective approach to discovering and nurturing talent.

One evening, Nick visited me at the studio and over drinks, he excitedly played me a new record that Beggars was gearing up to release. The track was titled "I'm A Wanker" by Ivor Biggun, although its original title had been "The Wanker's Song" it was altered to *"The Winker's Song"* due to concerns that stores might refuse to stock it. The song faced a ban on UK radio, but through word of mouth it astonishingly made its way into the charts, peaking at number 68. It remained in the charts for an impressive 12 weeks, reaching its highest position of 22 on October 1st, 1978. This marked a significant achievement for Beggars Banquet Records, as it secured their first UK Top 40 hit.

Nostromo and the Theme From Alien

In 1979, I formed Nostromo - a studio-based band, with the intention of releasing a disco type single based on the theme of the movie *Alien*. Despite the single not achieving chart success at the time, it has since gained a devoted following, becoming somewhat of a cult record. It was prominently featured as the opening theme in numerous big club nights during the 80s. Following this initial release, I created two more singles with sci-fi movie themes, namely "The Black Hole" and 'The Empire Strikes Back'.
Interestingly, these singles garnered almost as much interest in their B-sides as in their A-sides. Over the years, I've received numerous questions about the band Nostromo and have come across many kind comments and amazing reviews of the recordings online, particularly on YouTube.

In mid-1979 my close friend Colin Hankins held the role of advertising director at 20th Century Fox in London. Colin graciously extended me an invitation to a preview of a film that 20th Century was gearing up to distribute, called *"Alien."* The movie had a relatively small budget and marked the directorial debut of Ridley Scott. Given budget constraints the only recognizable actor in the cast was John Hurt whose character met an unfortunate fate early in this chilling haunted house storyline, helping to keep within the movie's budget.

Before its release, no one could predict whether this film would achieve success, but without doubt it possessed the elements that could elevate it to cult status.

Colin and 20th Century offered me a modest budget to create an alternative version of the main theme for commercial radio. I eagerly accepted but opted to finance the project independently on the condition that 20th Century would provide their full cooperation, a condition they agreed to wholeheartedly.

To bring this vision to life, I enlisted the talents of Dave Lawson, a highly regarded music programmer of that era.

Dave was renowned for contributing synth sounds to the space bar scene in the movie *Star Wars* and was a true expert in the burgeoning world of synthesiser technology.

Since Dave hadn't yet seen the movie *"Alien,"* I delivered a cassette tape, containing the John Williams theme, to his production room in his North London flat.

It took about three or four hours to lay down the foundational structure of the music, followed by a couple more hours of selecting the right sounds. A few days later, we entered Studio 2 at De Lane Lea for a three-hour session, transferring the music to a 24-track two-inch tape.

At this point, I asked Colin about the possibility of incorporating some snippets of dialogue from the film into the track.

Everyone agreed except for Sigourney Weaver, whose agent demanded an exorbitant fee, a substantial percentage of the record's profits plus additional credits way beyond what was reasonable. With time constraints and a dwindling budget, I made the practical decision to personally deliver a few whispered and screamed lines, adding a cat meowing sound effect. This alternative proved to be both cost-effective and hassle-free compared to accepting Ms. Weaver's demands.

Colin graciously arranged delivery of the recording of the iconic Alien sound shrieking over John Hurt's face from the pod, a moment that was impossible to replicate and a crucial part of the film that didn't warrant any royalties or credits.

After completing the track, I shared it with my friend Alan Sizer, head of A&R at Polydor Records. Alan was thoroughly impressed and wasted no time in extending an offer.

On the same day, I played the track for another friend, Robert Lemon, who served as the head of promotion at Bronze Records. Robert asked me to hold off on accepting the Polydor deal until he could present it to the company's owner, Gerry Bron. Despite Bronze Records primarily specialising in heavy rock, Gerry was captivated by the track and the concept of an instrumental synth band. He proposed an offer with a smaller advance payment but included a guarantee of two additional singles.

Considering Bronze had fewer acts to manage than Polydor, I believed that our records would receive more attention, so I accepted their offer. In the process of formalising the deal and needing a name for the band, I settled on Nostromo, the same name as the spaceship in the movie.

Bronze Records paid £1,000 to 20th Century to use the Alien imagery on the single's cover. With the movie set to release in less than ten weeks, time was of the essence and I urgently needed a B-side. Lacking the time and funds to compose, record and mix something new, I opted to repurpose an old B-side from a track I had written and released back in 1975.

Although it had a funky vibe, I gave it a more cosmic mix and added some simple synth elements and thus, "Around the World In 80 Seconds" was born.

To bolster the promotion of the record, Bronze Records secured the Empire Cinema in Leicester Square every Thursday afternoon for a duration of six weeks leading up to the official movie release. Each Thursday at noon, a cosy room within the theatre hosted a buffet and drinks for a specially chosen audience, consisting of DJs, music press members and other invitees. This gathering was followed by an exclusive preview of the movie.

By the time the film hit theatres for its general release, I had become so familiar with it that I could effectively lip-sync the entire movie. Although the single didn't achieve massive sales, it did receive substantial radio airplay and garnered excellent reviews, much to the delight of 20th Century Fox.

As history would reveal, the movie eventually grossed an impressive $106,285,522 worldwide, transforming it from a mere cult favourite into an enduring classic.

The absence of a chart entry didn't discourage Gerry Bron in the slightest; he remained a firm believer in the band's concept. Soon after, our next musical journey led us to create "The Black Hole Single" from the movie of the same name.

The format for this recording remained largely the same, with the exception of Dave Lawson's increased fee but this time, we opted not to rent the cinema again.

The flip side followed a similar creative process, utilising a previous B-side and giving it a spacey remix treatment, resulting in "Gom Jabbar."

During that period, I crafted several versions of this track, each requiring distinct titles to distinguish them. Interestingly, years later, while revisiting some ancient tapes, I discovered my personal favourite mix, which I aptly named "Close Encounters of a Nostromo Kind".

The last Nostromo recording was to be based on a rather unappealing piece of music known as "Darth Vader's Theme" from the movie, *The Empire Strikes Back,* composed by John Williams.

Be that as it may, due to my contractual obligation to deliver a third recording for Bronze Records as well as my working relationship with Colin and 20th Century, I embarked on creating the track.

David Lawson's fees had skyrocketed and my personal aversion to the music led me to take a step back and let David truly earn his substantial payment.

His invoice paperwork sported a full keyboard at the top of the page. When I paid his invoice, I couldn't resist a bit of playful humour. I returned a copy of his paperwork to him, writing a monetary value to each note on the keyboard – £10 for a C, £5 for an A and so forth. Sharps cost an extra 50 pence. A complete chord could accumulate up to £30 each time he played one. David didn't find my joke amusing.

Gerry Bron insisted that we utilise his brand-new digital recording studio-this track. I had always relied on De Lane Lea and was entirely unfamiliar with Gerry's new studio's operation. It felt peculiar to produce a track without having any say in the arrangement or the sound, in a studio over which I had no control. In truth, everyone in the room merely stood by as the machines handled everything. This marked the definitive conclusion of my involvement with the Nostromo project, although I maintained a close friendship with Gerry until his sad passing in 2012.

The most memorable part of my involvement in these recordings was when I had the opportunity to take our six-year-old son to the premiere of *The Empire Strikes Back*. He got the chance to witness all the actors entering the auditorium; individuals he only recognised by the names of their movie characters. I'm quite confident that he was the sole child in the audience during this premiere.

After the movie ended, Colin was at the base of the theatre stairs engaged in conversation with various people. Behind him in the foyer, there was an imposing line of Stormtroopers. As we approached, he asked our son if he would like to meet the Stormtroopers.
Our son was left speechless as Colin took his hand and led him over to the line and from a distance, I observed as they graciously presented him with several gifts including the most incredible lightsaber. I can't express my gratitude enough to Colin for that unforgettable night and his wonderful friendship throughout that period.
Although none of the Nostromo records achieved significant sales, by today's standards, we would have easily made it into the Top 20.

Georgios Panayiotou

During my tenure at Wembley, I had the privilege of having an account with a nearby restaurant called The Angus Pride Steak House, which was fully covered by the studio. I frequented this establishment at least twice a week, entertaining my clients as a means to encourage them to continue to use our studios for their future projects.
At the beginning of the working week, I would reserve a table just for my wife Sue and me, often conjuring up fictional clients to meet the requirements of the studio's accounting department. A nice little perk of the job.

Most Friday nights I would reserve a table for up to six guests, treating my most cherished clients to a truly extravagant evening at the restaurant. But for really significant events such as an artiste's birthday, I would secure multiple tables and a bill to match.

As you can imagine these events earned me tremendous favour, not only with the clients, who relished the outings, but also with Jack, the owner of the restaurant. In the true tradition of exceptional restaurant owners, Jack cultivated a wonderful ambiance, ensuring that each and every one of his patrons felt exceptionally valued.

As time passed, our friendship with Jack and his wife Lesley deepened to the point where, on most nights, after the restaurant had closed and the last customers had departed, we would linger behind, drinking well into the early hours of the morning.

Now nearly everyone I knew seemed to have a family member or close friend aspiring to enter the music industry and Jack was no exception.

He approached me with a request to assist his son Georgios, who possessed a passion for singing and song-writing and harboured a deep desire to establish himself in the music industry.

Having met Georgios on several occasions, it was clear that he didn't fit the typical image of a music star. Georgios was an overweight, introverted young man with acne, often unkindly referred to by some as "Fat Georgie the Greek." Even though this was a different era, I still couldn't help finding this nickname rather cruel.

With a due sense of apprehension, I asked Jack if he could provide a cassette tape for me to evaluate. After listening to the material, taking into consideration that they were basic demos, I concluded that the songs and vocals didn't possess any remarkable qualities worth following up.

I made sure to clarify to Jack that the assessment was merely my opinion and I pointed out that, every week, the top 20 record charts featured artistes and songs that left me wondering who had signed them and why.

As a favour to Jack, I produced several copies of the cassettes and promised to share them with my A&R contacts. From that point onward, during our Friday night gatherings, Jack would proudly 'treat' us to one or two of his son's freshly completed demos.

One of my guests, who had also become a very close friend, was Sonnie Rae, a record promoter working for the highly successful Stiff Records label. Sonnie was affectionately known as "Sunshine" due to her cheerful and positive character. She held the prestigious position of being the top radio promoter in the country at that time. I approached her and requested if she could share Georgios's tape with her boss, Dave Robinson, the company's owner.

Sonnie graciously obliged, but Dave Robinson's response was reportedly, "Even with the lights dimmed low and the volume cranked up high, it's still no cigar."

I received numerous rejections from different companies, yet I chose not to share any of the casual dismissals with Jack, these responses were commonplace among A&R professionals at that time and I didn't want to dishearten him. Instead, I encouraged him to convey to his son the importance of persistence and resilience, emphasising that even the Beatles faced rejection from nearly every corner before finding a record company that believed in their music. In a world filled with record companies, all it takes is for one to become genuinely enthusiastic about your material.

After her stint at Stiff Records, Sonnie decided to venture into freelance work. Despite her impressive track record of hits, she still felt apprehensive about losing the security of a guaranteed income from a successful record label. Nevertheless, she took the leap and founded The Sunshine Record Plugging Company.

I paid her a visit at her recently acquired office near Ladbroke Grove, where she played me one of her first assignments – a single titled "Young Guns Go for It," by a new band called Wham! My initial thoughts were, it sounded decent but not remarkable. In spite of that, Sonnie's infectious enthusiasm and unwavering belief in its potential as a major hit were so convincing that I wholeheartedly encouraged her passion.

The following Friday, Sue and I were at Jack's place when he enthusiastically shared the news that his son, Georgios, had successfully secured a recording deal and was on the verge of releasing his debut single "Young Guns Go for It." Jack went on to reveal that Georgios had adopted the new stage name George Michael and the band was now known as Wham!

I was taken aback, but the shock was even greater for Sonnie when I informed her that one of the band members was none other than Georgios, the former waiter.

George, having undergone a remarkable transformation, had clearly worked with top-notch stylists, shed a significant amount of weight and received impressive dental work. He had evolved from the restaurant waiter with an unfortunate nickname into the persona we now know as George Michael.

After the band had a couple of hits, I spent several hours with Jack one evening, explaining the tricks and scams that record companies can use to camouflage royalty accounting and prevent payment to artistes. Jack grabbed a pen and paper and wrote down everything I told him. It could have been a coincidence but a few months later Wham! changed record companies.

The rest, as they say, is history, George Michael went on to sell over 120 million records worldwide.

One night after the restaurant had shut down, Sue and I were seated at the bar with Jack when he confided in us about George's desire to pursue a solo career and asked for our absolute discretion.

He proceeded to play "Careless Whisper" for us. Up until that moment, I had never been a fan of Wham! and had always associated George with his days as the chubby waiter.

Hearing the song for the first time, admittedly after a few drinks and in the late hours of the night, I still really wasn't impressed. It felt as though I was taking an elevator ride, with the music accompanying me with a soothing melody.

Sometime later, while working in Austin, Texas, I tuned in to the car radio and learned that the number one song in the USA was "Careless Whisper." It was during that moment I realised the song had transformed into a classic and the former waiter had become a genuine worldwide star.

In 1987 when I first heard and watched the music video for "Faith," I couldn't help but think it was one of the finest pop songs and videos I had ever come across. It's a testament to the old adage that "nothing succeeds like success."
Looking back, I'm genuinely glad that none of the people I shared the tape with chose to sign George. Perhaps, without the visionary guidance of Simon Napier-Bell (the manager and mastermind behind Wham!), George might have continued serving tables for the rest of his life. Success often hinges on the right opportunities and the right people at the right time.

During the late 80s, George and his cousin reserved time at my Chiswick-based studio in West London to collaborate on a track with the group known as Boogie Box High. Luckily, Ben Matthews, a skilled recording engineer, frequently worked at the studio when he wasn't occupied with his successful rock band Thunder. This stroke of luck meant he was available to handle the recording for the Boogie Box High sessions.

I intentionally decided to keep my distance from the studio during those sessions because my lack of faith (excuse the pun) in George's abilities during those early days would have made me feel awkward. Plus, let's be honest, I wasn't entirely convinced I could resist the temptation to ask him to fetch me a cup of coffee!

The last few photographs I saw of George carried a profound sense of sadness. It appeared to me that, in the time leading up to his untimely passing, he had reconciled with his true self, Georgios Panayiotou, choosing to let go of the persona of George Michael, allowing it to become a part of history.

John Richards

In my humble opinion, John stands as the greatest film score recording engineer of all time. With an aura of unflappable coolness, unwavering under any circumstances, he embodied the quintessential English gentleman in every aspect, right down to his consistently flawless hair. Not only could he coax the finest sound from any sprawling orchestra, but his personality could make any client feel both serene and content. Esteemed figures such as Henry Mancini and John Barry held him in high regard.

During a break in a recording session with Johnny Dankworth and Cleo Laine, I ventured into the Studio One control room to confer with John about something. I inquired about how the session was progressing and in an unusual turn for John, he immediately launched into a playful imitation of Cleo singing, complete with whimsical vocalisations - "de da do da de dup, "Unbeknownst to John, Cleo had quietly returned to the room and was right behind him. He continued with his largely unflattering impersonation for a few more bars before turning around to

discover her standing there. With his signature cool composure, John promptly halted and said to Cleo, "Wonderful arrangement, Cleo, one of Johnny's?"
It was a moment of remarkable poise and extremely quick thinking.

Whenever I mentored young engineers, I made sure to impress upon them that knowing the ins and outs of the soundboard and microphones accounted for only half of the job, the crucial half was making the client feel at ease. In this regard, John Richards was a true master in all aspects of recording.

James Garner

James Garner, a seasoned American film and television actor, enjoyed a remarkable career spanning over five decades. With a prolific portfolio of more than 50 movies and memorable roles in television series such as *Maverick* and *The Rockford Files*, he distinguished himself as a pioneering figure who excelled in both spheres, playing a pivotal role in uniting Hollywood's grand cinema and the world of television.

In 1981 I had the privilege of being scheduled for a recording session in Studio Two alongside Gigi Garner, James' daughter. Given my profound admiration for her father I couldn't help but hope for a chance to engage her in conversation about him.
To my delight, a few days into the session, her father made a surprise appearance to check on our progress.

At that time, he happened to be in the UK for the filming of *Victor Victoria*, a new movie in which he shared the screen with Julie Andrews. Interestingly, Henry Mancini, the composer behind the film's music, was coincidentally working in Studio One right next door, crafting the movie's score with John Richards, the studio's esteemed film recording engineer.
Garner was every inch the true Hollywood icon, his commanding voice filling the room with a deep resonance, he was both charming and warm with everyone in the studio.

While we were all engrossed in the playback of his daughter's recording, it was evident that he was genuinely impressed with her performance.
During a break, as I was jotting down notes on the track-sheets, I inadvertently overheard Gigi recounting a dispute she had at the reception desk earlier with our all-knowing security guard, Albert. Gigi expressed her desire for her father to address the issue with him. Garner handled this delicate situation with his daughter masterfully.
Before approaching the security guard, he inquired about the precise details of how and why the argument had started, methodically dissecting every aspect of the story with her. It transpired that she had requested access to the phone line for a call and Albert had asked her to wait momentarily as he was arranging a cab for a client. The situation had escalated from there.
After patiently listening to the entire account, Garner kindly explained to her that he believed she might have been somewhat in the wrong and took the time to

explain why he felt that way. Eventually, she agreed with his perspective and later extended an apology to Albert.

While the recording sessions were undeniably enjoyable, the daily highlight for me was Jim Garner's arrival, typically occurring towards the end of the session. He was an easy person to get along with, insisting everyone call him Jim. It was like we had all known each other for years. There was no conceit, arrogance or ego that accompanied some of the lesser-known film actors that had visited the studios.

One night I told Jim how my young tape assistant Mark Philips, who was a wonderful, harmless but eccentric character, was aware that he'd played a part in a long running TV detective series, but had confused him with Rock Hudson.
Jimmy laughingly said, "He thinks I am that fag!"
It wasn't a well-known fact with the public at that time, that Rock was homosexual
Mark, being as unpredictable as ever, said to Garner, "Do you wanna see what a real star looks like?"
"Ok" he replied.
Mark walked to the corner of the room with his back to everyone, put on his leather jacket, turned up the collar in an Elvis style, put on a pair of mirrored sunglasses and ruffled up his hair. With his hands on his hips, he swaggered over to Garner and stopped directly in front of him in a statuesque pose.
Garner being taller than Mark, leaned down slightly to look directly into Mark's mirrored sunglasses, then running his finger across his eyebrow looking at his own reflection, Jimmy said,
"Yep, you're right, I guess that's what a real star does look like."
Everyone roared with laughter, but nobody laughed louder than Mark.

One evening, the session wrapped up ahead of schedule and the rest of the crew had departed early, as Gigi had to attend a photo session. I found myself alone in the control room, making a few phone calls, when Jim Garner walked in, wondering where everyone had gone. I filled him in on Gigi's absence and mentioned that she wouldn't be returning that night.

In a friendly gesture, Jimmy asked if I weren't too occupied, would I like to join him for a drink. I eagerly accepted the invitation and we made our way to the nearby local watering hole.
As we entered the bar, Jimmy inquired about my drink preference, but I insisted on buying the first round, sharing a peculiar story from my past when Jimmy had indirectly helped pay for my breakfast many years ago.
Baffled by this revelation, knowing we had never met before these recording sessions, he took a seat and I fetched the drinks. Jim's curiosity got the better of him and his first question was, "What's the story behind that breakfast?"

I proceeded to recount an adventure from my youth when, as a young hitchhiker with a couple of friends, we ended up in Southend-on-Sea. We used up nearly all our money on having a great time so ended up spending the night sleeping in a bus shelter.

The following morning, my friends decided to hitch back to London, but I wanted to savour a bit more of the seaside town - it felt like a vacation. The only problem was I was starving and the few pennies I had left wasn't enough to buy me any food.

Desperate, I sat outside one of the arcades. This arcade featured a machine with photos of six movie stars, each associated with a winning amount. Ava Gardner had a 10-pence pay-out, while James Garner was the jackpot at 12 pence. The machine had a flashing light behind each photo, stopping randomly on one of the pictures. If you could guess which star the light would land on, you'd win.

I watched those photos on the machine for a while, pondering what it must be like to be a movie star. Then, I noticed that the machine wasn't entirely random. There was a pattern. Every five minutes, the light would stop twice on Ava. After every second stop on Ava, the very next stop was the jackpot, James.

Taking a calculated risk, I invested a penny based on this pattern and within the next hour, I had won more than enough to treat myself to a substantial breakfast and secure a bus ticket back to London.

After hearing my tale, Jimmy laughed and said "Well, it looks like the rest of the night's on you."

The remainder of the evening was truly wonderful as we delved into discussions about movies, music and life. I mentioned one of my all-time favourite films, *Skin Game*, in which he starred alongside Louis Gossett, Jr. and Susan Clark. To my surprise, Jimmy mentioned that he had watched it for the first time in ages a few nights before on TV in his hotel room.

As we talked about music, I expressed my deep love for country music and Nashville. Jimmy casually revealed that one of his closest friends was none other than Waylon Jennings. He suggested as soon as we got back to the studio we should call Waylon, leaving me momentarily speechless.

Recovering slightly, I replied "Jimmy, I wouldn't even know where to begin in a conversation with him, but I appreciate the offer." Regrettably, today I wish I had taken him up on it.

Eventually, the evening drew to a close, leaving behind memories I would cherish for a lifetime.

Reflecting on that night, there was one more thing I wish I had asked of Jimmy and I'm sure he would have gladly obliged. It was the opportunity to record him for my answering machine message. Just imagine how amazing it would have been to have James Garner's voice on my answering machine, saying, "Hi, this is Jim Rockford. Kenny and Sue can't get to the phone right now, so please leave a message."

Little did I know, Jimmy had a conversation with Blake Edwards, the director of the movie *Victor Victoria* and recommended that I take charge of the music recordings. It was an incredibly kind gesture on his part, but it didn't sit well with the engineer at the time, John Richards.

I held John in the highest regard; he was undoubtedly the best in his field.

Assuring him that I had no intention of encroaching on his territory. I also made sure that I had alternative sessions that would allow me to decline the sessions with Blake Edwards gracefully.

Throughout my career, I've often been asked about the remarkable individuals I've had the privilege to meet and collaborate with. James Garner has always held a special place in my heart as one of the most genuine and genuinely nice people I've ever had the pleasure of encountering.

Chapter 10

Bill Haley

The Demise of Early Rock 'n' Roll

The emergence of rock 'n' roll music in the 1950s coincided with the rise of James Dean, who became a legendary figure in the youth revolution. Dean was a rebellious leader who encouraged young people to break free from societal norms and explore their individual identities. This shift in youth culture began to raise concerns for J. Edgar Hoover, the head of the FBI.
Hoover, known for his ability to influence presidents and governments, viewed this growing countercultural movement as a threat that needed to be quelled urgently. Consequently, in 1955, he made a deliberate decision to tarnish the image of rock 'n' roll and undermine the associated youth movement.

During the subsequent four years, Hoover's actions resulted in the gradual waning of rock 'n' roll and the diminishing prominence of its key figures. In 1958, DJ Alan Freed became entangled in a controversy in Boston when he uttered the words, "The police don't want you to have fun" when speaking to the audience. This declaration led to Freed's arrest and subsequent charges for incitement to riot. Shortly thereafter, he became embroiled in the payola scandal, an unlawful practice involving undisclosed payments to commercial radio stations for song airplay.

Around the same time, Chuck Berry faced imprisonment and Elvis Presley was drafted into the army. Meanwhile, Jerry Lee Lewis attempted to seize Elvis's musical throne, but his ambitions were swiftly derailed during his 1958 British tour. The media exposed a shocking revelation that Jerry Lee Lewis's wife was only 13 years old, causing public outrage.
As a result of this scandal, his British tour was cut short after only three performances. On his return to the USA, the scandal continued to escalate, leading to his blacklisting from radio and a significant decline in his music career.

Tragedy struck in 1959 when a plane crash claimed the lives of Buddy Holly, the Big Bopper and Ritchie Valens, marking a sombre chapter in the history of rock 'n' roll.
In the 1960s, notable developments occurred in the world of music and culture. Little Richard underwent a religious transformation, while Bill Haley faced legal troubles with the IRS that forced him to perform only outside the USA. Surprisingly, Haley only learned in the early 1970s that he had settled his IRS debt back in 1962.

During the 1960s, there was a shift towards a new generation of clean-cut male artists who embodied the "boy next door" image. Icons like Bobby Vee, Bobby Rydell and Bobby Darin emerged during this era, epitomising this wholesome image.
Some observers believe that J. Edgar Hoover's successful efforts to contain the

youth culture and its quest for individual identity contributed to the establishment of sensitive government operations like COINTELPRO and the CIA's MHCHAOS. These covert programs aimed to surveil and infiltrate various groups and movements, reflecting the government's concerns about social and political change during that time.

Bill Haley

Bill Haley was indeed a pivotal figure in the early days of rock 'n' roll. He achieved remarkable success and played a significant role in popularising the genre. Here are some key points highlighting his contributions:

- He sold over 150 million records worldwide, making him one of the best-selling artistes of his time.
- He is often credited as the first white artiste to record a rock 'n' roll single, "*Rocket 88*".
- He was the first artiste to popularise rock 'n' roll music, with his recording "*Rock Around the Clock*".
- Bill became the first major American rock 'n' roll singer to tour Europe, spreading this music internationally.
- He was the first to achieve the milestone of selling over one million records in both Britain and Germany.

Bill and his Comets also starred in one of the first rock 'n' roll musical movies, contributing to the cultural influence of the genre through film.
Haley's ground-breaking contributions played a crucial role in shaping rock 'n' roll and influencing countless musicians who followed in his footsteps.

Everyone Can Rock and Roll

In March of 1979, Sonet Records, a small London-based label, contacted me asking me to produce three or four tracks for their artist, Bill Haley. Despite Bill's relatively low sales over recent years, I eagerly embraced the chance to collaborate with a legend.
My first task was to get in touch with Bill's manager, Patrick Malynn. Our conversation turned out to be brief and somewhat awkward as he conveyed that I wouldn't be producing Bill. Instead, the job had been assigned to his assistant, Mal Gray, who also served as Bill's road manager. Bill had insisted that Gray oversee any recordings he made.
I promptly informed the record company about my conversation with Patrick Malynn and their response was clear; unless I produced the recordings, the sessions wouldn't proceed.
A few days later, I received a gracious call from Mr. Malynn, stating that if the record company had such faith in me, he and Bill had decided to grant me their blessing to produce the recordings.
Patrick also recommended that I speak to his assistant, Mal Gray, who knew Bill intimately and could offer valuable insight. Eager to ensure a smooth working relationship, I contacted Gray to glean any helpful advice he could provide

regarding recording with Bill.

During our conversation, Gray emphasised the importance of isolating Bill in a separate vocal booth from the band, as Bill was known to be quite temperamental, even the smallest disturbance could upset him. He also stressed the need to address him as Mr. Haley and not by his first name.
Gray went on to share several other nuances that I might encounter during the production process. At that point I began to wonder if I should have entrusted the production to someone who had a deeper understanding of Bill's personality.

The session was booked for Monday, March 26th and set to run from 3 p.m. to 8 p.m. in Studio 2 at De Lane Lea in Wembley.
Prior to the session I had only one telephone conversation with Bill. During our conversation he mentioned that he had rehearsed the material with the band, but there were no demo recordings of the songs available.

On the day of the session, I couldn't shake my apprehension about whether my producer skills would live up to the high expectations everyone had. The band, named the UK Comets, arrived with Jerry Tilley on lead guitar, Ray Parsons and Pete Spencer on rhythm guitars, Geoff Driscoll on tenor saxophone, Jim Lebak on bass guitar and Steve Murray on drums. Additionally, I had arranged for the talented session pianist Pete Wingfield to join us.

To my pleasant surprise one of the guitarists, Pete Spencer, turned out to be an old school friend of mine. We had initially met during guitar lessons at our secondary school and it had been over a decade since our last encounter. We quickly found ourselves reminiscing about the good old days.
As the session commenced, it became evident that Mal Gray had a strong influence over the band. While they were setting up, he cooperated with a friendly smile, but I couldn't shake a lingering sense of uncertainty about him.

At 2:45 p.m. Bill arrived accompanied by Patrick Malynn and Hugh McCullum, the president of the Bill Haley Fan Club. Bill's star presence and charisma were immediately apparent, radiating from his entire being.
He had a soft-spoken manner and a remarkably charming habit of addressing people by their names at the end of each phrase, making every interaction feel personal and friendly. I felt a bit foolish when he insisted I call him Bill rather than Mr. Haley. Glancing at Gray, I noticed a subtle smirk on his face.
Patrick was a flamboyant, loud character, while Hugh hardly spoke to anyone except Bill. As the session progressed, it became clear that Hugh was Haley's confidant.

After the initial introductions, we quickly moved into the first take but it was quite chaotic.
It became glaringly obvious that, apart from Bill's faultless vocals, the only true professional studio musician in the room was Pete Wingfield.
The rest of the musicians demonstrated competence, but the transition from live performances to the studio environment posed a different challenge.

Playing songs night after night on stage allowed them to work around imperfections, which often went unnoticed in live gigs but became glaringly obvious in the studio.
I faced the task of simplifying and altering each band member's part.

With every run through, the tracks gradually improved. After successfully capturing the first song, "Let the Good Times Roll Again", Bill expressed his desire to be moved into the studio with the band, saying, "I really dislike being shut away from the musicians."
It was becoming obvious that the advice I had received from Gray was designed to make me look silly. I could also see that he had a somewhat confrontational attitude - clearly he was an evenly balanced guy, he had a chip on both shoulders.

We continued to work on the next two songs, "Hail, Hail, Rock 'n' Roll" and a tricky one called "I Need the Music", followed by an even more challenging piece, "The King". Bill had a run-through of the last song before explaining that it didn't feel right for him, a sentiment I completely agreed with. Someone else provided a guide vocal and from that point on, I never played that particular multi-track again.
By the end of the first day, we had two satisfactory tracks, along with one more recording that needed further attention.

The following day, we reserved Studio 4 for backing vocal overdubs from 3 p.m. to 6 p.m. after which we would return to Studio 2 until 8 p.m. for guitar part replacements, this would continue until 8 p.m.

While we were in Studio 4, we had to take a short break to witness an interesting event.
Pickwick Sales Director, Alan Friedlander and Alan Whaley, the head of accounts for Sonet UK, presented Bill with a gold disc to commemorate the impressive achievement of 650,000 sales of his LP - *Rock Around the Clock*. This particular version of the album had been recorded in Sweden in 1968 for Sonet Records and released in the UK on Pickwick.
During the presentation, I found myself waiting in the reception area. It was then that I ran into my dear friend Dave Miller, who had been busy in Studio 1 producing a recording featuring a 100-piece orchestra.
Dave was Bill's original producer on those early recordings, including the historic rock and roll single, "Rocket 88".

During our conversation, I mentioned that Bill was currently in Studio 4. Dave's eyes lit up and he asked, "You're kidding me, can I go in?"
We entered the studio, where a Music Week magazine photographer was capturing some shots of Bill. Dave stood in quiet contemplation for a moment, gazing at Bill and then remarked, "Shouldn't Maxi Freedman get one of those?"
Bill, catching sight of Dave, inquired, "Dave, is that you?" Dave replied, "I can see you're busy; I'll catch you later," and exited the room. This brief reunion lasted less than two minutes and they never crossed paths again.
Later Bill asked me why Dave didn't stay longer, I explained that he had to rush

back due to his responsibilities in supervising the recording in Studio 1.

That evening, we completed the overdubbing and I informed Bill that I would soon remix the tracks, eagerly anticipating his feedback on the final product.

The advice I had received about Bill being difficult to work with in the studio turned out to be entirely misplaced. Nothing could have been further from the truth; his enthusiasm, involvement and warm, kind personality made the studio experience a real pleasure.

After completing his UK tour and recordings, Bill departed for a well-deserved break. flying back to his home in the USA. At that moment, I believed that may be the only time I'd have the opportunity to see or collaborate with Bill.

On the April 3rd, I finished remixing the tracks and promptly delivered the masters to Sonet. I thought I had finished but, several days later, a decision was made to further remix and replace the saxophone parts and the solo in "Hail, Hail Rock 'n' Roll", the chosen single. This session in Studio 2 was booked from 7 p.m. to 10 p.m. on April 10th.

By the April 14th, all three tracks had been sent to Bill in the USA.

To my immense delight and surprise, in early May, Sonet Records contacted me with the news that Bill was exceptionally pleased with the recording. He expressed his desire for me to join him in completing the album in Muscle Shoals.

Fame Studios

In June 1979, I set off for Fame Studios in Muscle Shoals, known for its exceptional studio musicians. to collaborate with Bill Haley. Rod Buckle, the Managing Director of Sonet Records UK, joined me on this journey to Alabama.

To my surprise, I found I was to be staying at a hotel in Huntington, a dry county with no bars, nor restaurants or stores that sold alcohol. Rod explained that Bill had struggled with alcohol in the past, making this alcohol-free environment ideal for our recording sessions at the renowned Fame Studios.

We arrived on June 25th, checked into the Howard Johnson Motel in Huntington and had a couple of days off to adjust to the time zone difference. During this time, I fulfilled a long-anticipated dream by visiting Graceland in Memphis, the cherished home of my personal hero, Elvis Presley.

On June 27th Bill Haley arrived, accompanied by his lovely wife Martha. Over the following two days, we embarked on the task of choosing the songs for the album from a vast selection of material. We were fortunate to have an array of strong options at our disposal, making the decision-making process quite enjoyable.

I had asked a couple of talented songwriter friends for contributions to Bill's album. Tony Wilson, of Hot Chocolate, penned the song "Everyone Can Rock and Roll" which eventually became the album's title.

I also asked Ronnie Harwood, a prominent figure in the world of rock 'n' roll song writing during that period he certainly delivered, crafting the memorable track 'God Bless Rock 'n' Roll' which became Bill's favourite song on the album. Later, Ronnie's career soared as he achieved recognition for penning "You Drive Me Crazy," a song performed by another good friend of mine Shakin' Stevens, who became the best-selling solo artiste in the UK throughout the 1980s.

I had aimed to record another 14 or 15 songs, providing us the flexibility to choose the very best tracks for the album. I especially wanted to record "Mockingbird Hill", originally a big hit for The Migil Five but, due to Bill's contractual limitations, we were only able to record nine titles.

Bill made it clear, saying, "We've already recorded three in England; I only get paid for 12 tracks, so I only record 12." It became apparent that this decision wasn't directed at Sonet Records in particular but stemmed from his long-standing dissatisfaction with the music industry that had treated him unfairly throughout the years.

From my perspective, the UK recordings had just one standout title, *"Hail Hail Rock 'n' Roll"* and I couldn't justify including any more inferior material on the album.

While I was content with the ultimate song selection, I did notice that Bill had opted for several tracks he had previously recorded, including "That's How I Got to Memphis", *"Jukebox Cannonball"*, *"Heartaches by the Number"* and "So Right Tonight".

Choosing familiar tracks did alleviate the pressure on Bill to learn new material in the short time we had for recording, but in retrospect, it might not have been the optimal path. Personally, I harboured doubts about the song *"So Right Tonight"* which Bill claimed to have penned for Elvis in the late 50s. To be frank I felt it was important not to end up with an album consisting of only 11 tracks due to time constraints.

Our recording sessions commenced on the 28th and we worked from 10 a.m. to 1 p.m, then from 2 p.m. until 6 p.m. We were joined by a talented group of musicians, namely Owen Hale on drums, Chalmers Davis on bass, Jimmy English on guitar, Walt Aldridge on guitar, Dave Baroni on piano, Ed Logan on saxophones and Wanda Hale contributing backing vocals and harmonica. Additionally, Chalmers Davis doubled on piano and all of these musicians participated in the backing vocals. The recording engineer overseeing the process was Mike Daniels.

While the recording sessions were enjoyable, I'd say the true highlights of the trip were the evenings spent having dinner with Bill and Martha. I would often ask Bill about his early career then I'd simply sit back and relish the delightful anecdotes he shared. It was evident that he was vividly reliving every moment of those stories as he recounted them.

Bill's Adventures

During one of our evenings together, I brought up my recent visit to Graceland, which naturally led to a conversation about Elvis. I asked Bill about the last time he had seen Elvis, he mentioned that it was in Germany in the late 50s.

It seems that during that period, Bill was going through a challenging phase in his life. At one gig he had made it clear that he didn't want anyone to come backstage for the usual meet-and-greet, this was quite a departure from the norm so it must have been a trying time for him.

After the show Bill's road manager came into the dressing room to tell Bill there was someone outside who would like to say hello.

Bill reacted angrily - "I said no one's coming back here!"

"You may wanna see this guy." The road manager replied.

Bill looked up to see the head of Elvis Presley peaking around the door.

"Hi Bill, I brought some friends who would love to meet you."

Bill immediately invited them in.

He told me how good he felt. It was clear that their reunion brought immense joy, allowing them to chat, reminisce and momentarily forget about the challenges Bill was facing during that period in his life.

I asked Bill about the rumours that he and Elvis had met in the early 70s, he told me this never happened.

Instead, Bill shared a touching story about contacting Elvis during a difficult period in Elvis's life in the early 70s. He sent a heartfelt letter to Graceland, offering his support and letting Elvis know that he would be there as an old friend if he ever needed to talk. It's unfortunate that he never received a reply, but Bill's gesture of friendship and support was a kind and sincere one.

Bill shared another intriguing story from the mid 50s when he believed he had saved Chuck Berry's life during their tour in the Southern States.

During this era, several artistes of the same genre would tour together. They would all travel on one tour bus and stay at the same hotels to keep costs down.

Chuck had a penchant for spending time with young white girls after the show leading to one rather tricky incident. After one particular show, everyone was sitting on the tour bus waiting for Chuck to get on so they could leave. After some time, they all agreed they couldn't wait any longer for him. Just as the bus began to drive away, one of the Comets spotted Chuck in his distinctive bright pink suit, white shirt and white shoes, running hastily across the parking lot toward the bus. The bus stopped to let Chuck on and he climbed aboard, clearly flustered and out of breath.

A few miles down the road the bus came to an unexpected and sudden stop, its path blocked by two pickup trucks. From these vehicles emerged several menacing-looking rednecks. Recognising that these were not friendly autograph hunters, Chuck quickly ran and hid at the back of the bus.

The rednecks began to board the bus and as the tension mounted. Haley stood up and addressed them, saying, "Hi, I'm Bill Haley. Can I help you guys?" One of the unfriendly individuals inquired, "We're looking for the n****r in the pink suit." Haley swiftly responded, "Do you really think we would let one of them travel with us?" Diverting their attention and protecting Chuck from a potentially dangerous situation.

It's fortunate that Bill's quick thinking and response managed to defuse the situation. The rednecks apologised for stopping the bus and left without causing further trouble. Chuck Berry must have been incredibly grateful to Bill for his actions, which likely saved them from a dangerous encounter. It's a testament to the camaraderie and support that can develop among musicians on the road.

Bill also shared another fascinating story involving Chuck Berry and the legendary Jerry Lee Lewis during one of the rock 'n' roll revival tours. Chuck and Jerry Lee devised a clever plan to capitalise on their popularity and address, what they felt were, years of promoters taking advantage of them.

Their scheme involved arriving at a venue and checking whose name was billed at the top. The one with the lower billing would refuse to perform, arguing that he was the bigger star and deserved top billing. The issue was easily resolved with a substantial cash payment, which they both split after the show.

This strategy continued throughout the tour, allowing them to pocket significant sums while also asserting their status as rock 'n' roll legends.

The Session Comes to a Close

The recording sessions proceeded smoothly and on Sunday, July 1st Bill left the studio to head back home to Texas. I remained behind to complete some overdubbing and create safety copies of the multi-track masters. Once that was completed, I decided to pay a visit to Nashville. Bill had kindly shared some names and contact numbers of his friends in the city and I was eager to connect with them.

As soon as I arrived in Nashville, my first call was to the legendary Porter Wagoner, also known as Mr. Grand Ole Opry. His syndicated television show, "The Porter Wagoner Show" had graced screens from 1960 to 1981.

I told Porter that I had just wrapped up recordings with Bill at Fame in Muscle Shoals and Bill had recommended I get in touch with him.

Porter wasted no time and invited me to his office on Music Row making me feel right at home from the moment I arrived.

Here I had the pleasure of meeting Carla Scarborough and their young assistant, Walter Hale. They were all part of Porter's team at the Owe-Par Music Publishing Company, partly owned to the legendary Dolly Parton.

Numerous rumours have circulated about the subject of Dolly's song, "I Will Always Love You." Interestingly, I later discovered that Dolly penned the song for Porter Wagoner.

Porter went on to introduce me to the other individuals on Bill's list, including a very pleasurable lunch with Wesley Rose. He was running Acuff Ross, one of Nashville's legendary music publishing firms owned by his father. After our meal, Wesley invited me to join him at a recording session with his friend Kenny

Rogers. I declined, as visiting a studio without working was a busman's holiday for me. Nevertheless, Wesley graciously gave me a VIP pass to the Country Hall of Fame.

In the days that followed, I experienced the warmth of true Southern hospitality. Nashville had won my heart, as the city pulsated with music and energy.

Over the course of the following month, I worked on remixing the album back in the UK at De Lane Lea. Then, on November 17th, I had the opportunity to meet Bill Haley again at The Venue in Victoria, London, where he was performing on stage with the UK Comets. It was also my first glimpse of the finished record and album cover.
I have to admit to being somewhat disappointed with David Oxtoby's artwork on the front cover.
Worse still, the back cover contained only photos and credits for the Fame musicians, with no mention whatsoever of any of the UK guys. This must have been a frustrating and unexpected oversight, considering the contributions made by all the musicians involved in the project.

Walking into the dressing room labelled "The UK Comets," I encountered a very tense atmosphere. It was clear that the band members were harbouring feelings of anger and disappointment regarding the album sleeve, but worse of all these emotions seemed directed at me. I felt about as popular as Hillary at a Trump rally.
I attempted to clarify my role, explaining that I had no involvement in the album cover design but sadly my efforts to provide a reasonable explanation fell on deaf ears. Their hurt and frustration were understandably hard to mend.
Realising I would never be asked to be best man at any of their weddings, I returned to the auditorium to watch the show.

The following Monday, Bill, the UK band and I met up at the BBC to record tracks for the Stuart Coleman Radio show.
Despite the atmosphere with the band still being a little frosty, the recordings went well.

One Great Day Out

Receiving a call from Bill the next morning to be invited to have lunch was a delightful surprise. I picked him up at his hotel in Swiss Cottage and the two of us headed into Central London. It turned out to be a truly memorable experience, just the two of us, making it the finest day I would ever spend with Bill.

During our time together, the conversation covered a wide range of subjects, including discussions about Dave Miller, owner of Bill's early record label, and those crazy early days recording Bill and the Comets.
Apparently over time, Bill's relationship with Dave deteriorated as Dave spent more and more time in Europe.
He mentioned that it was challenging to get paid by Dave, who had often spent

the money before it had arrived.

Dave had told me that there were no royalties payable, as Bill received a flat fee of $25 for each recording, with The Saddlemen, soon to become the Comets, receiving $15.

On the morning of Saturday, November 10th, Bill was busy rehearsing for the Royal Variety Show. He asked and me to join him and his wife Martha for lunch at his hotel after the rehearsal.

Following our enjoyable meal together, we spent the rest of the afternoon in Bill's hotel room. We discussed the completed album and briefly touched on plans for the next album. During our time together, Bill graciously signed several promotional posters for the album *Everyone Can Rock and Roll*. We also went through the photographs taken at Fame Studios.

In one of the pictures, Bill burst into laughter and pointed out that, due to the angle taken, it appeared as if my arm was stretched around both Martha and him. This wonderful photo became a cherished favourite among all of us, capturing a delightful moment of friendship and laughter.

Bill extended a generous invitation for me to bring our family for a holiday at his home in Harlingen, Texas, where we could spend time working on the project together. Regrettably, due to work commitments, I couldn't take him up on this offer.

In the following week, I had another meeting with Bill and Patrick to discuss plans for the next album. Sadly, this would be the last time I would see Bill in person, although I did have a couple of phone conversations with him over the next few months. My privileged time with Bill Haley was at an end.

During 1979 there were rumours that Haley was losing his faculties. This was untrue. He was in complete control of his artistic ability and showed no signs of vagueness in any situation during our time together.

When Bill died on February 9th, 1981, The Daily Mail newspaper wrote - "He died a bitter man."

I don't think so! He knew he was the first and as the first he influenced an entire generation. He was a modest, gentle and courteous man, who throughout his career, encouraged every change and newcomer in music, never criticising anyone.

Bill Haley and Dave Miller were both extraordinary men.

Every era produces such people but it's not often you have the chance to meet, work and become friends with them. I consider myself truly fortunate.

Patrick Malynn - Bill's Manager

Patrick was a tall, elegant Irishman and what one would call a dapper dresser with the ability to speak at a volume most people couldn't even shout at.

Many believed this was due to a slight hearing impediment, though he would never admit to it.

Malynn was commonly known in the industry as Paddy Malynn, but if someone ever made the mistake of calling him Paddy to his face, he would go absolutely ballistic.

During a phone conversation with him one day, I attempted to address him as Patrick but the moment I uttered "Pat," he began talking over me, mistakenly believing I had said "Pad," he promptly hung up.

His touchiness was certainly a recurring trait throughout our numerous interactions over the years with this remarkable, larger-than-life character.

One of my cherished tales featuring Paddy, oops, I mean Patrick, unfolded when my wife Sue and I received an invitation to dine with him at his preferred restaurant. Our rendezvous point was his top-floor apartment in Clifton Gardens, Maida Vale. The residence was comfortably furnished, its walls were adorned with valuable paintings by renowned artists.

We were scheduled to convene at his flat at 8 p.m. on that Saturday evening.
On our arrival, Patrick promptly inquired about our drink preferences. Sue responded, "I'll have a glass of medium white wine, please."
"Suzie, I only have champagne. What type of champagne would you prefer?" he replied, in a characteristically extravagant manner.

The TV was on, and Dallas was playing in the background. Patrick, fixated on the screen, speculated several times about the favours he could offer the more glamorous female cast members.

While intermittently gazing out the window, he shared that his girlfriend had been at his apartment for the past 24 hours and she had to return home this afternoon to rest due to complete exhaustion.
His insinuations implying that the past 24 hours had been a continuous indulgence in physical pleasure for both of them.
For the subsequent hour, Patrick maintained a watchful eye out of the window, reiterating his narrative about his girlfriend's exhaustion and emphasising,
"If she doesn't arrive within the next ten minutes, we'll have to go; otherwise, we risk losing our restaurant table reservation."

Ten more minutes elapsed until Patrick at last declared, "Well, that's it let's go. Leave your car here, we'll take my Rolls-Royce."
As Patrick locked his apartment door, I went ahead, down the stairs with Sue following closely behind. Once we reached the ground floor and opened the main front door, we encountered a stunning young lady adorned in a mink coat, her finger poised to press one of the doorbells.
She gazed at me and introduced herself, saying, "Hello, are you Mr. Malynn? I'm your escort for the evening."
Patrick's hurried descent down the stairs could be heard as I responded, "I believe Mr. Malynn will be here any moment."
Patrick, arriving behind me at the front door, appeared flustered and evidently

embarrassed as he urged, "Kenny, take your car and follow me."
It was apparent that Patrick's sudden change of plans regarding transportation was motivated by the need to privately explain to the young lady the events of their eventful last 24 hours together.

Although we arrived at the restaurant a bit late, our table wasn't ready, so we took a seat in the bar and perused the menu. Patrick and the young lady skillfully maintained the facade of being long-time friends when Mario, the maître d', approached to greet Patrick.

"Hello, Patrick, how are you?" Mario asked, shaking Patrick's hand. Patrick promptly introduced the rest of us to the maître d', who proceeded to playfully touch the top of Patrick's head, messing with his hair. In a booming voice, Mario exclaimed, "This is incredible Patrick! My friend had a similar procedure and his head was swollen for weeks, but yours... it's remarkable, Patrick, it looks so real the best I've ever seen no one would ever know."
This incident marked the first and only time I witnessed Patrick rendered speechless. Shortly thereafter, we placed our orders and enjoyed a splendid meal accompanied by fine wines. Sue and I had a wonderful evening, but it was clear that it just wasn't Paddy's night.

Chapter 11

Hercules The Bear

Hercules, a trained grizzly bear, achieved fame when he managed to escape during the filming of a TV commercial in the Outer Hebrides. After being missing for a tense period of 24 days, he was eventually located, rescued and reunited with his owner Andy Robin, a professional wrestler. This daring escapade catapulted Hercules to international stardom, garnering attention from media outlets worldwide. His face graced the cover of Time magazine and he played a role in promoting the Miss World contest. Hercules even had the unique honour of caddying for Bob Hope and appearing alongside Roger Moore in the James Bond film *Octopussy*. Beyond the silver screen, he featured in numerous television commercials and took on various small film roles. Notably, he was once honoured as the 'Personality of the Year' by the Scottish Tourist Board and received a telegram from none other than Ronald Reagan.

By the end of 1979, I found myself deeply immersed in a multitude of projects, leaving me with precious few moments spent with my family. Recognising that this situation was far from ideal, I made the decision to take all of us on a vacation to the USA. Regrettably, my timing couldn't have been worse, as this coincided with both putting a deposit on our first home and risking substantial sums of money on recording artistes and product development ventures I had recently discovered. My money was disappearing fast, in fact, my overdraft had reached such a staggering height that my bank manager began to suffer from vertigo.
Nevertheless, my family was important and so we embarked on a marvellous three-week journey, driving from New York down to Florida, with stops in Nashville and Memphis. Every day my credit cards were in a daily race to see which one would hit their limit first.
In the pre-electronic transaction era, I attempted the old trick of leaving the cards on the car dashboard in the scorching sun to slightly distort the embossed numbers, hoping they wouldn't register fully when swiped through the machines. This had worked by chance during a previous trip to Spain, but not this time.

On returning, the financial repercussions of our trip became starkly evident, adding to the already looming challenges. Yet, refreshed from our holiday, my fears melted away like a credit card left on a hot dashboard. All I needed to do was dive back into work and quickly. I immediately began the search for as much production work as possible.

After meetings and numerous phone calls, I learned about a couple of individuals in town with ready cash who were in search of a producer for what they described as "an unusual pop record." Little did I know.

Within hours, I found myself in a meeting with them at South Kensington's Blakes Hotel. They introduced themselves as Henry Spurway and Rudolf Huber, residents of Edinburgh and owners of a club named The Royal Chimes Casino. After some initial pleasantries they launched into the tale of Hercules The Bear, who had recently made the news with his escape in Scotland.

The extensive global attention garnered by Hercules led them to entertain the notion that the bear could achieve chart-topping success.

With this in mind, they made the audacious decision to record a rendition of Johnny Preston's hit song, "Running Bear," featuring Hercules as the artist. It was a risky venture, involving a Houdini-like, nine foot tall, 30 stone grizzly bear. What could possibly go wrong?

Having secured an agreement with Andy Robin they established their own record label, Royal Chimes Records with the sole purpose of releasing this single.

During our discussions, my initial reaction to the proposition of producing a record with a colossal grizzly bear was one of total disbelief. I half-expected hidden cameras to reveal that I was unwittingly participating in an episode of *Candid Camera*. Worryingly as no one arrived with the famous words, "You're on Candid Camera," it became increasingly clear that they were deadly serious about this venture.

Once we had settled the matter of my financial compensation and discussed the substantial budget allocated for producing the record, I began to tackle the logistical challenges of recording their newly signed artist.

They enlisted the services of the publicist Max Clifford. Max and I were scheduled to fly to Scotland on October 14th to pay a visit to Andy and Hercules at their residence in Dunblane, Stirlingshire. Although Max and I first met at the airport, by the time we touched down in Scotland, it felt as though we had known each other for ages.

Max proved to be a no-nonsense, straight-talking professional with a genuinely pleasant personality. He possessed a soft-spoken voice that exuded charm and charisma, undoubtedly befitting of a publicist. His persona bore no resemblance to the character I would later read about in the years to come.

For this adventure I was armed with nothing more than a battery-operated Nagra portable tape recorder and my self-confidence and was well aware that neither of these would be of use if our artiste turned out to be somewhat temperamental.

Arriving at Edinburgh airport Henry, the record label representative, greeted us and drove us to our hotel. Following a swift check-in and depositing our bags, we set off for the trip to Hercules' home.

After an hour's drive through pristine moorlands, rolling hills and breath-taking landscapes, we arrived at our destination - the Sheriffmuir Inn, a beautifully preserved three-hundred-year-old stone building painted in striking white.

Waiting for us in the inn's car park were Andy and his wife, ready to extend a warm welcome. The atmosphere here was incredibly serene and tranquil, you could hear an approaching car from miles away. At night, the echoes of a grizzly bear's growls carried even further.

With introductions complete we all gathered in the lounge, where Andy's wife, Maggie, graciously served us tea and sandwiches.

Andy eagerly shared the story of Hercules, affectionately known as Herky, his

remarkable history and how they ended up with this surrogate son.
He emphasised Hercules's unique distinction as the only bear ever to wrestle his trainer without a muzzle. My attention was particularly piqued when Andy mentioned the impressive set of teeth that Herky possessed.

With Andy briefly leaving the room, we continued our polite conversation with Maggie. Before long, this tranquillity was suddenly shattered by a thunderous sound increasing in volume until it reached a climax right in front of us. Hercules had made his entrance, settling down in front of the television, like a child eagerly awaiting a cartoon.
In that moment, the sheer enormity of this magnificent creature became undeniably clear It was an incredibly unsettling experience causing even the typically composed Max to break into a sweat.
There was a slight relief when Andy entered the room shortly after and gave the big old softie a cuddle - not Max, the bear.

It was time for me to record Herky, so Andy led him back to his spacious enclosure. Clutching my Nagra recorder tightly, I nervously followed them both into the bear den.
Andy started to talk to Hercules, encouraging him to produce grunting noises and grizzly growls.
With utmost caution, I nervously positioned the microphone as close to the bear's mouth as I dared, recalling Andy's earlier remarks about the sharpness of his teeth.
We followed Herky as he roamed around the enclosure, capturing audio until the tape ran out. Andy inquired, "Do you have enough to work with?" Whilst I knew that Hercules would never sing like Baloo from the movie *Jungle Book,* I was content with the recordings I had gathered. Even more satisfying was the prospect of getting out of Herky's den.

We retreated to the bar, where Hercules joined us for a pint of beer. Yes, you read that correctly, a pint of beer! There were obvious risks associated with offering alcohol to a nine-foot grizzly, but I could only hope he was a happy drunk.
It was certainly a remarkable spectacle, although a grizzly bear gulping down a pint was a very messy affair.

Relieved to still be in one piece after this bizarre but incredible adventure, Henry, Max and I returned to Edinburgh for a celebratory champagne dinner at the casino where we discussed our game plan for the weeks ahead.

Returning to London the next morning, I immediately focused on securing musicians and studio time, while Max was generating excitement in the Fleet Street newspapers by sharing a photo of Herky enjoying a pint of beer.
The very next day, several national newspapers featured the story of Hercules embarking on a recording venture, accompanied by a snapshot of him indulging in that pint. Everything was going to plan.

The record was successfully produced at Pye Studios the following week, with the lead vocals and harmonies performed by Suzie Mack, a talented young session singer.

The tapes were dispatched to the pressing plant for the vinyl manufacturing process. Soon, the record "Running Bear" by Hercules & The Three Bears on the Royal Chimes label would be available for purchase.

A week later, on a Friday evening, I received a phone call from Max. He informed me that he had secured a spot on the *Russell Harty* TV show to perform the song live the following Tuesday. Unfortunately, Suzie Mack, the original singer, was on a brief tour in Germany and wouldn't be available for the show. Somehow, Max managed to find three girls to replace her, but they wouldn't arrive in the UK until Sunday evening, leaving them just Monday to learn the track.

During the first rehearsal at the TV studios on Tuesday morning, Max and I watched as the girls performed. As the song concluded, I asked Max what he thought. He turned to me and said, "Do you have your passport with you?" It was clear this wasn't the greatest of performances.

That evening, when the show aired, Russell Harty briefly chatted with Andy, who had Hercules by his side, shortly afterward the 'three bears' delivered their rendition of the song. While the girls did their best under the circumstances, as performances go, they sounded like a zoo burning down.

On November 7th, Max organised the single launch, featuring a champagne lunch at the Café de Paris in Leicester Square. Hercules made a grand entrance on Regent Street, arriving in his own vibrantly adorned, air-conditioned coach. By the time Hercules and Andy arrived at the Café de Paris, Max had ensured the venue was packed with press and celebrities.

Within an hour, the RSPCA arrived and removed Herky from the premises, effectively shutting down the spectacle. It seemed that 'someone' had tipped them off about the event's location and timing. Well Max was brought on board with the specific mission of generating maximum publicity for the project.

The following day, the news captured the front pages of national newspapers across the country. On November 13th, the Daily Mirror published a headline that read "Hercules barred from the BBC," detailing how a vet named James Hadley had cautioned that the planned television appearances could breach the Dangerous Wild Animals Act of 1976. According to the act, wild animals were only allowed to perform in circuses. This event signalled the conclusion of Hercules's career in the recording industry.

I believed this would mark the end of the bear saga, particularly for Henry and Rudi, who had invested a significant amount of money in this project. But as I often say: in life, the next phone call can change it all.

Sure enough, a little later on I received a call from Henry, who inquired whether I'd be interested in selling my production percentage of the record in exchange for a one-time payment.

This proposition could only signify one thing - they had a genuine chance of selling a substantial quantity of Hercules records.

They went on to explain that a client at the casino called Giovanni had run up significant gambling debts that he couldn't cover. Giovanni happened to be a high-ranking lieutenant in the Moonies, a nickname for the controversial Unification Church.

It was suggested, or perhaps it was an offer he could not refuse, that a practical way to settle his debt with the casino would be for the Moonies organisation to purchase 250,000 copies of the Running Bear single from the Royal Chimes record label, at a rate of £1 per record.

These records would then be distributed to Moonie recruits to sell on the streets of the UK, in this way everyone involved emerged as a winner.

Giovanni agreed to the arrangement, which not only settled his debt but also returned Henry and Rudi's investment and yielded a substantial profit. Andy and I were pleasantly surprised when we both received an unexpected cash bonus.

Although Herky never achieved chart-topping success, he did manage to sell an impressive 250,000 copies of the single.

Chapter 12

Louis Clark

Louis or Lou Clark was born on February 27th, 1947 and sadly departed on February 13th, 2021. He was a remarkable English music arranger and keyboard player who also happened to be a dear friend. His legacy is most prominently associated with his contributions to ELO and his work on *Hooked on Classics*. Throughout his career, he collaborated with a diverse array of artistes, including luminaries like Roy Orbison, Ozzy Osbourne, Roy Wood, and the renowned band America.

Although working on the ELO album Eldorado wasn't exactly my favourite gig, it did introduce me to Lou Clark.

During the mid to late 70s and into the early 80s, Lou and I collaborated as partners on numerous music projects. It was during this time that I introduced Lou to my close friend and manager, Stuart Taylor. Remarkably, Stuart and Lou immediately formed a strong relationship.

Stuart, a maestro at pitching creative concepts to record companies, came up with a ground-breaking idea: Lou would craft arrangements of ABBA songs for a 100-piece orchestra paired with a rock rhythm section.
The envisioned album was supposed to bear the title *ABBAPHONIC*. Unfortunately, despite Stuart's determined efforts, finding a record company that shared his enthusiasm for this innovative project proved elusive.
In no time, Stuart came up with an alternative concept: to reinterpret Status Quo songs aptly naming the new project *Quophonoic*.
He managed to secure sufficient funding from Quo's management and publishers to record a couple of tracks, which he intended to use as a persuasive tool when approaching record companies. The hope was that these recordings would demonstrate the album's sales potential.
Lou diligently set to work on composing the arrangements and an impressive orchestra and rhythm section, featuring two drummers, were booked for EMI's Studio One at Abbey Road.
Just as the first run-through of the music had commenced, Francis Rossi and Rick Parfitt from Status Quo walked into the control room.
Lou's brilliant arrangements had seamlessly melded the sounds of ELO and Status Quo with a massive rock orchestra, creating something truly astonishing. As the final chord reverberated, Francis was so impressed that he exclaimed, "Jesus, did I fucking write that?"

Despite the exceptional quality of the recordings, Stuart's efforts to interest major record companies, once again, led to disappointment. We could only surmise that any reluctance stemmed from concerns about the high recording costs and uncertainty regarding potential sales.

It's worth noting that Lou eventually brought this unique project to fruition, albeit some years later after achieving success with *Hooked on Classics*.

By 1978, Lou became increasingly disheartened with the music industry. This became evident during my next meeting with him.

I gave him a call, informing him of my upcoming album project which I really needed his arrangement skills for, so we arranged for me to visit him.

I arrived at his home in Birmingham and pretty soon Lou opened up to me about his grievances with how Jeff Lynne was treating him and the rest of the band. It appeared that Jeff was claiming credit for everything on ELO singles and albums.

Over lunch, we discussed my forthcoming album project. He agreed to work on the project and I was pleased to hand him a cheque in advance, which he greatly appreciated. It was evident that he was facing financial difficulties, he had even mentioned the possibility of returning to teaching.

After lunch at a nearby restaurant we went back to his place. Lou surprised me by playing a single he had just completed with The Royal Philharmonic Orchestra, titled *Hooked on Classics (Parts 1 & 2)* due to be released shortly.

While the music itself was impeccable, featuring various famous classical masterpieces with Lou's signature string arrangements, the underlying rhythm track consisted of a simple budget-level bass drum, snare and handclaps from a drum machine, which detracted from the overall quality.

I couldn't help but wonder if Lou might indeed return to teaching sooner than expected. Nonetheless, I wished him the best of luck with the project and looked forward to our future recordings.

To my utter astonishment, the single I had reservations about skyrocketed in popularity. A few months down the line, it climbed to number two in the UK charts and later secured the tenth spot on the Billboard Hot 100 in the USA.

It dawned on me that Stuart's original idea, proposed some time before, had paved the way for this triumphant project. This newfound success provided Lou with the opportunity to break free from the confines of his ELO chains.

Around the same time, ELO was gearing up for a USA tour and Jeff Lynne extended an invitation for Lou to join them on the road. I recall that Lou seemed somewhat indifferent as to whether to accept the offer or not. But now, with Lou's newfound success as an artiste in his own right, he found himself in a position to make certain demands that had previously been denied to the band members.

Traditionally, Jeff would fly first class while the rest of the band travelled in coach, but for this tour, this and many of the usual rules were relaxed, perhaps reflecting the changing dynamics within the group.

Lou had extended numerous invitations to me over the years to attend ELO concerts at various venues, yet somehow, there was always a valid reason preventing me from going.

While I was working in Nashville, ELO happened to be in town for a one-night performance so I decided to give Lou a call at his hotel for a catch up. During the call he graciously invited me to the gig that evening. He promised to leave a ticket at the box office in my name.

I explained to him that I was currently tied up with a recording session in a local studio but promised that I would make every effort to attend if the session wrapped up on time. Unfortunately, that night, we didn't finish until around 3 a.m. making it impossible for me to make it to the concert.

When I returned to my hotel room, I noticed a blinking red light on the phone, indicating that I had a phone message. Considering the late hour, I decided to leave it until the following morning and retired to bed.

First thing the next morning, I called the hotel reception to retrieve the message. The receptionist, speaking with a pronounced Southern accent and in an entirely deadpan tone, relayed, "The message is from a Mr. Louis Clark, he says, 'Bollocks to you, you wanker for not coming.'"

I nearly fell off my bed. I was laughing so hard. I immediately dialled Lou's number. When he picked up, I was still in hysterics. Before I could get a word out, he said, "So, you got my message then?"

Still laughing, I replied, "Not only was it hilarious, but you should have heard the young girl delivering your message in her perfectly innocent Southern drawl."

Lou continued with a grin, "They have no clue about the meaning of those two words either, I've used one or the other in many a TV and radio interview."

I asked Lou if he'd like to grab lunch which he agreed to. Although, he emphasised that he absolutely had to be back at his hotel by 2 p.m. at the latest because the band had a flight to catch to Atlanta for their evening performance.

I drove round and picked him up from his hotel around noon and we enjoyed a fantastic lunch, leaving the restaurant at around 1:30 p.m. To our shock, we discovered that my car had been towed away. I can still vividly recall the expression on Lou's face at that moment.

Desperate to make it in time, we ended up sprinting five or six blocks through the sweltering heat to the office of a music publisher I was very familiar with where I knew I could borrow a car.

Having secured a car, our mad dash across town resembled a scene out of *Starsky & Hutch*. Just as we were approaching the hotel, the traffic lights abruptly turned red. We could see the black limousines lined up, engines idling, clearly waiting for Lou.

Without a moment's hesitation, Lou sprang out of the car and exclaimed, "I'll see you back home." Then, he bolted away, moving at a pace that would have given Usain Bolt a run for his money. As the lights changed to green, I watched in relief as Lou hopped into one of the waiting limos, knowing they were all bound for the airport.

Several months later, ELO concluded their tour at Wembley Arena in England. I received an unexpected call from Lou, who informed me that he had arranged six tickets for Saturday night, left at the box office for Sue and me, with a couple of extras for any friends we might want to invite.

Due to a busy week, I had somewhat forgotten about it until Saturday afternoon when, to my dismay, Lou called again, saying, "I'll see you tonight. I've also left backstage passes for you and your guests for the after-show party."
Panic set in! We lived an hour and a half from the venue and on such short notice, we quickly needed to find a babysitter and four additional friends to join us. No easy task but we managed to pull it off.

Arriving at the venue we picked up the tickets and passes and found we'd been given fantastic front-row seats.
It turned out to be one of the best rock 'n' roll shows that Sue and I had ever witnessed. No elaborate stage sets or over-the-top theatrics, just a band delivering pure rock 'n' roll.
After the show, we had a wonderful time at the backstage party. While I didn't quite get a kiss from Jeff, I did receive a polite hello, but Lou and the rest of the band were absolutely great.

In 1988, drummer Bev Bevan approached Jeff Lynne with the idea of recording another ELO album. Unfortunately, Lynne declined to participate. In response, Bevan decided to continue with the band without Jeff, but this move sparked objections from Jeff regarding the use of the ELO name.
After some negotiations, an agreement was reached between the two, resulting in the official disbanding of ELO in 1989. Bevan then formed a new band called Electric Light Orchestra Part Two, with an arrangement in place for Jeff to receive a percentage of their record royalties.
Bev set out to assemble the new band and whilst co-founder Roy Wood was asked to join, he declined. Bevan recruited various musicians, including Lou, although Lou was actually never an official member of ELO.

After a decade, Bev struck a deal to sell his rights to the ELO name back to Jeff Lynne. Consequently, the band couldn't use the name ELO Part Two. The remaining band members wished to continue with the name, leading to a legal battle that lasted for several years.
I remember Lou calling me when the court finally reached its decision, informing me that they had won. I congratulated him, thinking it was a great result. Sadly, he revealed, "Not really. We kept the name, but the American court ruled that we had to cover all the costs." Ouch!

As the years passed, Lou returned to touring with orchestras, showcasing his exceptional talent. Living on different continents, we spoke only occasionally in later years, but his health was declining and he took a step back from performing to spend more time with his family.

Lou Clark was an immensely talented musician and a truly wonderful person. I miss him to this day and am grateful for the great times we had and the friendship we shared.

An Era Ends

During the early years of the 1980s, my presence at the studio became less frequent as my work as a freelance producer and engineer saw me working in Europe and across the USA. By 1983, all the familiar faces I had known at De Lane Lea had moved on to different studios or freelance ventures.

During my visit to the studio, it became apparent that I had become somewhat of an anonymous figure, a few individuals even confused me for a client.
As my salary continued to be deposited into my bank account a sense of guilt washed over me, now was the right moment to say goodbye to De Lane Lea.

I scheduled a meeting with Peter Harris, who served as both the studio manager and director. During our discussion, I candidly expressed my concern that I might be causing inconvenience to him and the studio. As the last remaining original staff member, I asked if he had considered the possibility of letting me go. His eyes sparkled like a tray of diamonds and readily agreed it was a good idea.

A couple of weeks later, I received a summons from Peter. He informed me that, after reviewing the situation, he was willing to offer me £2000 redundancy payment. Given that I was already earning a substantial income as a freelancer and with nothing to lose, I explained to him that as I had dedicated most of my working life to the studio and that I had a wife and two children to support, I felt the offer was insulting. To my surprise, he responded with, "Let me think it over and I'll get back to you."

Two weeks later, we reconvened and instead of presenting a "take it or leave it" scenario, he proposed £4000. Finding some amusement in the absurdity of the situation, I reiterated my loyalty to the studio and my personal circumstances. Once again, to my astonishment, he said, "Let me see what I can do." My wages continued to be deposited into my bank account while several more weeks passed before our next meeting.
This time, the offer was £6000 and Peter stated that it had been sanctioned by the Chairman of the company, Mr. Ebbits.
I requested to speak with Mr. Ebbits emphasising my dedication to the studio, surprisingly Peter relented once more.

A few weeks later, I received another call asking for a meeting. The offer had now risen to £7500. By now I was starting to feel a bit guilty so I agreed to this sum. The cheque would be ready on the October 26th, 1983.

On the morning of the scheduled cheque pickup, I contacted the accounts department. The head of accounts, Peter Klyn, explained that Peter Harris had overlooked the fact that, in addition to the redundancy payment, he needed to include a month's wages for every year I had worked there. Peter Harris was concerned about potential repercussions from the board, as a final amount had been agreed. I offered to accept half of the additional payment and after checking with Peter Harris, Mr. Klyn confirmed the arrangement. That day, I collected nearly £10,000 and received an offer to return and work on a freelance basis.

Had Louis Elman, the former MD, or I, been in Peter Harris' position, we would have demanded that I come to the studio daily, even when there are no sessions scheduled as my wages were still being paid. Otherwise, termination of my employment would have been the only option.

Whilst I never actively took part in any other sessions at that location, I did manage to make a few visits and catch up with friends who were recording there. Eventually, in 2004, the building was demolished as a part of the redevelopment of Wembley Stadium.

The period that holds the fondest memories of my time at the studio spans from 1974 to 1978, a period often fondly referred to as the "glory years" by those that worked there. During those years, the studio was bustling with work and I had the privilege of collaborating with a remarkable team of colleagues and artistes.

Chapter 13

The Sonet Recordings

Augie Meyers

Augie Meyers, renowned in Texas music lore, gained fame as the keyboardist for both The Sir Douglas Quintet and The Texas Tornados.
Bob Dylan once said of Augie.
"Augie's my man, he's like an intellectual who goes fishing using bookworms. Seriously though he's the shining example of a musician, Vox player or otherwise, who can break the code.
His playing speaks volumes, speaks in tongues actually. He can bring a song, certainly any one of mine, into the real world. I've loved his playing going all the way back to the Sir Doug days.
What makes him so great is that internally speaking, he's the master of syncopation and timing and this is something that cannot be taught.
If you need someone to get you through the shipping lanes and there's no detour, Augie will get you right straight through. Augie's your man."

In 1981, I found myself producing an album at Pye Studios in London for Sonet Records, Sweden when an interesting opportunity arose. The record company informed me that one of their artists, Augie Meyers, a talented American artiste known for his keyboard and accordion skills, was passing through London. They inquired if there was a way to involve him in the album I was working on. Despite our tight budget and schedule, I initially expressed hesitation, feeling that we didn't require additional musicians.

Despite that, the record company was persistent, offering to cover any extra costs and studio time. They assured me that I could decide not to use Augie's performance if it didn't fit the session. Intrigued, I contacted Augie and invited him to the studio for the following day.

The next afternoon, as I was working on a track titled "Cruisin' on a Saturday Night" when the control room door swung open. In walked a towering six-foot-two Texan, Augie Meyers, with his accordion in hand. He greeted us with a simple, "Hi, I'm Augie Meyers, am I in the right place?"

Augie entered the room with a slight limp, his weathered face revealing a life rich in experiences. Beneath his Stetson hat, a three-foot ponytail cascaded down his back like a dookie rope. Little did I know then that this encounter would mark the beginning of a deep friendship, making Augie an honorary member of my family to this very day.

Following a cordial "howdy," Augie retrieved his accordion from its case and began playing along with the track in the control room. To my astonishment, the instrument's tone and Augie's skilled performance harmonised perfectly with the track. Although, I had some reservations about the rhythmic aspect.

In an attempt to convey the rhythmic vibe I had in mind, I played the track and positioned myself in front of Augie, playing air accordion, looking totally ridiculous, with my arms flapping up and down like an overweight chicken attempting to take flight.
When the track concluded and I had finished my demonstration, Augie gazed at me and remarked, "Man, you make it look so easy."

Augie, being the consummate professional, persisted and after a few attempts in the control room, we achieved the perfect feel. Augie ventured down into the studio and we began rehearsing with the track playing.
During the initial run-through, Augie voiced his frustration about his headphones only working in one ear. I promptly had the assistant swap them out for a different pair. On the second take, the same issue persisted.
"I can still only hear the track in one ear," Augie informed me again. Concerned, I had the assistant change the headphones once more. Once again, on the third take, the problem recurred.

Frustrated, I descended into the studio, donned a further set of headphones and had the assistant run the tape. Finally, I confirmed that the headphones were working flawlessly on both sides and handed my functional set to Augie.
He put them on, glanced at me and remarked, "Nope, still only working on one side," before promptly returning them. I couldn't understand what was going on, I had just tested them myself and they were functioning perfectly on both sides.
"Augie," I said, puzzled, "They're working on both sides."
"Oh, it's okay, Kenny, it must be me," Augie replied casually. He then swept his hair back from over his ear, revealing to my astonishment that he was missing an ear.

This marked my initial encounter with Mr. Meyers' wonderful sense of humour. Later, I learned that his limp and the absence of his ear were the result of his battle with polio during childhood. My initial reservations about having Augie participate in the recording turned out to be entirely unfounded, his contribution to the track exceeded my expectations.

My next encounter with Augie would take place in San Francisco during the recording of The Sir Douglas Quintet album titled *Midnight Sun*.

After the release of that album, Augie and I maintained an ongoing collaboration, working together on many projects. I had the honour of producing two of his solo albums, namely *August In New York* and *Augie's Back*. Additionally, I enlisted him as a session musician for recordings in the UK, Sweden and Nashville.

In 1984, I set out on a journey to Nashville with the purpose of recording four tracks for an album featuring the country singer Joe Sun at Glaser Sound Studios. Before my trip, I invited Augie to join me and lend his piano skills to the recording sessions.
Unfortunately, once the sessions began, it became painfully apparent that the Nashville session musicians were not particularly welcoming to outsiders.

Despite Augie's undeniable talent and warm personality, he encountered indifference and rudeness from these session players throughout the process, when they weren't ignoring him, they treated him with total disrespect. Consequently, I made the decision to exclude Augie from the live sessions and recorded his parts after the other musicians had departed.

Memorable Augie Moments

During a night out in San Antonio: Augie and I found ourselves in a nightclub, enjoying the music and sipping on beers. As the night progressed, a burly redneck approached us at the bar, clearly looking for trouble. He directed his hostility towards Augie, saying, "Hey man, what are you doing here? We don't like your kind in our club," all while glancing over at his three equally imposing friends.
The tension in the air was electric and I feared the situation might escalate into something quite dangerous, seeing that most people in Texas owned a gun or two. To my relief, Augie responded with remarkable composure, saying, "I'm just having a drink man and enjoying the music." The redneck, still eyeing his friends, reiterated his disapproval of "hippy long-haired types."
Although Augie was significantly taller, this redneck was as wide as Augie was tall and he had backup. Augie maintained eye contact, leaned down and calmly suggested, "Sir, would you like to quietly step outside and show me your ID?" The redneck, thinking Augie might be an undercover cop, promptly raised his hands in surrender, palms out and walked backward, apologising, "I'm really sorry, man. I thought you were someone else." I said, "Augie, that was amazing." With a large smile he whispered in my ear, "Kenny, it will never work for you."

The Drunken Skinhead

While enjoying a drink in a London pub, Augie and I encountered a drunken, tough-looking skinhead seated next to us at the bar, clearly seeking trouble. He questioned Augie, "Oi mate, how come your fucking hair is so long?"
Augie, ever the master of wit, responded, "I was kinda wondering why yours is so short." The skinhead replied "fuck off, I asked you, why don't you get your fucking haircut?"
Augie, maintaining his calm manor, said, "Well I'll tell ya, when I was a little bitty boy, I had my hair cut and the barber cut off my ear." Augie then revealed his missing ear by pulling back his hair.
The skinhead was taken aback and asked, "What the fuck did you do?"
Augie, in a low, menacing voice and unwavering gaze, replied, "Well, I killed that son of a bitch." The skinhead's reaction was swift; he nervously downed the rest of his beer and hastily exited the pub; he didn't look back.

The Sir Douglas Quintet

The Sir Douglas Quintet was led by Doug Sahm, who hailed from San Antonio, Texas. The group blended blues, soul, Texas swing, a hint of doo-wop, Tex-Mex and Cajun influences, establishing themselves as pioneers in the world of rock 'n' roll music. Augie Meyers's entrancing Vox Continental organ rhythm is the key feature of their acclaimed 1965 track, "She's About a Mover."

I first met Doug in 1982, at Sonet Records' offices in Lidingö, just outside Stockholm. He had a resemblance to John Lennon, complete with a cowboy hat. Our paths often crossed at gigs and various Sonet Records events. Doug had a rapid-fire way of speaking, mostly about himself, with a vocabulary that seemed straight out of the late 60s, using phrases like "Far out man" and "He's a groovy cat." Our conversations were largely one-sided, as he showed little interest in me and honestly, I felt the same about him. This is where I learnt that you can always tell a Texan but you can't tell him much.

Then, Dag Häggqvist, one of the MDs at Sonet, approached me with the idea of producing an album with The Sir Douglas Quintet. I'd heard stories about Doug being a challenging collaborator, but having worked with some formidable artists in my career, I didn't anticipate it being too tough. Plus, the recordings were set to take place in San Francisco, a place I'd always wanted to visit and my good friend and long-time member of SDQ, Augie Meyers would be there to lend support. How difficult could it be?

I was entrusted with $50,000 in cash to cover studio expenses, musicians, hotels and other expenses during my stay. I was aware of the rule about carrying more than £10,000 into the USA without declaring it, but since I had nothing actually illegal with me, I figured it should be fine.
I departed from London to Seattle in early December, where I would clear customs before catching an internal flight to San Francisco. As I filled out the standard USA entry form on the plane, I confidently checked the "No" box for carrying more than $10,000.
Once I landed and stood in line at customs, my stomach started sending distress signals, insisting that bringing this amount of money into the USA might not be such a good idea. My mind argued with my stomach to hold on for just a bit longer.
Finally, it was my turn at the customs desk. The officer asked me the standard questions from the form. "Do you have any fresh fruit?" "No." "Have you been on a farm in the last three weeks?" "No." And then came the crucial question, "Are you carrying $10,000 or more?" I instinctively said, "No."

At that moment, when the officer opened my briefcase, she discovered two packs, each containing $10,000 and confronted me with an assertive tone, demanding, "What is this?" After a brief hesitation, I admitted, "Um, well, that's $20,000." Without hesitation she pressed a button triggering an alarm, the echoes of which I can still hear to this day.

I glanced back to see everyone in the queue behind me trying to see what was happening. Two imposing security guards appeared out of nowhere and escorted me to a small room and proceeded to do things that I wouldn't even have let my wife do to me. You'd think they'd have at least taken me out for dinner first!
They continued searching my briefcase, finding the rest of the cash and then meticulously inspected every inch of my suitcase, all while questioning me.

I insisted there was no more cash, but these officers were genuinely intimidating. They pressed me for the purpose of the money so I explained it was for a recording session in San Francisco. Immediately, one of them pointed out, "That's funny, on your entry form, you ticked that you're on holiday. You know you need a green card to work in our country?"
Things were not looking good. They looked at my passport, which showed multiple entries into the USA and began to suspect me of money laundering.
Their interrogation became even more intense. There was no bad cop, good cop they were both just seriously bad.
After a gruelling three hours, they reluctantly accepted my explanation that I was simply delivering the money on behalf of the record company to ensure all bills were paid correctly, so technically I wasn't working. I was fined $5,000 and released.

I caught the next flight to San Francisco, where I picked up a rental car. To my dismay, the rental company had no record of the record company reserving a vehicle for me. Exhausted and frustrated after the day's events, I demanded the best car they had, which turned out to be a beautiful, brand new, white Camaro Chevrolet with blacked-out windows.

Driving over the Golden Gate Bridge, the sun shining and with the car radio blaring, I was finally heading for the motel in Mill Valley and things finally began to feel a bit better. But it wasn't long before I was met with yet another hurdle: my motel room hadn't been booked either and there were no rooms available.
Utterly drained, I inquired if they had a broom cupboard I could stay in. After an hour or so, they managed to find me a room. I got in the room, collapsed on the bed and passed out until the next day.
I had arrived a couple of days ahead of the band to adjust to the time difference. Finally, it seemed like things were taking a turn for the better.

On my second day at the motel, as I sat in the restaurant feeling rather alone, when I noticed a familiar figure through the glass window – a rather tall guy wearing a large cowboy hat. To my relief, it was Augie Meyers.
Augie, known for avoiding flying anywhere due to a recurring plane crash dream, had just arrived on a Greyhound bus from New York. He joined me at my table, ordered a meal and listened as I recounted my unfortunate encounters with customs, rental cars and hotel bookings.

Augie, in his typical storytelling fashion, shared a recent stroke of luck he'd experienced just before leaving New York.
"Kenny, I was heading to catch the bus when I walked into this new snack bar called, *Aim to Please*. They had a challenge – if they couldn't make a sandwich of your choice in two minutes, they'd give you 50 bucks. So I ordered an elephant's ear on rye."'
In astonishment I said, "So what happened?" He replied, "Yeah they had to pay me 50 bucks - they were all out of rye."
I should have known.

Shortly after Augie looked over and said, "Hi Ry," to my amazement, Ry Cooder had walked into the restaurant and came to join us at our table.

Being a huge fan of Ry I told him that, just a few nights before my departure to the US, I had watched the movie *Southern Comfort*, for which Ry had composed the Cajun music. After this introduction, Augie joined in and announced my Grammy nomination for the Queen Ida Cajun album. Ry seemed genuinely impressed, yet my level of excitement was way beyond that - here I was, seated in the presence of the great man himself.

A little later, we were joined by Huey Lewis, who I discovered was in town to collaborate with Ry on the music for a new movie.

This experience truly stood out as one of the highlights of the project I was working on. Almost every morning, I would cross paths with Ry either in the reception area or the car park. Each time, he'd ask, "How are the sessions going?" Thinking about it now I wondered why I never invited him to the studio to perhaps contribute to a track or two. It turned out it may have been a blessing in disguise as I was about to encounter Doug Sahm and the chaos that surrounded him.

Soon enough, Doug and the rest of the band arrived, with the exception of the drummer, Dougie Clifford. The backbeat of the band Creedence Clearwater Revival.

We had the rehearsal studio booked for the upcoming Saturday and Sunday, followed by five days in the recording studio to cut the album. My plan was to return to the UK with the finished recordings for mixing and eventual release.

Rehearsal Studio Antics

Our first day at the rehearsal studio, around 11 a.m. quickly revealed that there wasn't much rehearsing going on. Everyone lounged around, smoking pot and chatting. As the day progressed, I got the impression that Doug assumed I was there to be his errand boy.

At one point, Doug turned to me and said, "Kenny, go get me a Coke from the machine." I returned with a Dr Pepper; the only option available.

He shouted, "What the heck is this, man? I wanted a Coke."

I explained, "That's all they had."

He retorted, "Well, go find me a Coke somewhere else."

Not eager to wander around an unfamiliar area in search of a soda, I firmly replied, "I don't know the area well enough and I won't be able to find my way back, so it's Dr Pepper or nothing." He wasn't pleased.

Around 4 p.m. having observed everyone smoking and chatting all day, I decided to join in and take a hit of the marijuana.

After one puff, within seconds, I had totally lost all feeling in my limbs and my head was spinning like a roulette wheel. Panic set in as I prayed no one would try to speak to me or ask me anything. I wondered if I could even make it to the nearest chair.

Stumbling almost unconsciously into a dark corner, I sat there, amazed at how the others managed to stand up, let alone engage in conversation.

By around 6:30 p.m. as the numbness began to subside, Dougie Clifford finally arrived and started setting up his drums. It was decided that we would continue the next day.

Doug suggested we all go to Fisherman's Wharf for dinner. Clifford, who had $5,000 in cash, wanted to check into the hotel and secure his money in the safe first. Doug chose to ride with me in the car, claiming he knew a shortcut back to the hotel. Clifford, unaware of our hotel's location, followed us with the rest of the band in his truck.
I followed Doug's directions until we ended up in a cul-de-sac. Clifford jumped out if his truck infuriated and yelled at me, "What the fuck are we doing here?"
I simply pointed at Doug, who calmly got out of the car and remarked, "Well, we're at Fisherman's Wharf now, we might as well eat."
Clearly, that had been his plan all along.

Sunday mirrored the disarray of Saturday, it seemed like nobody cared about the upcoming album. We had little material to work with apart for a couple of covers of old songs. Doug claimed he was still writing one song, ironically entitled "Let's Don't Waste a Minute."
With each passing moment, my disdain for Doug intensified. His treatment of me as his subordinate, with orders instead of requests, left me deeply frustrated and angry.

Arriving at Different Fur Studios on that Monday, I realised we had only five days to record the album. To expedite the process, I relied on the resident studio engineer, Stacy Baird, to handle the recording side of the project.
Once we had the band set up and ready to record, it soon became apparent that everyone, except for me, was thoroughly stoned again.

After a few attempts at rehearsing the song, it was clear that things weren't going well. I suggested we lay down a track so the band could listen and discuss any necessary changes.
Everyone gathered in the control room for the playback. To my shock, Doug Sahm and the band thought it was fantastic. Doug declared, "Let's move on to the next track."
For a few seconds I thought it must be me, even though they were all stoned how could all these people think this piece of shit was anywhere near acceptable?
I realised this was a circus that needed a ringmaster, I had to gain control. I told Doug,
"This is not good enough, the band's playing out of time, out of tune and, it sounds like, out of desperation!"
Doug looked at me with bewilderment and commented, "Man, this is how we make our music."
With raised intensity, I responded, "Well, you're making it fucking wrong. I'm the one who has to sit in the office in Sweden, play the finished album and account for the record company's money and this isn't good enough."

Reluctantly, like a chastised child, Doug agreed to do a few more takes until I was satisfied.

We had already lost valuable time by arriving late at the studio on Monday and Tuesday due to the lackadaisical attitude of Doug. It was clear that he operated in his own time zone.

On Wednesday morning, at breakfast, I informed everyone that we'd be leaving for the studio promptly at 11:30 a.m. sharp, to start recording at noon. Doug wasn't present at breakfast, so I knocked on his door at 9:30 a.m. to remind him of our schedule.
He answered the door wearing only long-johns underwear. I emphasised the importance of punctuality to him, to which he replied, "Sure, I'll be ready."

At 10:30 a.m. I knocked on his door again to reiterate the schedule. Still in his underwear, he asked me to put a letter in the mailbox for him.
I replied, "Why don't you do it.? He shouted back, "What's wrong with you man it's no big deal, just do it."
"If it's no big deal you can do it yourself."
"It's nothing, man." he insisted.
I decided the best thing to do was to just walk away.

At exactly 11:30 a.m. I knocked on Doug's door once more, only to find him still in his underwear. I reminded him, "It's 11:30 Doug, so I'm leaving for the studio." As I began walking down the hallway he just stood there, screaming at the top of his voice, "You crazy English fuck," along with a string of other obscenities.
Hearing the commotion, the rest of the band emerged from their rooms. I stood at the end of the corridor and declared, "If anyone wants to come and make a record, I'll be outside for two minutes, then I'm leaving for the studio."

Finally, a minute later, the wonderful Louie Ortega, the guitarist, came downstairs and joined me in my car. I confided in him that Doug had accomplish something in 27 seconds that no one had managed to do in 27 years, and that was make me lose my temper.
We waited a few more minutes but no one else had turned up so I decided to leave for the studio. Doug arrived around 2 p.m. with the rest of the band, as if nothing had happened.

The rest of the day proceeded smoothly until Patrick, the studio owner, approached me. Doug had apparently cancelled the last two days of studio time, claiming we wouldn't need it.
This raised a red flag for me, as I realised that any leftover budget would likely go to Doug. I asserted my authority over the project to Patrick, stating that we needed every minute of the time we had booked.

Returning to the studio, I confronted Doug about the studio time issue, resulting in the first and only heated argument with an artiste in my entire career. During our dispute, Doug lit a massive joint, disappearing in front of my eyes behind a cloud of smoke. I could only hear his voice, but I knew he was in there somewhere.

Once we reached an understanding, I made it clear to Doug that I wouldn't release any money to him until Friday, after we had completed the recordings. From that point on, he became more cooperative.

Dag Häggqvist called me later that day from Sweden, to check on our progress. I confided in him, saying, "This is undoubtedly the toughest gig I've ever worked on. Doug doesn't need me; he needs a yes-man or a gofer who also happens to be a psychiatrist."

By now, I was so distressed, my next call was to my wife Sue back in England. After explaining the situation, I asked her to arrange for our children to stay with my mother and to fly out to meet me immediately.

Knowing that Sue was on her way provided me with some sanity, enabling me to continue the sessions without resorting to violence against Sahm.

The band's recording process was entirely live, with Doug taking on a lead vocal role, which we could redo at a later time.

In the midst of recording, Doug would occasionally shout out someone's name without warning, signalling them to take a solo. The sequence of names varied from one take to the next, keeping everyone on their toes.

Typically, the band had up to three attempts to lay down the foundational track. After that, Doug would declare, "I'm kinda burnt out with this one now, let's try something else."

Louie Ortega once shared a secret with me: "I stand so close to Doug during recordings so I can anticipate the chords he's going to play next."

On the final day, we were still missing one track for the album. Doug suggested we tackle a version of "Sugar Bee." Surprisingly, this became my favourite track on the album.

During this recording, Doug sang live with the band, with a massive joint hanging from his lips. Under normal circumstances I would have redone this vocal later but as it turned out this added a distinctive quality to the vocal sound, which complemented the recording perfectly. It is truly worthwhile listening to this track while picturing Doug singing with a big joint hanging from the side of his mouth. I think you will understand why I kept this vocal.

Once I returned to the UK, I took on the task of mixing the album, which they named *Midnight Sun* and promptly sent it off to Dag in Sweden. I believe Dag had some reservations based on our phone conversation, perhaps doubting if there was enough quality material for a full album.

To his pleasant surprise, I delivered 11 fully polished tracks. His response left me astonished - he loved the album and it went on to exceed all expectations in terms of sales.

With the success of *Midnight Sun,* I was approached to produce a second Doug Sahm album. After careful consideration and armed with the knowledge of what

I was getting myself into, I agreed. I also knew that I would have the unwavering support of the band.

During the recording of this subsequent album, I began to decipher the enigma that was Doug Sahm and learned to navigate his peculiar behaviour.
This allowed me to uncover the true depth of his artistic talent. Furthermore, his respect for me grew over time.
In total, I worked on three albums with SDQ, though it often felt like six, each marked by its own set of eccentric Doug Sahm quirks. Through it all, I developed a deep affection and admiration for Doug, a uniquely bizarre, complex and incredibly talented individual. To this day, I continue to miss him dearly.

Memorable Moments With Doug Sahm

On the first day of recording The Midnight Sun Album, Doug proposed that we visit a nearby restaurant close to our hotel in Mill Valley for breakfast, lured by their reputation for serving excellent omelettes. Since there were eight of us, we split into two cars. When we arrived at the restaurant, we found it bustling with activity. It took some time, but we eventually secured a table and discovered that the food was well worth the wait.
A few days later, we decided to return to the same spot. This time, Doug promptly hopped out of the car, expressing his intention to check for available tables. As we waited in our cars, five minutes passed with no sign of Doug. Curious, I went inside to investigate. To my surprise, Doug was comfortably seated at a table, happily indulging in a huge omelette. It seemed Doug wasn't willing to wait in line this day for his breakfast. When the rest of the band eventually entered the restaurant and saw Doug, there was not a lot of love in the room.

Recording the Hits

During the first day of recording our second album, *Rio Medina,* Doug had an unexpected idea. He turned to Augie and said, "You know, Augie, let's record the hits tomorrow. How about we do some of your songs today?"
I roared with laughter and asked Augie "How do you put up with things like that.? He replied, "That's just Doug man!"

Swedish TV

We had a rehearsal for a Swedish TV show scheduled to be broadcast live, but true to his character, Doug arrived late.
The Swedish TV director was organising camera shots and explained that Doug should enter the stage from the left after his introduction. Doug insisted, "No, that won't suit me. I'd rather come out from the right." After much discussion, the director, aiming for an easy resolution, adjusted the camera positions for Doug's entrance from the right.
Rehearsal went smoothly. Naturally, when the live show aired that night, the host introduced Doug with the cameras aimed at the right of the stage, Doug, of

course, entered from the left.

While touring in Scandinavia, the band always travelled light, having their clothes cleaned on the road. In contrast, Doug insisted on bringing six or seven suitcases with him to ensure he had clean clothes without dealing with laundry expenses. This often meant that the band members ended up acting as porters for Doug, carrying his luggage for him.

Trains, Cards and Helicopters

One memorable incident occurred in Trondheim, Norway. Everyone from the band, except Doug, arrived early at the station to catch the train for the next town on the tour. They were playing cards in the train compartment when Doug finally showed up and asked for their help with his luggage. Although reluctant, they agreed. When they attempted to load his bags onto the train in their compartment, Doug suddenly changed his mind saying, "No, I think I want to be in the carriage behind." Augie said, "But Doug, we're all in this one." But Doug insisted on moving his luggage to the other carriage. After complying with Doug's request, they returned to their card game.

Just as the train was about to leave Doug's face appeared at the compartment window, shouting frantically to Augie and the guys saying,
"They've unhooked the back part of the train; quick I need you all to help get my bags." Everyone remained seated and continued playing cards as the train pulled out of the station, with Doug's image slowly disappearing from the window as he was left standing on the platform.
With no other options available, he had to arrange for a helicopter to transport him and his luggage to the next gig - That's Doug for you!

Who would have guessed that I would end up developing a deep affection for this eccentric Texan?

Joe Sun

Born James Paulsen on September 25th, 1943 and passing away on October 25th, 2019, Joe Sun stood as a distinguished American country music singer-songwriter. Throughout his career, he recorded for both Ovation and Elektra Records, achieving an impressive 14 singles on the Hot Country Songs charts. Sun's musical odyssey encompassed the release of 15 albums, delivering captivating performances across the USA and Europe. Notably, his voice resonated in national radio advertisements for Budweiser. Beyond his musical journey, Joe Sun made several television appearances, gained recognition for producing two Grammy-nominated foreign albums in 1989 and 1990 and explored acting, portraying Tommy Fratter in the film Marie alongside Sissy Spacek and Morgan Freeman.

My initial encounter with Joe Sun took place in early 1984, when Sonet had just signed the country singer. They approached me with the task of producing an album with Joe, to be recorded in Nashville.

Before committing to any project, I had a personal rule: Wherever possible I should meet the artiste in person to ensure we clicked and were on the same creative wavelength.

So, since I was already visiting Joe's hometown of Nashville, for other business, Sonet told Joe that I would be staying at the Maxwell House Hotel, which was my preferred choice back then.

I was in my hotel room when Joe called, saying he'd come over in about an hour. I agreed and told him to ring my room when he arrived and I would come down to greet him. True to his word, an hour later, the phone rang and without waiting for my response, Joe declared, "OK, I'm here. I'll come up to your room."

When I opened the door a few minutes later, I was met with the imposing figure of a man who had the stature of an American football player. "Hi, Joe. I'm Kenny," I began, but he cut me off, walking straight into my room and asked, "What does an English guy like you know about country music?" I couldn't help but think, "Nice to meet you too."

Swiftly, I responded, "Nowhere near as much as you do, but that's not my job. Your job is to know the music; my job is to bring out the best in you."

This seemed to defuse the tension a bit and over the next few hours, our interaction became somewhat less strained.

The following day, I visited Joe's home, where he played me some of the songs he had written and intended to record. In his performance, I detected shades of Jerry Reed, one of my all-time favourite country acts and songwriters. Jerry had numerous hits and also penned chart-toppers for others, including two classics for Elvis, "Guitar Man" and "US Male".

After each song, Joe would confidently declare, "Now, that's one hell of a great song." While I didn't entirely agree with his assessment, there was some solid material to work with. I asked him if he could provide a tape of the songs he wanted to record so that I could take them back with me. Additionally, I mentioned that I'd like to send him a couple of songs from the UK for his consideration. We spent the rest of the day discussing dates and studio options.

Despite my initial reservations, perhaps stemming from our awkward first meeting at the hotel, I began to feel more at ease working with Joe.

Joe had mentioned an event called The Bluebird Cafe, where emerging songwriters could showcase their original material alongside a successful guest artist. He invited me to join him and I eagerly agreed to pick him up later in the evening.

The Bluebird Cafe was Situated in Nashville's Green Hills neighbourhood and had become a world-renowned listening room over its 39-year history. It's a place where the unsung heroes behind hit songs share their stories and perform their own creations.

When I arrived at Joe's house, he was ready with his guitar, clearly prepared to make an impression.

As we rode to The Bluebird, Joe told me about his past successes and it became very apparent that he had an ego larger than Carnegie Hall.

The Bluebird had a charming ambiance with seating for about 80 people. We found a couple of seats at the bar since we arrived early, affording us a good view of the stage. Before Joe took the stage, a couple of up-and-coming songwriters performed, then finally, with his guitar case and ego wide open, Joe confidently graced the platform.
He certainly demonstrated his craft well and the audience responded warmly.

After his performance, there was a short break, we were at the bar having a beer when an intimidating individual, looking like a troublesome Redneck, approached and locked eyes with me.
He menacingly declared, "I'm kinda in the frame of mind to punch you in the face."
I knew talking my way out of this was not gonna be easy but it really was my only option.
My initial thought was to humorously say, "I never get into fights with ugly people because they have nothing to lose," but I decided against it.
Instead, I attempted to disarm him with humour, asking, "Why would you want to do that? Unless you're the guy who wrote the sign over the front door of this place." Confused, he grumbled, "What do ya mean?"
I continued, "The sign over the front door, the one that says, 'Hey, pick up your teeth come on in and let's be friends and you can buy me a beer and we can make amends.'"
To my relief and surprise, he grunted, almost like laughter hidden beneath a cough. Capitalising on this, I swiftly added, "So, can I buy you a beer?"

At this point, I hoped for some backup from Joe, but all I saw were his broad shoulders turning away from the situation. The confrontation continued for about five minutes, during which I kept up the humorous banter.
I told him, "I'm a lover, not a fighter. Though there was a time when I was a boxer," quickly adding that I wasn't a very good one. This seemed to ease the tension further.
"In fact," I continued, "I was so bad that my manager decided to make some money by advertising on the soles of my shoes. And to make it easy for the corner men to carry me out of the ring, he put handles on the sides of my shorts."
By now, he was on his third beer and appeared to have relaxed a bit. Fortunately, the break in the music ended and another performer took the stage.
My newfound sparring partner grabbed his drink and, without a punch, a kiss, or a cuddle, disappeared into the audience.
At this point, Joe was busy networking, so I decided to call it a night and hailed a cab back to my hotel.
Only as I write about this encounter years later did it cross my mind that Joe may have orchestrated the entire episode, perhaps to test my confidence or see how I would handle a challenging situation.

The day prior to my departure from Nashville, I contacted Joe to arrange picking up a tape of the songs. We planned to discuss the final recording decisions over the phone.

A few weeks later everything fell into place. The material was confirmed, recording dates were set and we had booked Glaser Sound Studios in Nashville for the sessions. Additionally, I contacted Augie Myers, who was residing in New York at the time and he enthusiastically agreed to be part of the project.

On returning to Nashville, I allocated a couple of days for rehearsal before the official recording sessions commenced. Augie would join us the evening before the sessions began.

Joe had assembled a talented backing band of young musicians known as Solar System and we dedicated a few lengthy afternoons to rehearsing the four songs we were to record. Everything was coming together wonderfully.

The day before the sessions began, we found ourselves spending a considerable amount of time at the local Musician's Union office. There was an array of paperwork and agreements to be read and signed, some of which were unique to this situation.

On the morning of the recording, I arrived at the studio bright and early. I had instructed Augie to join us around 9:45. I never handled engineering duties in unfamiliar studios; there was already enough pressure on me to get the music just right, let alone navigating an unfamiliar recording environment.

As I entered the studio control room, I noticed the engineer in the studio setting up microphones for the musicians. I greeted him and supervised the mic positioning. While he was friendly and laid-back, I observed that he had placed the drums in the middle of the room.

I had to intervene, explaining that this setup wouldn't work for me. I needed the drums in a separate booth for the sake of sound separation; otherwise, every instrument track would be contaminated with drum sounds. Together, we moved the mics to the drum booth. Unfortunately, the pace of communication between us and his working tempo didn't align with the tight budget I had to adhere to. I knew this engineer wasn't right for the job.

I felt uneasy, something I had never experienced in my entire career and had to approach the studio manager to explain that I needed a different engineer. Being a professional studio, they swiftly arranged for a replacement.

The musicians began to arrive. They were not the same musicians I had seen playing in Joe's band earlier so I started to doubt whether I was at the correct studio until they inquired, "Is this the Joe Sun Session?"

The drummer began setting up and, since the new engineer hadn't arrived yet, I took the initiative to position some microphones around the drum kit.

The drummer then informed me that he was only booked for the morning session, as he had another gig later that day. This meant we would have to invest additional time setting up for another drummer in the afternoon.

I began to grow slightly agitated as the new engineer had yet to arrive and I had this inexplicable notion that we would be working with Joe's band and not these session musicians.

When Joe finally arrived, I couldn't contain my bewilderment. "Joe, what's happening here, why aren't we using your band?"

He responded, "Kenny, you don't get it, man. When this record is released, it has to feature the big names of Nashville playing on it. There's no way I could use my band."

Perplexed, I said, "Joe, why did we rehearse the songs with your band?"

His response, dripping with condescension, was, "So you could hear what the songs sounded like with a band."

By 9:45, all the musicians had assembled and the new engineer was enroute. Joe commenced running through the first song to allow the session musicians to jot down the chords.

I went to grab a coffee and to my surprise; I found the engineer I had dismissed seated in the lounge area. Despite feeling terrible about it, I apologised to him and tried to clarify my decision. I explained that due to our tight budget, I needed to work at an exceptionally fast pace and I didn't believe we would be compatible in that regard.

He seemed understanding, but given his laid-back attitude, I couldn't tell if he had fully accepted my apology or if it hadn't quite sunk in yet. Glancing at the wall, I was stunned to see three gold discs recognising his work on Elvis's albums. It was a shame I didn't have Presley's budget.

Returning to the recording session, I noticed that Augie had arrived and was encountering difficulties with the Nashville music community. It was evident that they were not welcoming of out-of-town musicians, especially those from Texas. I advised Augie to remain in the control room with me and we would add his parts later.

Finally, we began the recording process with the new engineer, who became a pain in the ass expressing after each and every take, "That's the greatest thing I ever heard," and then looking at me, adding, "Isn't it?"

More often than not, I would respond, "No, we'll need to do it again."

After painstakingly working through the sessions, we had the basic tracks and vocals completed, along with overdubs. Joe started reaching out to his contacts for backing vocalists.

I suggested to Joe, "Hey, Joe, let's bring in your band. They're familiar with the songs and harmonies and when you hit the road, the band will sound much closer to the recordings." He reluctantly agreed.

When his band members arrived, they couldn't stop expressing their gratitude for the opportunity to be in a professional studio and to contribute to this record. I pointed out to them that, as Joe's band, they should have been playing the backing tracks from the beginning.

Once I returned to the UK, I called Sweden and spoke with record company executives Dag and Gunnar. I explained that I couldn't continue the album in

Nashville because Joe's approach to making a good record didn't align with mine. To ensure a quality result, I proposed recording Joe outside of Nashville.

Dag suggested to Joe the idea of finishing the album with his band at the Sonet studios in London and possibly performing some gigs in Sweden and around Europe.

With Joe now in my territory, I knew I would have the full cooperation of his band. We agreed that this was a good way to complete the album. I don't recall much about the London recordings, except that there was significantly less pressure. Joe and the band performed admirably and professionally and the tracks came together without any issues. The Album, now entitled *The Sun Never Sets*, was finally ready for mixing.

A Monumental Disaster

I was tasked with mixing the album at Sonet's Park Studios in Sweden. My usual routine involved working late into the night. Despite the studio's excellent noise gates, I had a preference for meticulously cleaning each track on the multi-track recording, removing any unwanted noises, breaths, or guitar hums by recording over them with silence. This meticulous process made the mixing phase much smoother.

One night, around 2 a.m. while editing Joe's harmonica track for the song titled "The Light That Shines the Brightest," my mind wandered and before I realised it, I had accidentally erased his entire harmonica solo. Oops!

With Joe in Nashville and me in Sweden, this was a disaster of monumental proportions. After the initial panic subsided, I decided to salvage the situation. I scoured the recording for harmonica phrases Joe had played in the verses and painstakingly pieced them together to form a solo. This took hours before I had something that could pass as a reasonable solo.

Once I had a few bars that worked for the opening, I repeated the same phrase three times and then spent more time crafting the final few bars. I was convinced that Joe would notice when he heard the final mix, but luckily for me, he didn't so much as raise an eyebrow when he heard it. I guess he either thought the solo was so amazing it was well worthy of his talent, or it was so bad it was best not to draw any attention to it.

In fact, no one else seemed to notice either; it would appear I got away with it.

The album didn't achieve significant sales, but managed minor success in the Billboard Country charts with the single "Bad for Me". Recently, I listened to this album for the first time since I finished the recording and, to my surprise, it wasn't as 'bad for me' as I had thought at the time.

I couldn't help but wonder if our initial fraught meeting had set a different tone, perhaps we would have had more mutual respect and the recordings might have captured something significantly better. Even during subsequent visits to Nashville, unlike many other artistes I had produced, I never spoke or stayed in touch with Joe once the album was completed.

Joe Sun, finally arrived at the place where the sun never sets on October 25th, 2019, in Palm Bay Florida. RIP

Kinky Friedman - Too Much Ain't Enough

Kinky Friedman is a versatile Texan artist, excelling as a singer, novelist, songwriter, humourist, he also ventured into politics.

One evening in the early 80s, during a trip to New York City, I found a review in a local paper of a notorious Texan hangout called The Lone Star Cafe.
This place was renowned for embodying Texan-style rowdiness in the heart of the Big Apple. It was a bustling, often packed, joint with flowing tequila, delectable barbecue and an impressive line-up of performers such as Willie Nelson and Roy Orbison. I couldn't resist the allure of an evening in such a venue.

When I arrived at The Lone Star, the building's exterior seemed oddly out of place in the upscale neighbourhood. A colossal 40-foot iguana statue adorned the roof, with a sign below it that boldly declared, "Too Much Ain't Enough."
Inside, it was cosier than expected. The bar area was very busy, so I ventured upstairs to find a circular balcony with tables that overlooked the modest stage below.

That night's entertainment featured none other than Kinky Friedman & the Texas Jewboys. I grabbed a table with a great view, almost right above the stage and while waiting for Kinky's performance, I ordered a beer and some food.
On the next table was a young couple. I could hear the young man continuously raving to his lady friend about Kinky Friedman and what a great show we were about to see. He sounded like he was Kinky's biggest fan. His enthusiastic remarks continued until Kinky and his band arrived on stage.

As I finished my meal, leaning on the balcony with crossed arms, I had a front-row seat as the band launched into their first song, "They Ain't Makin' Jews Like Jesus Anymore."

The song finished and, after the applause waned, Kinky lit a huge cigar and proceeded to insult various audience members to the amusement of most but not those he targeted. This monologue was punctuated by frequent cigar puffs and persistent invitations to catch his show at 53rd and 3rd on the following Friday.

After about ten minutes and after the umpteenth time of Kinky telling everyone, if they wanted to see a great show he would be appearing at 53rd and 3rd on the following Friday, the young man on the next table lunged out of the dark and shouted," HOW ABOUT A FUCKING SHOW TONIGHT?"
Before disappearing back into the darkness as swiftly as he had appeared.

Still leaning on the balcony with my arms crossed, Kinky looked in my direction, our eyes met with laser precision and without breaking eye contact, removed his guitar and uttered, "Someone up there don't like me." The entire venue turned its attention to me.

From the audience below, a voice shouted, "I don't like you either, Kinky." The place erupted, but moments later, the same person yelled, "Cause Kinky, I love ya!" The crowd went wild.

By this point, a massive bouncer had joined Kinky on stage, both of them conversing and gazing up at me. Kinky remained adamant about not continuing the show.

I noticed that the couple from the nearby table had quietly departed earlier than planned. There was no way to convey that the true rebel among us had, in true Elvis-fashion, left the building.

Sensing the mounting tension, I decided to slip into the shadows and search for the nearest exit. I settled the bill with the waiter and swiftly departed through the upstairs exit.

Luckily, a yellow cab was dropping someone off right outside so I jumped into it as fast as a striking rattlesnake.

As I headed back to the hotel, I couldn't help but feel a tinge of disappointment about the evening. The Lone Star had truly lived up to its reputation with its mouth-watering barbecue, wild behaviour, raucous atmosphere, abundant tequila and, of course, the music courtesy of Kinky Friedman.

I surmised that the slogan "Too Much Ain't Enough" on the establishment's exterior was probably intended exclusively for Texans.

That night, I had surely had my fill of good old Texas hospitality.

Chapter 14

Nashville and Jerry Foster

Walter Hale, was a delightfully eccentric character who I had the pleasure of encountering during my initial visit to Nashville, whilst he was working for Porter Wagoner. Over the years he became a dear friend. Affectionately, I dubbed him "Nutty Walt," and he, in turn, called me "Kinney Dinten, my bestest buddy in the whole-wide-world."

During subsequent visits to Nashville, Nutty Walt would pick me up at the airport in his open-top Jeep, usually with a joint in one hand and a glass of wine in the other. Our journeys across town were never straightforward as Walter would often stop his car in the middle of the street to strike up conversations with people on the sidewalk. It seemed he knew everyone in town.
On one of my trips, Walter had changed jobs and was incredibly enthusiastic about introducing me to his new employer, Jerry Foster.

Jerry Foster

Jerry Foster, a much-celebrated songwriter, has built an impressive career, contributing over 500 songs that have been recorded by highly successful artistes. Collaborating with Bill Rice, together they hold the distinction of receiving the most awards in a single year from The American Society of Composers, Authors and Publishers. Furthermore, they accomplished the remarkable feat of having ten songs concurrently on the Billboard Country Music Chart.

On entering Jerry's office, it was impossible not to be impressed by the numerous gold records and awards adorning the walls. My initial impression was a testament to the company's resounding success.
As I examined these accolades more closely, it became clear that every honour belonged to one person - Jerry Foster, an immensely accomplished individual.

After a brief wait, I was invited up to Jerry's office. There, I found Jerry seated behind a substantial desk, his shirt collar upturned, mimicking Elvis's iconic look in a prominent picture on the wall behind him.
It was somewhat reminiscent of the scene from the 1980 movie *Airplane*, except Jerry was seated, not standing.

Walter introduced me to Jerry, proclaiming, "This is Kinney Dinten, my bestest buddy in the whole-wide-world." Jerry rose to shake my hand and greeted me with, "Hi buddy, Walter's told me all about you." It quickly became apparent that Walter had embellished my profile significantly to Jerry, making it seem like I was responsible for every hit record and major artiste in the UK and Europe for the past two decades. Who was I to shatter the illusion?

Seated on the sofa to my right were four heavyweight individuals who comprised Jerry's entourage which I later dubbed the Foster Mafia. To Jerry's left sat an extremely large lady who remained strangely silent throughout the entire meeting.

Once the introductions were over, Jerry sat down, propped one foot on his desk. With his guitar in hand, played and sang for me for the next three hours. Occasionally, members of the Foster Mafia would chime in, urging Jerry to play one of his songs written for a successful artist.
At one point, Jerry took out a cigarette and two members of the entourage eagerly competed to light it for him - like children vying for their father's approval.

Eventually, Jerry stopped playing and offered to get some food for everyone. I eagerly accepted the offer, if only to give my ears and facial muscles a much-needed break. I had been forcing a smile for so long that I feared it might become permanent.
The Foster Mafia scurried off immediately to collect some food. Meanwhile, Jerry disappeared into a side room with the silent lady. This left just Walter and me alone in the office.

I asked Walter if this lady was Jerry's wife,
"No Kinney, she is his clairvoyant, he is now asking her if you are seen in his future."
Lucky for me, or maybe not, I was seen in Jerry's stars as the chosen one.

A little while later the Foster Mafia returned with every type of food imaginable, there was Chinese, burgers, pizza, enough to feed a small army.
When I asked why there was such an amount and variety, one of his entourage replied.
"Wasn't sure what you liked so we wanted to give you a choice."
Well, they certainly covered all the bases!

From that moment onward, Jerry's attention and generosity became overwhelming.
At the end of the meeting, I was given use of Jerry's chauffeur and stretch limo, and I was asked if I would like to move from my hotel into his house.
Having seen someone take Jerry's guitar to his car and thinking he probably had a few hundred songs I hadn't heard yet, I figured my hotel would be the best option.

We went on to have several meetings and in each of them Jerry would be seated behind his desk with his guitar, churning out song after song, telling me how and why he wrote it. Occasionally he would take a break to play me some of his recordings that had been covered by various Nashville artistes.
After a few of these meetings, I started wondering why I was actually there. I figured that crunch time had come,
"Jerry," I asked, "You have been very hospitable to me and I have enjoyed your company but I have to ask, is there something you want from me?"
"Well," he said, "Now you come to mention it, I would like you to help me become a big star in Europe."

My stomach sank. This guy was in his early forties and even with all his success in country music I couldn't see him storming the British charts any time soon.

"Mmmm, with respect, the European market is really tough, plus you are a little old to break in as a new artiste over there."

Suddenly, the atmosphere in the room shifted, becoming charged with hostility and darkness.

If you have ever heard real silence, it can be a very loud sound. At this point you could have heard a fly wearing slippers walking across the ceiling.

For a second I thought I had signed my death warrant. The deafening silence, which seemed to go on for an eternity was broken by Jerry leaning forward across his desk and with a smile wider than a Texas mile, said in a quiet voice,

"Yeah, but Kenny, I can still cut it."

The Foster Mafia went wild, rising from their seats, shouting and whooping, "Yeah, Jerry can still cut it."

I knew then I would live to see another day.

Jerry decided to put the guitar down and play me some of the recordings he had made. They had DJ Fontana on drums, Scotty Moore on guitar and backing vocals sung by the Jordanaires. With the original Elvis band and Jerry doing his Elvis interpretation on the lead vocal, it was a really good 50s Sun Studio type of recording.

One particular track stood out above all of the others; it was a song called "Don't Let Go."

At this time I had my own label in England called, A-Side Records, handled through Sonet Records UK.

I explained to Jerry that I believed we could have a chance with "Don't Let Go," but we would need to make the most of the fact that it was the Elvis backing band and mention it both on the label and in the sleeve notes.

I decided that, even if the track was rejected by the radio, I had a release that I would be very proud to represent.

In November of that same year, I presented the track to Rod Buckle, the Managing Director of Sonet Records UK.

While A-Side Records was my own label, Sonet handled the crucial tasks of promotion, distribution and placement of products across Europe.

During our discussion, I conveyed my belief that we could achieve reasonable sales thanks to the track's unique appeal. While Jerry Foster was unknown in the UK, DJ, Scotty and the Jordanaires had a recognisable profile. Buckle agreed, seeing the potential in the idea.

After the record was pressed, we provided several copies to Radio One producers for consideration during the Christmas season. Then, on the first Monday of the New Year, as I tuned in to the Radio One Breakfast show, I was taken completely by surprise when I heard "Don't Let Go" playing. DJ Mike Read was enthusiastically praising this new record by Jerry Foster.

On the same day, a few hours later as I was driving my car listening to Radio One, the track graced the airwaves once more, this time on the Simon Bates show. I promptly pulled over at the nearest telephone box to contact Sonet with the exhilarating news - we had a bona fide hit on our hands. I urged them to put 5000 copies of the single into production as swiftly as possible, ready to stock the record shops. The radio plays continued unabated, day after day.

Unfortunately, there was a notable absence of records available in the local record shops for potential buyers, reportedly due to some disruptions at the distribution depot. I explored the option of resupplying the shops through an alternative company, but the time required for this process would have made it impossible to sustain the momentum that had been generated by the extensive radio play.
Despite Radio One continuing to feature the record on air for three weeks, it failed to make an appearance on the charts. It appeared that both the producers and the DJs had miscalculated their audience's preferences, resulting in the record being removed from the playlist.
On a more positive note, in The New Musical Express weekly rock 'n' roll chart, "Don't Let Go" held the number one position for an impressive ten weeks.
While conveying this news to Jerry proved challenging, he handled it gracefully thanks to his professionalism, understanding of the music industry, and busy work schedule.
Jerry remained one of those remarkable, talented and unconventional characters that make the music industry endlessly fascinating. Once again, it was a reminder that in the world of rock 'n' roll, the hand of fate often dictates and there are indeed no rules.

Chapter 15

My Cajun Adventure

First a history lesson and I promise to keep it brief.
In 1605, French settlers first arrived in what is now Nova Scotia. By 1755 a significant number of these early colonists refused to pledge allegiance to the English Crown prompting their relocation to Louisiana. This migration led to the fusion of various cultures, giving birth to the Cajun culture.
In the early 1900s a pivotal moment occurred when the accordion was introduced into French Louisiana music, supplanting the fiddle as the primary instrument. As the 1920s rolled in, dances began to evolve with the emergence of two-steps and waltzes.
More recently, recordings like Jonnie Allen's rendition of "Promised Land" and Denise Lasalle version "Don't Mess with My Tu Tu" have brought Cajun music into the mainstream consciousness. Zydeco, which bears similarities to Cajun music, serves as the vibrant dance music of Louisiana. Its origins are attributed to Lafayette or Opelousas, blending old Creole rhythms with elements of blues and soul. This unique mixture, akin to Cajun music, results in infectious and uplifting tunes.

To safeguard the identities of those involved in this story, certain names have been altered.

Through my connection with Sonet Records in Sweden, I had the opportunity to collaborate with Rockin' Dopsie, a renowned Zydeco accordion player. I also had the privilege of producing Queen Ida's album, *On A Saturday Night,* which was later nominated for a Grammy award.
Both Dopsie and Ida were seasoned artistes with dedicated followings who revelled in this wonderful feel-good, foot-stomping, body-moving music.

Time To Follow Another Dream

In 1992, I had the idea of finding a young Louisiana musician or band merging the traditional Cajun sounds of Louisiana with a contemporary, computer-based, recording style tailored to attract a younger generation of music enthusiasts.
So, with a youthful naivety, I embarked on a journey to Southwest Louisiana to scour the clubs and bars for a promising candidate.

On my way to Louisiana, I made a pit stop in Austin, Texas, where I spent a few days with close friends. I shared my ambitious plan with them, but they expressed genuine concern for my safety, particularly regarding my solo expedition into Cajun territory.
To alleviate their worries, I promised I would call them each day to confirm where I was, that all was well and that I was still alive.

My journey led me to Louisiana with Mamou as my destination - a quaint town renowned as the epicentre of Cajun culture. I believed it was the ideal starting point for my quest to discover a young, talented artist.

I rolled into Mamou around 7:30 p.m. on a Saturday evening but the town was deserted, it was like a ghost town waiting for a ghost.
My search led me to Fred's Lounge Bar on Sixth Street and Chestnut, the very heart of the Mamou Cajun scene.
I parked my car and peered out the window, only to discover that Fred's had closed its doors. Evidently, this musical feast commenced early on Saturday mornings and concluded around lunchtime.

While I cruised through town in my shiny new red Chevrolet rental, the sparse onlookers couldn't help but gawk at me, an extraordinarily conspicuous stranger in their midst.
I felt as welcome as a steak at a vegan BBQ, an uncomfortable sensation in the less-than-hospitable atmosphere of Mamou.
With Fred's Lounge closed for the day and my weariness growing, I decided it was time to seek some accommodation for the night.
Unfortunately the only establishment claiming to be a hotel was a very run-down two-story building. Driven by both adventure and exhaustion, I took a deep breath and decided to spend the night there.

As I approached the entrance, I discovered with a due sense of dread that it too was shut.
Nearby, I spotted a shop with a sign that read *Honk and Go*, a drive-in store where customers could simply honk their car horns for service. I found out later these stores were also known as Stop n Robs. I gave a honk, ordered a Coke and a pack of cigarettes and inquired of the attendant if there was a hotel nearby.
"Wont somewar carlean?" he replied.
"I certainly do" I said,
"Wheel I be! Ya haff tar heyed back ta Lafayette."
As dusk was descending this seemed like a very good idea.
Just as I was leaving, I spotted another bar. It looked promising, proclaiming to have live music. After thinking about it carefully, the presence of pickup trucks with rifles hanging in their rear windows, coupled with the approaching nightfall and with nowhere to stay, dampened my enthusiasm for immersing myself in Mamou's nightlife. I decided to leave.

Heading back to the interstate, I became engrossed in the music blaring from my car radio. Although, I couldn't help but notice a large pickup truck up ahead. In the bed of the truck stood three locals and I couldn't miss the customary rifle swinging in the rear window. Their gestures and shouts in my direction didn't appear welcoming at all, resembling the friendliness of a shark with a leg in its mouth.
I had no desire to pass them, so I attempted to maintain a safe distance. Yet, whenever I slowed down, they matched my pace. After what felt like an eternity of this cat-and-mouse game, they finally made a left turn off the road.
With a tremendous sigh of relief, I stepped on the gas and didn't slow down until I reached Lafayette. It was only now the reality of how dangerous and insane this

task I was attempting began to dawn on me.

After a restful night at a "carlean' hotel, I rose early and tuned in to the radio. During the broadcast the DJ mentioned a Cajun event scheduled for that afternoon at the Triangle Club in a town named Scott.
After studying my map for a while, I decided this could be a good place to start my quest. I set off in the car and soon arrived at the club.

Pulling into the parking lot, the pulsating music emanating from the walls of yet another weathered building reached my ears. Despite the somewhat unwelcoming appearance and since I had travelled a considerable distance in search of a promising young artist, there was no option but to grab the bull by the horns and step inside.
As I entered through the front door, transitioning from the bright daylight outside to the dimly lit interior of the club, my vision temporarily suffered, I couldn't see properly at all. Luckily someone was leaving just as I entered and the encounter alerted me to a steep step down immediately inside the doorway, preventing what could have been a calamitous mishap. Tripping and careening toward the bar with my head down like a Matador's bull would have hardly been a dignified entrance. I maintained an air of casual nonchalance as I strolled toward the bar, striving to appear inconspicuous and in full command of the situation, while my eyes gradually adapted to the dim lighting.

A deafening band occupied the stage, their volume so overpowering that I couldn't discern if they were playing Cajun, reggae, or simply tuning their instruments. I secured a seat at the bar and, in the brief lulls between songs when the bartender could actually hear me, ordered a beer. Most of the conversations I caught were unfolding in French Creole.
Turning to the guy seated to my right, I queried in English if he knew the band's name. His curt reply was, "Don't know, don't care." As the band began announcing their next song, I took a generous gulp of my beer.
Right after I swallowed that sip, a woman positioned behind me leaned in, her mouth mere inches from my ear and unleashed the most thunderous rebel yell I'd ever encountered.
Had this happened a fraction of a second earlier, the beer in my mouth would have spewed out like a firefighter's hose, drenching the guy in front of me and likely sparking a chaotic brawl. I was certainly riding my luck that day.
The band on stage weren't burdened by talent and were less than impressive, leading me to believe that I had tested my fortune enough for now. It was time to finish my drink and make my exit.

After several more days of trudging through second-rate clubs, listening to third-rate bands, I came to the realisation that this wasn't the path to discovering the major artiste I sought. My trip to Louisiana had been far from enjoyable; it was undeniably disappointing. I made the decision to throw in the towel and head back to Texas.

During my return journey, I decided to tune in to a Cajun radio station. The DJ happened to be a guy named Camey Doucet. Suddenly it dawned on me, Camey would possess a wealth of knowledge about the local bands and artistes I was seeking. He could be the key to unlocking the door to my quest.

Realising it was time to take a break, I checked into a hotel in Lake Charles for the night and attempted to establish contact with Camey. I phoned the radio station and spoke with his secretary, introducing myself and explaining my mission in Louisiana. She conveyed that Camey was currently on air but promised to pass along my message and assured me that he would return my call once he finished his show.

Before too long, he returned my call and I recounted my entire story to him. Without hesitation, he responded, "Well, there's only one kid I can think of who fits the description you're looking for and that's Toby Tomera. He's 16 years old and incredibly talented." Camey generously provided me with a couple of contact numbers and suggested that I mention his name when calling them. I felt as though I had struck gold.

After my conversation with Camey, I promptly dialled Toby and introduced myself, detailing the project I was endeavouring to put together. Toby came across as a polite and easy-going young man. He asked if I could speak to his brother, Baloo.

As it turned out, Baloo not only played the role of the drummer in Toby's band but also acted as his manager. I called Baloo to arrange a meeting and present my idea. He proposed we meet at a club called Poets in Lafayette the following afternoon at four.

With an evening free, I asked the young hotel receptionist if there was a local spot where I could enjoy both great food and good music. She recommended a venue called "Cowboys" that evening as it was to be their *Uptown Country night*, where a $5 cover granted access to unlimited food and drinks and a live band and even better it was only ten minutes away. She told me it opened at 7:30 and kindly gave me directions.

I set out around 7 p.m. reaching the expansive venue by 7:15. Navigating a lengthy corridor lined with enormous glass windows on both sides, I encountered three or four doormen stationed outside the entrance. Peeking through the door, I observed a band tuning their instruments on stage, accompanied by a young girl conducting the customary mic "one, two" sound check. With everything appearing in order, I happily paid the $5 cover fee. The doorman marked my hand with a blue rubber stamp before granting entry.

Stepping into the sizable venue, which I guess was big enough for well over 150 people. I noticed long tables capable of seating around 20 people each. Opting for a spot in the middle of one of these tables, I enjoyed a clear view of the stage where the band was preparing for their performance.

Over the next 15 minutes, the place filled up faster than Paul McCartney's royalty account. I'd never seen so many Kenny Rogers lookalikes in one place.
The man sitting directly across from me took off his hat and set it on the table,

unveiling a head adorned with the most impeccably silver hair. Running his fingers through the strands that had been tousled by the hat, he seemed to revel in the moment.

I was stunned by the attention to detail to every attendee's extravagant western attire. The women adorned themselves in top-notch denim jeans, expensive snakeskin boots and eye-catching hats embellished with rhinestones and tassels. Meanwhile, the men engaged in their own subtle competition to outdo each other, donning denim and flannel shirts with plaid patterns, accented by embroidery and small waistcoats and, of course, the obligatory Stetson cowboy hat. Many opted for braided necklaces and bow ties, aiming for a sophisticated look. In contrast, I felt quite ridiculous in my simple T-shirt, white tracksuit bottoms and brand-new trainers.

As my table filled up around me, I realised I should have chosen to sit at the end of the table, not slap in the middle, it was bizarre, I hadn't wanted to draw any attention to myself and strangely it was almost like I was invisible, which felt odd but the incessant chatter simply drowned out my presence.

Two guys nearby engaged in banter, one asking, "What does a girl from Louisiana do if she's not in bed by 10 p.m.?" The response came quickly "Go home."
By 8 p.m. the emcee took the stage, announcing, "The bar and buffet are now open." A chaotic rush ensued as everyone stampeded toward the bar. Suddenly I noticed through the numerous glass windows that lines of police were assembling outside. It didn't seem like they were there for the $5 entry fee or to enjoy the band, this felt more like a night destined to end in a massive brawl. With my table now deserted, leaving became my priority. Exiting through the main door, once again observing the police presence, the guy who stamped my hand upon arrival asked, "Leaving already?" I replied. "There's just too many cowboys in there and not enough Indians" He laughed as I hastily retreated.
Returning to my hotel, I opted for the tranquillity of the restaurant, where only a couple dined. There, I enjoyed a peaceful evening, enjoying a generous steak accompanied by a delightful bottle of red wine before I retired to my room.

The next day I drove back to Lafayette to meet Baloo. I arrived at Poets only to discover it was closed. Peering through the glass front door, I saw the silhouette of a figure heading toward me, a figure so large that had me worried I was about to experience a solar eclipse.
As the door swung open, I was greeted with, "Hi, are you Kenny? I'm Baloo, come on in. It's strange, you sounded a lot taller on the phone." An intriguing opening line, I thought.

As our meeting progressed, it became apparent that Snow White must have had an affair with Dopey and I was sitting across from their offspring. The next few hours were devoted to explaining the entire concept to Baloo, which proved to be somewhat taxing, he seemed to struggle to grasp the nuances of the plan.
I continued to explain that by integrating computer technology and blending it

with Cajun music, we could make the music more appealing to a broader and younger audience.

It became evident that Baloo's primary concern revolved around himself, particularly his role as the drummer and his insistence on being involved in all recordings. While this was a discussion for later, my initial priority was to meet Toby and witness his musical abilities in action.

Finally Toby arrived carrying his school books and resembling a youthful Buddy Holly. This composed and softly spoken young man brought a welcomed layer of comprehension to our conversation. It was clear who had inherited all the intellect in the family.

The following evening, the band was set to perform their routine weekly gig at Poets. As I entered, I was met with a packed venue. Camey's assessment had been accurate - Toby possessed an extraordinary level of talent, coupled with a remarkable stage presence. I was thoroughly impressed by his vocals, accordion skills and utterly blown away by his guitar playing.

At one point during the show, four girls took to the dance floor and executed a perfectly synchronised dance routine, I assumed they were dedicated Toby fans who had rehearsed every step. Within minutes, a dozen more people joined in and, before long, the entire dance floor was a spectacle of synchronised dancing - lines of people moving in unison, each executing every move simultaneously. It was a mesmerising sight.

After the performance, I quizzed Toby about this remarkable dance routine. He seemed surprised and asked, "Man, you've never seen line dancing before?"
"No," I admitted, "but I have just witnessed the perfect idea for your first music video."
Regrettably, later that year, Billy Ray Cyrus pipped us to the post and managed to capitalise on a similar idea with his hit "Achy Breaky Heart."

That night, witnessing the excitement and adulation of the girls screaming for Toby, confirmed to me that he was indeed the artiste I had been searching for. It was one of the most electrifying gigs I had experienced in a long time.

Over the next 18 months, I would find myself gradually losing my sanity and parting with $50,000. The first six months were consumed by negotiations with Toby's family and their attorney. Given that Toby was only 16 his father had to sign the deal on his behalf. The contract we forged extended over five years, segmented into yearly options.

During our first year, we made numerous trips between Louisiana and my hometown. I often brought my wife, Sue, along to meet Toby's family and we attended several of Toby's gigs.

One evening, memorable for all the wrong reasons, Sue and I were graciously invited to Toby's home for a family meal. As we entered the house I could see into the kitchen, I couldn't help but notice the largest pot I had ever seen, brimming with the local delicacy, Jambalaya. It seemed this pot had a permanent spot on the stove, readily filled every day for the family whenever hunger struck. We all sat down ready to eat and a slightly smaller pot, filled to the brim, appeared on the table. Its appearance and aroma weren't exactly appetising.

Toby's mother took the lead in serving everyone and Sue, desperately trying to avoid a large helping, attempted to politely decline. Unfortunately for Sue, her efforts were in vain and a large portion was dished up for her accompanied by some soft buns. Sue's face was a picture; she could not hide the look of dread. She delicately placed the tiniest morsel of food on the tip of her fork, only to follow it with an enormous gulp of water every time.

I watched as she artfully rearranged her food on her plate, trying to make it seem like she had eaten more than she actually had.

As the meal neared its end, Toby's mother turned her attention to Sue, exclaiming, "Sue, you've hardly eaten anything!" With an unexpected lunge forward, she wielded two enormous spoons, dipping back into the pot and transferring more onto Sue's plate, insisting, "Let me get you some more gizzards." I couldn't help but worry that Sue might become physically ill from the situation.

Seeing her distress, I felt compelled to intervene. I apologised profusely, saying, "I'm truly sorry; I should have mentioned that Sue is a vegetarian." Shock and bewilderment enveloped the dinner table. Toby's mother exclaimed, "A vegetarian? How on earth do you survive?"

Quick on her feet, Sue came up with the excuse that her dietary restriction was due to a medical condition, not a mere food preference. This explanation appeared to resolve the situation.

As we drove back to our hotel, Sue sharing her thoughts, mentioned how passing a restaurant earlier that day with a sign that read, "From your grill to ours," had not been particularly helpful. It was a light-hearted nod to the concept of serving roadkill, which I found rather amusing.

To kickstart our musical odyssey, I flew Toby and Baloo to London, where we entered the studio to produce some tracks. Our aim was to record a standout single that would catch the attention of major record labels.

The fusion of computer-generated rhythms, live instruments and a sprinkle of Cajun lyrics transformed these tracks into unexpectedly commercial songs, exceeding my initial expectations.

I suggested to Baloo that we release a single ourselves to generate interest, labelling it as a preview from Toby's forthcoming album.

To this, Baloo responded with, "That won't work, Toby hasn't released the first three albums yet." I couldn't quite discern if he was joking or not, though I suspected not.

Armed with this fantastic new material, I successfully arranged meetings with the heads of nearly every major record company in the UK. I presented this idea as a comprehensive package, a fresh and exciting concept that must have seemed like a dream scenario for a PR company. It featured innovative music, untapped Louisiana heritage, Cajun cuisine and song lyrics partly in the Creole language all from a young good looking talented artist.

Regrettably, my enthusiasm wasn't entirely shared by these record companies but each rejection only fuelled my determination to make this project a success. One managing director of a record company asked me, "I love the music and the idea, but how do we categorise him?"
I countered with, "How did they pigeonhole Elvis, The Beatles, David Bowie?"
"That was then, this is now," he replied.
After several encounters like this, my persistence eventually paid off, securing a deal with a record company.
Unfortunately, by that point, I was 11 months into my contract with the artiste and to activate the second-year option, I needed to come up with $15,0000 which I didn't have.

My only recourse was to fly to New Orleans for an urgent meeting with Toby, Baloo and their lawyer. I intended to discuss the need for a brief extension of my contract without paying the second advance, which would allow me to complete the paperwork with the record company. I arrived in New Orleans on October 10th, a Sunday evening and we all gathered for dinner. We shared the fantastic news about the major record deal that had finally been offered, everything appeared to be on track.

The following morning, Baloo and Toby were supposed to meet me at my hotel at 10:30 a.m. and together, we would head to the lawyer's office for an 11 a.m. meeting. As the clock ticked to 10:45 a.m. with no sign of Baloo, I began to grow concerned.
I decided to call him at home but to my astonishment, his wife answered and informed me that he had gone directly to the lawyer's office for 10 a.m. meeting. Furious, I hastily hailed a cab and headed straight to the lawyer's office.

Arriving at the meeting, I sensed a tense atmosphere in the room. It felt very sombre and I could almost smell treachery and greed lingering in the air. I raised the issue of the meeting time, but Baloo vehemently denied that we had arranged to meet at the hotel and insisted that he had informed me the meeting was at ten.

I conveyed my need for a six-to-eight-week extension on our contract to finalise the deal with the record company. The lawyer replied, "This is something I would need to discuss with my clients."
Fuming with frustration, I clenched my teeth and said, "Well, you'd better discuss it with them now. I've flown in from the UK to sort this out. I've also devoted the last 18 months of my life to this project I've even re-mortgaged my home for $50,000 to make this happen."

It was decided that another meeting would take place later that week, scheduled for Friday afternoon. Feeling utterly despondent after the meeting, I checked out of my hotel and took a cab to New Orleans airport. From there, I called Sue and informed her that I was returning home immediately, as I had strong suspicions that they were plotting against me.
Sue, as always, managed to calm my nerves and wisely suggested that considering the significant time and money we had invested in this project, it was

best for me to stay in New Orleans until Friday for the meeting.

I decided I didn't want to spend any more time than necessary in New Orleans, a place I was beginning to hate so I opted to take a flight to Austin, Texas and book a room at the Embassy Suites Hotel. It was a place I was familiar with and quite fond of. Despite having many friends in Austin, I didn't feel much like socialising, so I remained in the hotel until Friday morning. Then, I checked out and returned to New Orleans.

A feeling of trepidation came over me as I arrived at the lawyer's office for the meeting. We engaged in about an hour or so of discussion. During that time, I was reassured that everything would be resolved. Everyone expressed their understanding of the immense time, effort and money I had dedicated to the project and we all agreed to move forward.

I flew back to the UK, realising that the trust had been irrevocably broken, even if we were to continue as planned.
My contract with Toby was set to expire on the first day of November.
On the morning of November 1st, right on schedule, my lawyer delivered the news, "Kenny, are you sitting down? I've just received a fax from Toby's lawyer stating that they no longer require your services and they will sign with the record company directly."
I was deeply hurt, though not entirely surprised. Greed had taken over and the inevitable had occurred. I sat down and contemplated what had driven me to embark on such an absurd adventure with such baffling individuals. There were many uncomfortable situations I had encountered in Louisiana.

One particular afternoon, after having lunch with Baloo in Lafayette, he told me he wanted to drop in and see a friend of his.
We arrived unannounced and entered the house, there were several guys in the living room. It felt like we had interrupted some sort of meeting.
I was offered a coffee and asked a series of stupid questions,
"Does it ever rain in England?"
"Have I ever met the Queen?"
Then one particularly unpleasant character asked,
"Do you have black people in England?"
"Yeah" I replied,
"Do they cause all the trouble?" he continued,
"Some do, some don't." I answered.
He looked me straight in the eyes and then said,
"I'm a racist, I hate all blacks".

I felt extremely uneasy, I had no desire to spend another moment in that house with those individuals.
Politely declining a refill of coffee, I explained that I needed to return to my hotel urgently, awaiting an important phone call. With that, I made a swift departure and headed back to the car.

During the drive back, Baloo, who had a knack for saying peculiar things daily, turned to me and asked, "Hey Kenny, do you know how to identify a good Cajun woman?" I responded with a sense of indifference, "No idea." To which he replied, "Well, she can look at a field of rice and tell you how much gravy it needs."

The conclusion to this adventure was that Toby did sign the record deal and proceeded to record the album with his band, but they omitted two crucial elements: the modern computer-techno style and my involvement. They received their advance and used the remaining funds to produce an unremarkable, ordinary Cajun album that was never released in the USA and only saw a few minor releases in Europe.

As for Toby, I am aware that he continues to perform in local bars around Louisiana and Baloo? Well, who knows or perhaps, who cares?

It's worth noting that when artistes sign with a major label, they often proclaim that they've secured the best contract ever, emphasising artistic freedom and a guaranteed five-album deal.

But, when they eventually part ways with the label, they tend to insist that it was the worst contract ever and request to be released from it. Such is the nature of the music industry.

Chapter 16

Alisha's Attic

Alisha's Attic were a successful duo during the mid-1990s, consisting of sisters, Shelly and Karen Poole. In 1997 they earned a Brit Award nomination for Best Newcomer and interestingly, they are the daughters of Brian Poole, renowned for his hits in the mid-60s with his backing band, the Tremeloes.
From 1996 to 2001, they secured nine singles in the UK charts. The internet is rife with various accounts of how Alisha's Attic secured their recording deal, this is the truth about what happened.

After my Cajun adventure, I found myself bouncing back when an old colleague, Laurie Jay, approached me wanting to connect me with two talented female vocalists he knew. Laurie possessed an impressive musical background, having served as a drummer for icons such as The Shadows, The Echoes (from 1960 to 1962), Dusty Springfield, Chuck Berry, Gene Vincent and Jerry Lee Lewis. Additionally, he led the Laurie Jay Combo from 1962 to 1965.
He eventually transitioned into artiste management, representing talents such as Elkie Brooks, Billy Ocean and Shirley Bassey.

Laurie was considering extending a management offer to Alisha's Attic and inquired if, assuming I enjoyed their music, I'd be interested in producing some tracks for potential presentation to a record label with an aim to secure a recording contract.
He explained that if a record company expressed interest, I would have the opportunity to oversee the production of their album.
Despite Laurie's reputation for being a 'challenging' collaborator, something I encountered personally, he undeniably stood out as a distinctive figure with an exceptional ability to spot promising artistes. I had the honour of working alongside Laurie on numerous occasions throughout the years.

Shelly and Karen paid a visit to my studio. Our connection was instant and we engaged in lively conversations about our musical tastes and life in general. Amidst our discussion, I opened up about the recent let-down I had faced with my Cajun artiste.
Karen expressed her empathy. "How could he do that to you?" she said.
In hindsight, I wish I had had the prescience to respond with, "A few years from now, the tables will turn and you'll do exactly the same.

The two girls possessed striking beauty and abundant charm, complemented by their incredible singing voices but it couldn't be ignored, the demos they presented were noticeably amateurish. Despite this, I made the conscious decision to zero in on one particular song, titled "Natural Thing".
For my next move, I contacted my immensely talented friend and music programmer, Danny Saxon. Danny and I had a long history of collaboration spanning several years, having worked with diverse artistes like Anthony Newley and Fleetwood Mac's Peter Green. His musical expertise and programming skills

had proven invaluable, especially on my previous Cajun recordings.

I got in touch with Danny, providing him with an overview of Laurie's new project and the overall plan. But I also had to caution him about the absence of a budget. Given his familiarity with Laurie, Danny approached the opportunity with a hint of scepticism but nevertheless, owing to our strong friendship, he agreed to join me in the recording endeavour.
Over the subsequent weeks, we worked diligently and successfully completed the track, earning a genuine satisfaction from everyone involved.

Then, a profound silence descended as nearly a year slipped by with only sporadic contact from Shelly and Karen or their management. Eventually, Karen made a phone call, asking if they both could come and see me.

During our meeting, they unveiled their frustration with their current management and their burning desire to return to the studio for new recordings. They brought along a cassette tape containing three demo songs, which had been recorded on a basic four-track cassette machine by Karen's boyfriend, Terry.
The quality of these recordings, as one might expect, left much to be desired. But there was no question, the songs possessed an undeniable spark of something special.
In one of the songs "Toy Box," one lyric, in particular, resonated deeply with me: "Dreaming with a capital D".

I promptly contacted Danny once again, letting him know of the girls' renewed interest and that they had some new material. I emphasised my belief in the potential of Shelly and Karen, convinced that we could secure them a record deal and share in the success.
Playing the demo to Danny he didn't really share my level of enthusiasm for the project. Nevertheless, he placed his trust in me once more, agreeing to work on the project without compensation, driven by his faith in my judgement rather than his immediate enthusiasm for the girls' music.

Initially, we had to take a rather ruthless approach, trimming bars and lines from their songs and lyrics. While their song writing displayed clear potential, the meticulous art of crafting a song still eluded them.
During this process, they remained quite content with our guidance, recognizing the necessity of these changes.

Ultimately, we polished three songs into shape: "Toy Box," "Alisha Rules the World," and "Air We Breathe".
We invested a considerable amount of time refining the girls' vocal performances. Danny skillfully arranged harmonies, ensuring they didn't resemble Wilson Phillips, another successful girl duo of that era.

While working on their lead vocals I dedicated substantial effort to imparting a crucial lesson about connecting with the audience. I'd often tell them, "If you don't believe in what you're singing, how can you expect anyone else to?"

In my view, the distinction between a great vocalist and a cabaret singer lies in this: a cabaret singer merely delivers the melody and lyrics, while a great singer conveys not just the melody but also the true meaning behind the words.

After the recording and mixing process concluded, we emerged with three outstanding tracks, certainly deserving of a substantial record and publishing contract.
The girls approached me with a request for assistance in securing a record deal. I suggested that it would be wise for them to approach the record companies personally and I offered to help them assemble a polished package. This would consist of a well-crafted letter, a couple of high-quality photos and a tape containing the music. I explained that I would include just one song on the cassette, as record companies typically inquire about additional material if they like what they hear initially and we would be ready with a couple of songs in reserve.

Before long, A&R representatives started contacting the girls desperate for a meeting. I spent hours on the phone with the girls, often late at night, and several times a week. First, Karen would call and shortly after Shelly, both seeking reassurance and morale boosts. I gave them the encouragement they needed, assuring them that things were looking promising and that they must be patient. During a conversation with the girls and Terry at a BBQ hosted at my house, they insisted that Danny and I, were as integral to Alisha's Attic as they were.

As more record companies expressed interest in the band, the girls eventually asked if I would consider managing them. I admitted that I had no prior experience in management, so I advised them to visit management agencies and select one that they would be happy with, then return to me with their decision.
In a matter of weeks, they contacted me to inform me that they had made progress in their selection process but were grappling with a decision between two potential managers.

One of these candidates had a roster of a dozen successful artistes. The other contender, Paul White, had previously overseen a prosperous duo act but had taken a break from the industry and was making a comeback into management.
I recommended that they seriously consider Paul White's candidacy. My reasoning was that by choosing him, they would have the advantage of his undivided attention, as opposed to becoming a small fish in a large pond with the other manager's extensive roster. Ultimately, they heeded my advice and opted for the candidate returning to full-time management.

With a couple of potential deals on the horizon, the new manager was enthusiastic about a meeting at my studio with Danny and me. Naively, I assumed it might relate to our future collaboration with the girls.

As the meeting got underway White told us he had received an offer of a publishing deal with EMI worth £125,000 and a serious proposal from Mercury Records for a record contract. He added "that to really seal the deal with a major

record company, under his terms and in the best interests of the girls" he would require us to produce three additional tracks for Karen and Shelly.
Unfortunately, for these new recordings, he was only willing to offer us a paltry £600.

I shared a knowing look with Danny and grinned as I turned to Paul. I went on to describe how, for the past few years, we had been wholeheartedly dedicated to the band without any compensation and that we were ready to maintain that dedication for these new tracks. I then said that I acknowledged the record label might prefer to have a well-known producer complete the album; however, we were only seeking an assurance that he would use his best efforts to secure at least two songs on the album for us to produce.
In response, Paul firmly stated, "I am not going to make any promises on that."
The conversation grew tense. I reminded him of his earlier statement, "To really seal the deal with a major record company under his terms," suggesting that his terms could include a small two song production deal for us.
"£600 and that's final," he said.
I then asked if he could at least promise to present the idea to the record company. It was only at this point that Karen spoke up, saying, "Paul told us that if we give everything away now, we will end up with very little."
I agreed but added, "We've been baking this cake for a long time, long before Paul entered the picture, and now we're not even being offered the crumbs."
Shortly thereafter, the meeting came to an end.

That marked the final occasion I would ever meet or communicate with them in any manner. Once the Mercury Records deal had been finalised, I contacted the record company to inquire if they were interested in acquiring my multi-track recordings.
It turned out that their legal department promptly conveyed their disinterest in these tapes. Moreover, since I had no official paperwork with Alisha's Attic, I was warned that any use of the tapes could result in a lawsuit from Mercury Records.
Reflecting on my past experience with legal issues while attempting to safeguard my interests with my Cajun artist, which ultimately yielded no benefits, I mistakenly chose not to formalise an agreement with these friendly young, talented girls who were in need of assistance, hence the absence of documentation.
Danny's contribution with the girls was nothing short of remarkable; he possessed a genius for extracting the best from their material. This fact was subsequently confirmed when Dave Stewart replicated the string lines, various instrument sounds and riffs from our version in his hit rendition of "Alisha Rules the World". Looking back, it's clear that Dave Stewart's version of "Air We Breathe" could have benefited significantly had he applied the same approach to that track as well.

Every time I heard "Alisha Rules the World" playing on the radio, it was a painful reminder. But I assure you, the true pain ran much deeper, realising that Danny and I had been taken advantage of by individuals we had regarded as friends and even family.

It was disheartening to witness the girls moving forward and seemingly forgetting about both of us. Equally regrettable was the fact that, despite their success, they appeared to have overlooked the valuable lessons we had imparted to them. Had they retained and applied those lessons, they could have achieved even greater success and that's the undeniable truth.

I taught them everything they know, but not everything I know - James Brown

Chapter 17

Fleetwood Mac's Peter Green

Peter Green achieved legendary status during his career, most notably as the co-founder of Fleetwood Mac alongside Mick Fleetwood and John McVie. In 1968, the band found success with Green's hits such as "Black Magic Woman" followed by "Albatross", "Oh Well", "Man of the World" and "Green Manalishi".

Eventually the overwhelming success took its toll on Peter, leading him to experiment with LSD, which is believed to have contributed to his battle with schizophrenia. Consequently, in 1970, he made the difficult decision to part ways with Fleetwood Mac and embarked on a tumultuous journey haunted by personal demons.

Peter Green's struggle led to periods of hospitalisation in psychiatric facilities undergoing electroconvulsive therapy. Despite managing to resurface several times over the years, he often melted back into obscurity once more.

Peter Green and the Splinter Group

In the 90s I owned my own recording studio in West London. It was here I received a call from my close friend Stuart Taylor, who was managing a band named The Splinter Group featuring Peter Green. He wanted to schedule studio time to mix a recording of their instrumental track, "Walk Don't Run."

This recording had been initially produced by the renowned drummer, Cozy Powell at a different studio but Cozy had grown dissatisfied with the band's overall situation and decided to part company. As a long-time admirer of Peter Green, the opportunity for me to collaborate with him was a genuine honour.

Despite my knowledge of Peter's eventful history, I was genuinely taken aback when I met him. Instead of the image of a legendary guitarist, he resembled Mr. Smee from Peter Pan. His wispy sideburns peeked out from beneath a tightly fastened bandana around his head and his clothing, draped over his slightly overweight torso, looked like they had been discarded by Oxfam.

Initially, engaging in conversation with Peter was quite challenging for me but, as our acquaintance deepened, I encountered a remarkable individual with a genuinely warm and gentle character. He had a profound passion for music as well as a mind deeply immersed in a world of his own creation. I couldn't help but develop a deep admiration for him.

His constant musings on life always fascinated me. I once asked Peter whether he believed in an afterlife. After a lengthy silence, during which he gazed at the ceiling, he responded, "I'm not certain I believe in this one."

My initial responsibility as the engineer was to prepare the multi-track for mixing. The first ten tracks were dedicated to drums, bass and rhythm guitar, all of which were in good shape.

Peter had recorded various takes of his guitar solos, so I meticulously listened to each one and selected the most exceptional sections. I then combined these sections into a single cohesive guitar solo.

With the backing track sounding complete, I began to integrate Peter's guitar into the mix. While adding reverb to the guitar using one of my many electronic effects units, Peter inquired, "How many different types of echoes does the module have?"
I replied, "There's over 200 in this one."
Peter decided he wanted to hear every one of them. So, with the multi-track machine set to loop, playing the track repeatedly, I changed the reverb setting every ten or 15 seconds. We carefully listened to every variation, noting down the ones Peter favoured.
After a thorough exploration of reverb options, Peter settled on his preferred choice. I then carefully balanced the level of his guitar with the rest of the instruments.
Following this adjustment, Peter remarked, "The drums are too loud." I promptly reduced the drum volume.
He continued, "Now the bass is too loud, can we lower it?" I complied and decreased the bass level.
Then he mentioned, "The rhythm guitar is too loud, please bring it down." At this point, Peter's lead guitar dominated the mix. As a result of the changes he wanted me to make, he soon realised that his guitar was excessively loud, prompting us to backtrack on all our previous adjustments.
As time progressed, I pulled Stuart aside, and together we discreetly devised a plan to reach a settlement. We would finish this mix with Peter then, later I would remix the track again by myself.
When the finalised master was delivered, everyone appeared more than happy with the result.

The Robert Johnson Songbook

Not long after, Stuart approached me once more with a proposal. He asked if I would consider producing an album featuring Robert Johnson songs for Snapper Records. The unique twist was that it would be a collaboration between Peter and the other guitarist from the Splinter Group.
Despite my prior experiences with Peter this project didn't appear overly complicated. I had worked with many challenging artistes throughout my career and I saw this as an intriguing opportunity.
Little did I know that this album would be my introduction to the maelstrom that constantly surrounded Peter Green.

Initially, the plan was for Peter and his colleague to record the album.
We had the studio booked for three-day sessions spread across a four-week period.
On the first day, we kicked off by listening to various Robert Johnson tracks from two CDs. We carefully compiled a list of the songs that Peter and his colleague wanted to record.
After a discussion, we decided to adopt a straightforward approach. As our plan was to record both musicians simultaneously, so I set out two chairs, positioned

microphones for the guitars and live vocals and provided music stands for the lyrics.

Performing a live duet of the material became quite challenging for Peter and his colleague, mainly because they had not made any preparations. This lack of readiness led to tension between them, as they struggled to determine who would sing lead vocals and who would take the solos.

After a few hours, it became evident that this method of recording wasn't effective.

Over the following days, we experimented with different techniques. We attempted to record one musician first and then overdub the second. I then tried introducing a metronome into the mix, hoping to maintain some consistency in timing.

One of the more unusual approaches I tried was recording the original Robert Johnson tracks from the CD onto the multi-track and overdubbing them playing along with it. I added a count-in at the beginning of the Johnson recordings, aiming to guide Peter and his colleague in and when to start playing. As it turned out none of these methods proved successful. In reality, this album should have been recorded, overdubbed, remixed and delivered within seven to ten days.

After several frustrating days, I nervously contacted Stuart to discuss the need for a project re-evaluation as our current recording approach was leading nowhere. I suggested the possibility of bringing in the rest of the Splinter Group to the studio to assist in completing the album. Stuart agreed to visit the studio and discuss this idea with Peter and his colleague.

Peter expressed genuine interest in involving the rest of the band and was intrigued to hear about offers from well-known artistes to contribute to the album. But Peter's colleague adamantly opposed anyone other than Peter and himself being part of the recording process.

I started to notice that Peter's colleague had a Svengali-like influence over him, also possessing a child-like manner that could quickly transform into explosive anger when things didn't go his way.

Ultimately, we decided to press on and complete the album without additional musicians. Stuart explained to Peter that the decision not to include guest artistes or the Splinter band was likely influenced by the terms of the recording deal.

The album advance was meant to cover recording and mixing costs with any leftover funds to be split between Peter and his colleague. Involving others would eat into the recording budget, reducing the potential surplus.

What should have been a straightforward recording had now devolved into chaos. Peter's colleague's constant interference and "that'll do" attitude was hindering Peter's creative process significantly.

A producer's role is to extract the best from an artiste and although I witnessed genuine moments of brilliance from Peter, I was often denied the opportunity to fully capitalise on these exceptional moments.

There were times when I contemplated resigning, but I chose to stay for my own peace of mind, unwilling to abandon the situation.

As the session progresses it became obvious that Peter's colleague was determined to keep others from getting too close to Peter.
For instance, if Peter's colleague couldn't make it to the studio on a particular day, Peter would express a desire to work with me alone, but this request was consistently denied.
After several more sessions, I decided to involve someone from the record company to witness the unfolding debacle, but my concerns were not taken seriously. While we managed to salvage a couple of usable tracks, we still needed many more to complete an album.

As we made headway with the recordings, Peter's colleague approached me and said, "I realise you're the producer for this album, but I'm contributing a lot of ideas, so I think I should also be credited as a producer."
I responded, "That's fine by me, I'm not taking all the blame!"
He was so pleased that I didn't argue with his request, he missed the point completely.

One evening, during a break from the session, Peter and his colleague were sitting in the reception area, while I stepped into the studio office next door to make a telephone call. After a few minutes, I heard their voices escalating in the other room. I promptly ended my call and rushed to find out what was causing the disturbance.
As I arrived, I discovered Peter and his colleague embroiled in a heated argument. I attempted to mediate, but it became clear that, in their anger, they were oblivious to my presence. Peter had been informed, though not by me, that his colleague was pushing to wrap up the album quickly to save on production costs.

Peter was vehemently accusing him of excluding other musicians from the recording to ensure that there was more money left to be divided between them once the album was delivered to the record company.
This information had really infuriated Peter; to him the quality of the music was paramount, the money meant nothing.
This argument went on for at least half an hour with Peter shouting and slamming his hand on the table screaming, "You will send me back to the madhouse."
I had never seen Peter so angry; I'd not even heard him raise his voice before.
Once his colleague realised he had pushed Peter to the limit and that he wasn't going to get his own way, he started to back down, saying,
"Ped, you've got it all wrong I'm your best friend, I don't care about the money, if you want other musicians on the record that's fine by me."
"In that case, we will give what money is left over to Kenny." Peter said.
I quickly interrupted, saying, "Peter, I don't want the money."
"Are you rich?" he asked. I told him 'No, but I am being paid as the producer and I'm truly happy with that."

This marked a turning point for the album. Within days, the Splinter Group began collaborating on the tracks and we introduced backing vocalists into the recording.

We had the talented Linda Lewis visit the studio to contribute a few lines to the song "Kind Hearted Woman," without any interference. Nevertheless, Peter's colleague continued to press for haste, exclaiming after each take, "That's it, that's great, that will do." Clearly, he was trying to minimise studio time expenses.

Having come this far, I was determined not to let anything slide until it met the standards it deserved. I now had the support of Peter and the band but most importantly, everyone could hear the album was finally coming together.

Once the band finished their recordings and the backing vocals were complete, I believed it was a good time for all of us to take a couple of weeks off, allowing us the space to listen to our progress. Afterward, we could assess if there were any remaining tasks to address before diving into the mixing phase.

I ran the tracks through once, creating rough stereo mixes of the entire album and recording them onto DAT. Subsequently, I made cassette copies for each of us to take home and listen to.

During the rough mix of "Sweet Home Chicago," I found myself in a dispute with Peter's colleague regarding renowned singer Paul Rodgers' vocal performance. There were two vocal takes: one was the final master take, the other was a playful, unserious take where Paul was improvising – the one that Peter's partner preferred.

I explained, "We can't use this track. Paul isn't singing the correct lyrics; he's just messing around, singing things like "two and two is four, four and two is eight."

His response was, "Why can't we use it? It sounds good to me."

I raised my voice in frustration, stating, "Because it just doesn't add up."

But he still didn't get it.

A few days later, I received a call from Dougie Dudgeon, the MD of Snapper Records, the label funding the recording. He asked if I could send over the finished master tapes.

I explained to him that the album wasn't actually finished yet. Apparently, he had received a call from Peter's colleague, who claimed that the album was completed and ready for the final steps.

I implored Dougie to come to the studio and listen to what was labelled as the "finished" mixes. Remarkably, Dougie arrived within the hour.

While we sat in the control room, Dougie acknowledged that he understood this project had been exceptionally challenging and that he had been aware of the difficulties but believed that his presence during the recording sessions would not have alleviated the tension; in fact, it might have worsened it.

I clarified that the rough mixes we had were far from usable; they were merely reference tracks, a foundation for applying last-minute overdubs to prepare the songs for proper mixing.

To illustrate this, I inserted the DAT containing all the tracks into the machine and asked Dougie to choose a number between 1 and 18.

He picked "Number seven," and I initiated the automatic search, causing track seven to play.

After just a minute or so, Dougie abruptly stood up, covered his ears and shouted "TURN IT OFF!" He panicked as he explained that the album had to be completed and sent to the USA within ten days to meet the American release date and that it was also scheduled for release in Europe in six weeks.

I proposed a solution to Dougie: if he allowed me to work on the album for one week without any interference, I could guarantee delivering the finished product on time, ensuring we could meet all subsequent release dates.

Dougie agreed and I successfully completed the final mixes as scheduled. Dougie later called to express his admiration for the album.

I waited, fully anticipating the inevitable phone call. As expected, roughly four weeks later, Peter's colleague unleashed a tirade over the phone, accusing me of ruining the album and conveying Peter's profound dissatisfaction.

I calmly explained that the record company was dissatisfied with the rough mixes he had provided, which had led them to request that I rework them.

At that point, he told me that Peter expressed a desire to speak with me, although it was evident, as I had witnessed so many times before, I could tell he was being prompted with words he didn't seem to genuinely endorse.

I interrupted Peter to emphasise how proud I was of the album and how I had ensured that every aspect of the mixes I believed was representative of the project we had envisioned. I conveyed my belief that it would be well-received.

In an unexpected turn, Peter suddenly, as only he could, changed subjects and said "Kenny, if I come over one night, can we go for Chinese?"

I replied, "Of course, we can," and we bid farewell.

As you would expect, the story didn't conclude there. Peter's colleague raised concerns about the album cover artwork, particularly the contrast between Peter's name in bold white and his partner's name in less bold red. This issue was eventually resolved through a financial settlement, oddly easing his objection.

This marked the last collaboration I had with Peter. Although I was offered the opportunity to work on the next album and was even offered a higher fee, my decision to decline was not motivated by money.

I felt that everyone sought a piece of Peter Green and producing this album with him had been my small piece of that rather complex puzzle.

The *Robert Johnson Songbook* went on to receive enthusiastic reviews and even won the prestigious W.C. Handy Award in the USA. It would be many years before I finally unwrapped my copy of the CD to have a listen and I was genuinely pleased with the outcome of Peter's performances.

Chapter 18

Anthony Newley

Anthony Newley was a global celebrity whose illustrious career stretched over five decades. He landed his first major film role as The Artful Dodger in David Lean's 1948 film adaptation of *Oliver Twist*. Newley's trajectory took him from a child star actor to a rock 'n' roll icon, a prolific songwriter, an accomplished author, a revered West End actor and a film director.

He established himself as one of Broadway's most esteemed leading men, amassing a truly international fanbase. Newley's distinctive vocal style left an indelible mark, notably influencing David Bowie, evident in Bowie's song "The Laughing Gnome."

For many years, Newley collaborated with Leslie Bricusse, creating a rich body of work that encompassed theatrical productions and numerous musical film scores, including the beloved 1971 classic, *Willy Wonka & The Chocolate Factory*. Together, they crafted one of the most recognised James Bond movie themes ever in "Goldfinger."

Their profound impact on the world of music earned them a place of honour in the Songwriters Hall of Fame in 1987, an accolade previously bestowed only upon British luminaries such as Noel Coward, John Lennon and Paul McCartney.

My First Meeting

My first encounter with Anthony Newley took place during the recording sessions for the movie *Quilp* at The Music Centre in Wembley, England. As a long-time admirer of Newley's immense contribution to the entertainment industry, meeting him really was a dream come true. Although my role in the recording was limited to a few minor overdub sessions for the film, it granted me the privilege of collaborating with someone I had revered for so long.

I held high hopes for the title song "Quilp" believing it had the potential to become a musical classic. But the movie didn't fare well and neither did its music. Seventeen years passed before I had the opportunity to reconnect with Tony. By that time I owned a recording studio in Chiswick in West London. He booked a couple of days to record some piano and vocal demos.

Once he had arrived and the sessions were underway, during a break, I used the opportunity to mention our previous encounter at Wembley in the 70s. Although he remembered that time at the studio, he had no recollection of me. Nevertheless, we spent two fantastic days recording together.

Tony was delighted with the results, and this led to him booking the studio for several more sessions. Over the following years, we forged a strong friendship that endured until his passing in 1999.

Around that time, Tony received an offer to record an album under the PolyGram TV label, but he felt uneasy about the negotiations, he felt the people involved were from the film industry and lacked any true understanding of the music business. Concerned, Tony asked me if I could speak with PolyGram on his behalf.

I explained to him that it was impossible for me to intervene, as the deal was already in progress. Several weeks later Tony shared the news that the deal had been cancelled because PolyGram had signed the actor Ian McShane instead. We both knew that McShane wasn't known for song writing or singing, but he had a higher TV profile.

As an alternative, I offered to cover all the expenses and produce the album with Tony in my own studio. We arranged for me to visit Tony's new house in Esher to discuss the details.

As this was my first visit to his home, I had terrible trouble trying to find it. I made several phone calls to Tony, explaining that despite following his directions, I kept driving round and round the one-way system, ending up in the same place.

In response, he advised me to give it another try, suggesting that once I spotted a small park, I should be on the lookout for two narrow slip roads. He instructed me to park on the one on the right and patiently wait there, which I did.

A few minutes later, I spotted a rather peculiar sight at the top of the street: Anthony Newley, wearing a dressing gown and slippers, strolling towards me.

I drove forward to meet him and said, "Tony, hop in the car." To my surprise, he replied, "No need, just follow me."

It was a rather surreal scene; for the next few minutes, I found myself slowly driving behind Tony as he walked ahead of me in his night attire, looking just like Wee Willie Winkie, all he needed was a candlestick.

We spent the morning discussing how we would go about making the album and settled on a plan. We were both eager to start.

During this period my son Nathan was working with me, so I entrusted him with the task of driving Tony to and from the studio.

On the first day of recording, I brought Nathan to Tony's house to introduce him. As we sat sipping tea, Tony read his horoscope from the daily paper, which ominously stated, "The project you are about to embark on will be difficult and demanding and only with luck will it be successful."

Tony looked up from the newspaper and asked, "Well, what shall we do?" Without missing a beat, Nathan said laughingly, "Buy another newspaper." Tony burst into laughter, from that moment on Tony and Nathan's friendship was sealed.

Tony felt very comfortable around Nathan, who, due to his age, wasn't in awe of his remarkable career and so they became true friends. He often affectionately referred to Nathan as his adopted son due to his incredible ability to make Tony laugh in an instant, they genuinely enjoyed each other's company.

We made the choice to record a collection of fresh songs, intermingled with re-recordings of a few timeless classics. Once we had selected the material, we dedicated time to selecting the appropriate keys and deliberating over the arrangements. Following this, I embarked on the task of recording the backing tracks.

The recording sessions were proceeding smoothly until we reached the point

where we needed to record "Who Can I Turn To?"
At this point things took an unexpected turn; I had made the error of providing the arranger with a copy of Tony's original recording from the 60s.

When it came time to record Tony's vocals, after the first run-through it was immediately apparent that the key was completely wrong. Despite Tony's best efforts, the result was less than satisfactory. Tony explained, "Kenny, this is the key I used to sing it in 30 years ago. It's much too high for me now."

I found myself in a predicament as I not only needed this track due to its status as a classic Newley song, but also to fulfil the necessary song count for the completion of the album. With my fingers crossed behind my back, I reassured Tony, "That didn't sound too bad at all. It's definitely worth giving it another shot."
The second attempt was slightly improved but still far from usable. Trying to boost Tony's confidence, I exclaimed, "Tony, that was fabulous! We're getting closer." Nevertheless, Tony's confidence was waning and he expressed his doubt, saying, "Kenny, I really don't think I can do this."
I persisted with genuine enthusiasm, saying, "Well, even if you're not enjoying it, I absolutely am. It sounds amazing. If you're up for it, let's give it one more try."
In the next take, Tony poured his heart and soul into the performance, exceeding both of our expectations and really nailed the performance. I was elated, not only because I needed this track to complete the required number of recordings but also because I couldn't imagine the album without this timeless classic.

The album took several weeks to complete, affording me a wonderful opportunity to delve deeper into the persona behind this extraordinary and multifaceted talent. What I discovered was a remarkably complex individual, whose emotions could shift from hearty laughter to a stream of tears in a matter of minutes. Oddly, when referring to himself as an artiste he always used the name Newley and spoke of him in the third person. This was particularly noticeable in the messages Tony left on my answering machine. If he simply said, "Hi, it's Tony," I knew it was a personal matter. But should he say, "Hi, it's Newley," I immediately understood it was business-related.
Our first recording for the album was a rendition of the song "Why", which had been a chart-topping hit for Tony in 1960. We decided to transform it into a duet with his daughter, Tara. Tony's performance leaned towards the operatic and it became evident that I wasn't entirely pleased with the result.
When I explained to him that it didn't quite match my expectations and that his voice seemed too grand for the track, he responded with a smile and said, "Ah, you want more Newley." With that, he returned to the studio, stepped up to the microphone and delivered a flawless rendition as Anthony Newley.

When I had finished mixing the recordings, Tony arrived at the studio for a playback of the entire album. As the final notes of the song "Nearly Wonderful" echoed, I turned my gaze to Tony and observed tears streaming down his cheeks. Intrigued, I asked about the source of his emotional response.

He then revealed that the song carried profound meaning as it was dedicated to his third wife, Dareth Rich, with whom he shared 18 years of marriage. Their love story commenced in 1970 when they first connected, ultimately leading to their union in 1971.

In 1978, Tony and Dareth, bought 426 N Bristol Avenue, Los Angeles 90049, the former residence of the American dancer, singer and actor Donald O'Connor and had once belonged to Joan Crawford. He had no knowledge of its appearance in the notorious book and film, *Mommie Dearest,* penned by Christina, Joan Crawford's daughter.

Being very familiar with the plot of the movie and curious about the property's history, I asked Tony if he had ever ventured into the basement of the house. To my surprise, he admitted to being entirely unaware of the book or the movie's existence. Surprisingly, he did share that, following their acquisition of the property, they invested a staggering $1,000,000 in refurbishments over the course of a year. During this extensive renovation process, they uncovered a deeply unsettling atmosphere within the house, leading them to the decision not to make it their home.

In 1989, after parting ways with Dareth and finalising their divorce, Tony returned to England with his mother Grace and settled in Esher Surrey.

He mentioned that the subsequent owners of the property took the step of having the house exorcised to address the eerie presence they had encountered.

During their time together, Tony and Dareth had two children, Christopher and Shelby. We had the pleasure of meeting Shelby on multiple occasions and she left a lasting impression due to her wonderfully charming personality.

Christopher, on the other hand, we encountered only once and he struck us as a well-mannered and grounded young man, earning praise from those who knew him.

Notably, both Christopher and Shelby chose to distance themselves from the industry that had brought their father fame, opting not to use the Newley name.

With the album completed, I presented it to several record companies. Unfortunately, securing a major release proved challenging, primarily due to Newley's limited media presence at the time. Faced with this situation, I made the decision to release the album independently.

Sadly, with limited financial resources for promotion and that elusive stroke of luck needed in the music industry, the album fell short of the success we had envisioned.

Tony Newley was intrigued by Tony Bennett's successful comeback in the early 90s and once asked me why the public had embraced him so readily. In response, I explained, "Beyond his remarkable talent, Tony Bennett is accessible, whereas you, Tony, lead a more secluded life. People don't know how to reach you, they're unsure whether you reside in the UK, Hong Kong or America."

At the time, I wasn't aware, but I later discovered that Tony's manager, Peter Charlesworth, kept a tight control over Tony. I learned that Peter had turned down several offers that could have undoubtedly advanced Tony's career. It was revealed to me that Dawn French and Jennifer Saunders had repeatedly requested for Tony to appear on their highly successful TV show but, for unknown reasons, Peter declined the offer each time.

I remember being in Tony's dressing room after a live show, where I witnessed him asking Peter for his thoughts on the performance. Peter replied, rather cruelly, "Well, the audience was great." I was told that Tony had been considering changing his management during the last years of his life but became too ill to implement this change.

I regularly met up with Tony and it always fascinated me how his introverted lifestyle would lead to him asking questions like, "Kenny, who is Morrissey?"

"Well," I'd explain, "he's a singer, songwriter and a highly successful one at that. Why do you ask?"

Tony replied, "I've been asked to present him with an Ivor Novello award. I think he's either dedicated a song to me or is a fan, something like that."

Tony did go on to present the award, although I'm quite certain he still had no real grasp of who Morrissey was.

During our conversations, Tony once remarked, "The movie business is the only industry where you can see your entire life play back to you with precise ageing."
I responded, "That's true, but only if you achieve success at an early age."

Throughout our years of friendship, I would often asked him why he hadn't considered writing a book. His response was always, "I can't remember anything." Nevertheless, I never found that to be an issue once I got him reminiscing.

I once asked about his thoughts on Frank Gorshin's impersonation of him and it seemed he wasn't particularly fond of impersonators. He had this to say about Frank: "When I first saw him perform, it was awful, I couldn't move my hands on stage for the next year." Surprisingly, they later collaborated and formed a close friendship.

He also remarked on others who imitate him, expressing that Rich Little, although a close friend of his, did the least unattractive impression and felt it to be rather unkind.

"After witnessing these impersonations of myself, I must confess that I require a moment or two alone in my room to sulk. It's fascinating because one never truly considers how one appears, moves, or sings. Observing someone imitating you is genuinely astonishing. I recognise it as the highest form of flattery, yet it remains quite a shock. Witnessing oneself replicated in that manner would surprise anyone.

They tend to exaggerate a bit, I suppose. Initially, it genuinely caught me off guard and I found it rather unkind. Of course, I understand that exaggeration is necessary for instant recognition. It's all part of the performance."

Dr Dolittle

While working with Tony, he shared some great stories about the making of *Dr Dolittle*, the 1967 movie in which he played Matthew Mugg.

Rex Harrison, a big star at the time, was given the lead role. Despite being considered for the role, the producers and director had their doubts about casting him and these reservations would soon become apparent.

Once cast as Dr Dolittle, Harrison's first move was to dismiss the director and rewrite Leslie Bricusse's screenplay, giving himself all the best lines and making everyone else's dialogue monosyllabic.

During these alterations, Rex chose to sit out his contract. He made unreasonable demands such as replacing Sammy Davis Jr., who was to play Bumpo, with Sidney Poitier, who wasn't known for musical roles. Eventually, the part of Bumpo was removed entirely. The producers grew impatient with Rex and decided to hire Christopher Plummer to replace Harrison, but Rex agreed to cooperate and Plummer was paid his full fee to exit the production.

Rex's knack for irking everyone on set was met with retaliation, but only from the animals in the film, who seized any opportunity to bite him, much to the amusement of the cast and crew.

Harrison and Tony had a strained relationship throughout the filming, with Rex attempting to belittle Tony, making comments such as, "Where is the little Jewish boy from the East End?" This naturally didn't sit well with Tony.

At one point during filming, Rex was dating a German woman who disapproved of his drinking habits. To appease her he went through a period of abstinence, which contributed to his edgy character on set. Near the end of filming, during a social gathering, Tony noticed Rex looking uncomfortable holding a glass of orange juice whilst all around him were enjoying a glass of something stronger. To help him out, Tony instructed a waitress to bring Rex a clean glass and a full bottle of bourbon.

Unable to resist temptation, Rex consumed the entire bottle. Tony was well aware that Rex's intoxicated return home that night would result in his mistress, as Tony put it, "kicking the shit out of him." It was a bit of payback from the little Jewish boy from the East End.

Grace Newley

We met Tony's mother, Grace, when she was in her later eighties, petite and sprightly, her high-pitched Cockney lilt held a disarming honesty and she possessed a charm that defied her years. No topic was off-limits for Grace and her down-to-earth perspective, seasoned with wit and warmth, could elicit a smile from even the most hardened soul. This vibrant spirit remained unflagging until her sad passing, just shy of her 100th birthday. I was very privileged to get to know Grace and over the years both my wife Sue and I became great friends with her. Tony and Grace lived together in a beautiful house in Esher, Surrey.

It was during my first visit to their home that Grace's vibrant personality made its mark. "Would you like a cup of tea?" she asked, a glint in her eye. "I'd prefer coffee," I replied. "Coffee?" she said in mock horror. "What's a Cockney boy like you want with that American stuff?" I decided to opt for the tea.

On another occasion I had been invited to breakfast. As we were all sitting at the dining table eating, Tony inquired of Grace, "Did you see that letter today from my old teacher?" Grace replied, "No, which teacher are you talking about?" Tony clarified, saying, "You know, she was the lesbian." Grace, her voice filled with surprise, exclaimed, "Tony, you dun'arf know some funny people."

Harvey Wallbanger

On April 6th, 1996, I was working on a Saturday afternoon in the studio when my wife Sue came in to inform me that Tony was on the telephone. I immediately inquired whether it was Tony or Newley, to which Sue replied "It's Tony." This signified that it was a personal call, not a business matter, although I would have taken the call regardless.

Tony asked when my session was scheduled to finish, I informed him it should be around 6 p.m. He then revealed his plan to take Grace, or 'the Duchess' as he referred to her, out for dinner that evening.

He added he would like to invite Sue and me to join them. We gladly accepted his invitation. He mentioned that he had never been to any of the restaurants in Esher and asked Sue if she would be kind enough to find a restaurant and book a table.

Sue made the effort to call every restaurant in Esher listed but only to find that they were all fully booked.

After finishing the session, I called Tony to explain the situation and suggested ordering a takeaway. After a moment of silence, he said, "No, I have an idea, so just come on over."

When we arrived at his house, Grace was upstairs getting ready. I explained to Tony that due to the short notice, finding a table locally was impossible. He assured me it wasn't a problem but still didn't reveal his plan.

We all got into my car, and for the next ten minutes Tony provided directions. We eventually arrived at a small, almost deserted high street. We parked and noticed that the only open place was a fish and chip shop. Tony led us past a small queue of people waiting to order takeaways and directed us to the back of the shop where there were five small tables, only one of which was occupied by a young couple. The situation was becoming increasingly surreal.

Once we were seated, a waiter handed us menus and asked if we would like a drink. Grace immediately said, "Yes, I'd love a Harvey Wallbanger." Tony advised her, "Mom, they don't serve them here."

Grace then asked for a Screwdriver, but the waiter regretfully informed her that they didn't have an alcohol licence. So, she asked for a glass of "Cockney champagne." otherwise known as Coca-Cola.

We had a delightful evening and once the young couple left, against all odds on a Saturday night we had the entire place to ourselves. As we chatted about the first time I met Tony and how much I loved the song "Quilp," he began singing the first few lines and I joined in. It was a bizarre but incredibly special moment, sitting in a chip shop in the middle of nowhere, singing a duet with Anthony Newley.

During the evening, Tony confided that he was scheduled to perform in Atlantic City the following week for ten days, from April 12th to April 21st but wasn't looking forward to it due to his declining health. Undoubtedly pulling out of the booking would have resulted in financial repercussions as the casino would have sued. He decided that the show must go on.

The next day, Tony called to check if we had enjoyed the evening. I responded, "We both had a great time, but Sue was surprised by the venue. "Tony laughed and said, "I think Suzie thinks I'm a little more classy than I am."

The Last Great One-Man Show

On October 6th, 1992, Newley was scheduled to perform his one-man show at the prestigious Langham Hotel in London and my wife and I were fortunate enough to receive an invitation from Tony to come and watch the show.

The venue was brimming with luminaries from all corners of the entertainment industry. Seating was meticulously arranged based on one's level of fame, which meant my wife and I found ourselves seated near the exit at the back of the room.

Newley stepped onto the stage to a three-minute standing ovation After that he mesmerised the audience, holding them spellbound throughout his performance. Following several encores that garnered further standing ovations, Newley left the stage, navigating through the crowd. He exchanged handshakes and warm embraces with the guests. As he reached the spot where Grace was seated, he bent down and asked her, "Did you have a good time, Mum? This is what I do in the evenings."

As he approached our spot near the exit, he spotted me and enthusiastically shouted, "KENNY!" Making his way over to our table, he enveloped me in a heartfelt hug and asked, "Where's Susie?" Spotting Sue, he went over to her, giving her an affectionate hug and kiss.

This was an incredibly special moment that left us feeling truly cherished; one that will forever be etched in our memories.

Tony then asked us to join him upstairs in his dressing room and hospitality suite where a private party was to be held.

That night, I believe we all witnessed the final brilliant live performance of Anthony Newley's one-man show.

During the 1990s, Newley made appearances in various TV shows and took on the challenging lead role in Leslie Bricusse's *Scrooge: The Musical*. Sadly, during this period, his health began to deteriorate as the demands of the gruelling stage production became too overwhelming for him.

There were rare instances when Newley's health was so compromised that he couldn't perform, necessitating his understudy to step in for him. This situation led to hate mail from fans who had anticipated seeing Newley onstage, not an understudy. Tony was deeply hurt by this and couldn't fathom how people could be so unkind.

During this period, Tony and Gina Fratini reignited their romantic relationship. Gina, Tony's girlfriend in the mid 50s, had previously ended things due to the excessive attention from other women and the immense pressure of dating such an icon. However, in an unexpected twist in the early 90s, mutual friends brought them back together. This time, Gina became an integral part of Tony's life, assuming the role of his caregiver while reigniting her profound love for him. They became inseparable once again.

A little over a year before his passing, Tony called me with one of his typically curious questions, asking, "Kenny, what's Eastenders? I explained that it was a highly successful BBC TV show and inquired why he wanted to know. He revealed that he had been offered a short contract to appear in the programme.
Within weeks of his appearance on *Eastenders* he was elated by the outpouring of admiration he received. It had been quite some time since he had garnered this much attention from the media.
As Tony approached the end of the initial contract, he received an offer for a permanent role on the program. Unfortunately, his health further declined before he could finalise the new agreement, making it impossible for him to commit to such a demanding project.

On Boxing Day in 1998, Tony left the UK for the last time, accompanied by Gina, to seek specialised medical treatment for renal cancer in America.
He had pre-recorded a small part as the Bishop in the TV drama *The Lakes*, which aired two months before his passing on April 14th, 1999.

On the evening of Sunday, February 21st, 1999 Sue and I watched exceptional portrayal of the Bishop in TV drama *The Lakes*. It was a remarkable performance and, in many people's opinion, his finest acting achievement. I believe that had it not been for his declining health, Newley could have once again become a household name.
Some years later, Gina Fratini shared a wonderful insight with me. She said that when Tony had finished filming this role, he told her, "At last, I have finally got it. I now understand how acting works." Unfortunately, this turned out to be his last performance.
As we were watching the end of the program, the telephone rang, it was Grace on the line. She was in uncontrollable tears as she had just had the devastating news that her son was terminally ill.
While Tony's deteriorating health was known to many, Grace had been somewhat shielded from the full extent by Tony and Gina.
It was nearly impossible to console her so I offered to have us come over to be with her. But given the late hour Grace declined, stating that she would attempt to get some rest. I suspected that she would have appreciated our presence but didn't want to burden us so late on a Sunday evening. Nevertheless, I promised to help her book a plane ticket as early as possible the next morning.

The following day at 10.a.m. I contacted Tony's secretary, Vivian, regarding Grace's urgent call and inquired about arranging her immediate departure to America. Vivian explained that Grace would need someone to accompany her. I

suggested the possibility of asking Tony's daughter, Tara, to assist her.
A few hours later, the secretary returned my call to convey that Tara couldn't accompany Grace as she had her hands full looking after her four-month-old baby, Miel. I couldn't cancel my studio sessions since I was in the midst of finishing an album for a client.
I asked Sue if she would be willing to accompany Grace and she agreed without hesitation. I provided my credit card information and requested the secretary to book a flight for Sue, with a return flight scheduled for the following Wednesday night. She promised to call back and confirm all the details.
A few hours later the secretary called back to confirm that first class tickets had been booked and that both Sue and Grace were to meet at Tony's residence at 9 a.m. The following morning a car was arranged to take them to Gatwick.

I had asked Sue to phone me from her hotel once Grace was with Tony and Sue was settled at the hotel. On the morning of Wednesday, the 23rd, around 4 a.m. Sue called and was visibly upset.
She told me on arriving at Tony's Condo in West Palm Beach, Sue was taken aback and, frankly, furious when Gina said, "What a shame you just missed Tara." Sue inquired if Tara had her baby with her, to which she was told that it would have been too much for Tara to take the baby on the trip.
I urged Sue not to get upset and advised her to get some rest and relax.
The next morning, having had no sleep, Sue returned to the airport, only to find that her flight had been delayed due to a severe storm, compounded by the arrival of the US President. This delay led to her missing the connecting flight. After finally reaching New York and after several hours of further delays, she was eventually offered an alternative flight back to Heathrow.

While the outbound flight was in first class, offering Sue larger seats, edible food and the prospect of rest, her return flight was in economy. Sue finally arrived at Heathrow at 9 a.m. the following morning, relieved to be home but still very upset with Tara for not wanting to accompany her 96-year-old grandmother to see her dying son.
When my Amex bill arrived, it revealed the cost of the flight amounted to £4,500. Although we never requested reimbursement, several years later, following Grace's passing, Tony's estate contacted me. They asked if I still had my Amex statement indicating the ticket price, which I did. To my delight, I received a full reimbursement.

Tony Or Newley

Tony's artistic side had always been his alter ego which he referred to as "Newley" In his final years Tony began to scrutinise Newley the artist, leading to a profound sense of confusion. This uncertainty cast a shadow over his creative spirit. I remember a moment when we were listening to one of his old hits and he startled me by saying, "Listen to that vowel sound I'm making, why didn't anyone tell me?"

Regarding his relationships with women, he once confided, "Every woman I've ever known has brought me to my knees."

It's my belief, they all fell in love with Newley and then fell out of love with Tony. One exception to this happened during the last few years of his life when he reconnected with Gina Fratini. Gina's love, care and understanding surpassed that of anyone else, effortlessly transcending the complexities of his character.

As Tony once put it, "Marriage is like getting in a bathtub. Once you're in, it's really not so hot."

On Friday, March 19th, 1999, I was preparing to leave my studio early for an extended weekend getaway. Just as I set the alarm, the telephone began to ring. I hesitated, torn between the desire to answer it and the promise I'd made to Sue about our planned weekend together. I didn't want to entertain any last-minute studio bookings.

Ultimately, my conscience compelled me to pick up the phone. To my surprise, it was Gina calling from Florida, saying, "Tony would like to talk to you." I was elated to hear from him. Sadly, our conversation took a sombre turn swiftly. He had called me to bid farewell.

I reiterated what I had told him so many times before: "Don't give up; keep fighting." In a feeble voice, he responded, "I have nothing left to fight with. I am needed in another place." We exchanged our goodbyes and I left the studio, wishing I hadn't answered the phone.

The following April 15th marked my birthday. When I awoke, I switched on the TV for the morning news. It was then I saw the heart-breaking announcement that Anthony Newley had passed away the night before in Florida. Sue and I were deeply saddened and I found myself grateful for the phone call that had unsettled me just a few weeks earlier.

Beyond the genius who had transitioned from child star to pop idol, composer, author, director and leading man, excelling in each of these talents, I knew a kind, compassionate and emotional individual. It was an absolute privilege to have known and collaborated with Tony Newley.

Grace Newley's Sadness

After Tony's passing in April 1999, Sue and I made it a tradition to take Grace out for her favourite meal every Saturday morning. Being a true cockney, her choice was always jellied eels, though Sue and I preferred our own personal favourite - pie and mash.

Following our delightful meal, we would embark on a mini-tour of the East End, Grace's childhood neighbourhood, which she held dear. Surprisingly, she could recall specific street names from her youth so we made it a joyful game to locate them.

On one occasion, we took Grace to Victoria Park in Tower Hamlets, enroute, she inquired if the bandstand was still there. To her sheer delight, it was. Grace began reminiscing about her father playing in the band on Sundays back in 1913 when she was a young girl. Her vivid memories of the entire area from those early days were astonishing, considering she hadn't visited in nearly 70 years. Listening to Grace's recollections of her life was an absolute pleasure.

During our conversations, it became evident that I was acquainted with several individuals Tony had known. People like Frankie Vaughan, with whom I had studio collaborations and maintained a close friendship with the family. On the other hand, there was Tommy Steele, with whom I didn't quite get along with. Grace simply assumed that I was familiar with most of Tony's circle.
She had a charming way of making us smile, often saying things like,
"Have you met Peter?"
"Peter?" I would inquire.
"Peter... Peter Sellers."
"No, Grace, but I would have loved to."
"He used to drop by whenever he had women trouble and he always had women trouble... always."
"How about Orson, Orson Welles?"
"No, Grace!"
"He was such a wonderful man, truly wonderful."

After taking Grace back home, our routine was to escort her to what was known as Tony's room. It was adorned with photos, awards, posters plus an extensive collection of memorabilia. Grace shared that she would spend the rest of the evening in that very spot, conversing with Tony, recounting her day to him.

Every Christmas Day Grace would have dinner with Tony's ex-wife Joan Collins, the following day she would come and have lunch with us.
During her visit to us on Boxing Day 2001 she told us she had a meeting with a nice man, Garth Bardsely, who was writing a book about Tony. I told her I had also made a small contribution to this book.
Grace went on to say.
"I told him everything you know, no good making stuff up, but when you read it, you won't ever want to talk to me again."
"Why not?" I asked.
"Well, I was a scarlet woman!" she replied.
Sue and I both roared with laughter and told her she really shouldn't worry, whatever was in the book, it would make no difference to us.

During lunch, Grace went on to tell us that Joan was getting married on February 17th and although she had been invited, she really didn't want to go.
She explained. "As I'm on my own, I will just be sitting in a corner somewhere with no one to talk to."
Then Grace surprised us all by asking if our son Nathan, who she absolutely adored, would be her chaperone. Nathan accepted gracefully, forgive the pun.

On Saturday, February 10th, just a week before the wedding, we took Grace out as usual and she appeared to be herself. But the following day, when I called to check on her, she sounded dreadful. Sue and I offered to come over, Grace replied, "I'd love you to, but I don't want to spoil your Sunday." But we insisted, and arrived within 30 minutes.
When we arrived it was obvious that Grace was not herself. She asked Sue if she

would prepare her some chicken stew for her, which Sue gladly did. After Grace manage a very small portion, she asked us to help her back to her armchair in Tony's award room. There, we sat and chatted with her until around 6 p.m.

Later, Grace requested that we assist her into her living room, saying, "You both should be heading home now; I'll be fine. Annie will be here soon." Annie was Grace's carer who visited in the morning and evening to assist her.

We called Annie to inform her of Grace's illness and asked if she could come earlier, but unfortunately, she couldn't. We decided to stay with Grace until Annie's arrival.

After a short while, Grace started coughing and much to our concern, she began coughing up blood. We immediately called Annie again, who reassured us, "She'll be fine; she's been through this before. You go on, I'll be there later."

During the next ten minutes, Grace's condition worsened, prompting us to call for an ambulance. We also contacted Annie to update her on the situation. The ambulance arrived the crew and attended to Grace. They decided to transport her to the hospital and placed her on a stretcher to take her to the ambulance.

Just as she was being placed in the ambulance, Grace extended her hands to Sue and myself and said, "Thank you both for everything. I don't think I'll see you again." I replied, "Don't be silly, you will and don't forget you have a wedding to attend soon."

At that moment, Annie arrived and questioned the ambulance crew about their destination. They explained that they were taking her to Richmond Hospital, an NHS hospital. We visited Grace on the following Wednesday.

Despite her own condition, the first thing she inquired about was my mother's health. We assured her that my mother was fine and asked about her well-being. Grace expressed her desire to go home so we assured her that she would when the doctors deemed it safe.

While we were there, Tara Newley arrived. Hearing Grace's wish to return home, Tara asked us to help her leave the hospital immediately. We suggested she speak to the doctors and, if they approved, we would assist with transportation but the hospital denied the request.

A few days later, Gina returned from the USA to organise Grace's return home, arranging for a hospital bed and an IV drip stand to be delivered. We sent a large bouquet of flowers, Gina conveyed that they were from us since Grace was too weak to ask.

It was clear that these were Grace's final days, we all hoped she wouldn't pass away before or on the day of Joan's wedding.

Grace finally passed away the day after the Wedding.

Rest in peace, Frances Grace Newley.

It was a privilege to have known Tony Newley but it was an honour to have known Grace Newley.

A short while after the funeral, Gina returned to her home in the USA and Several months later, Gina asked us if we could go to Tony's house in Esher and gather all of his 16mm and 8mm film cans, as the house was being sold. We stored these cans at our studio in Chiswick for quite some time because it seemed no one knew what to do with them.

With Gina's approval, I eventually made contact with the British Film Institute, who were delighted to house this valuable collection of material. We maintained a close friendship with Gina and saw her whenever she returned to the UK.

Gina passed away on May 25th, 2017 and was cremated at Kingston Crematorium. Her ashes were returned to the USA to be laid to rest alongside her true love, Tony Newley. Just like Grace, Gina never truly recovered from losing Tony. Her heart remained broken from the day he passed until her own last day.

With Gina's passing, an era of wonderful friendships came to an end – with Tony, Grace and Gina. These were years filled with good times and laughter, we miss them all dearly.

Chapter 19

Sir Thomas Hicks OBE

Thomas Hicks, professionally recognised as Tommy Steele, was an English entertainer celebrated as Britain's inaugural teenage heartthrob and pioneer of rock 'n' roll. Born in Bermondsey, London, he was the child of Thomas Walter Hicks and Elizabeth Ellen Bennett, who were married in Bermondsey in 1933.

Tommy Steele came to prominence when a freelance photographer named John Kennedy spotted his potential as Britain's answer to Elvis Presley.
In just six weeks, Steele ascended to top billing in numerous variety shows.
Following his discovery at the 2i's Coffee Bar, he swiftly delivered a string of chart-topping singles, including, "Rock with the Caveman" and "Singing the Blues".
During his early career, he released his first three singles at a rapid pace with a new one hitting the shelves every three weeks.
As the 1950s and 1960s witnessed a surge in homegrown musical talent, Steele transitioned to a successful career in stage and film musicals, leaving his pop-idol persona behind.

On the West End stage, he took on the lead role of Hans Christian Andersen. In the world of cinema, he reprised his stage role, from both London and Broadway, in *Half a Sixpence* and assumed character roles in *The Happiest Millionaire*, although some critics felt his on-screen persona was somewhat overpowering.
In *Finian's Rainbow*, what is likely his most recognised film performance, he shared the screen with Petula Clark and Fred Astaire.

From the mid-50s onwards, Tommy Steele became a master in every venture he pursued. He excelled as a singer, dancer, movie star, musician, composer, stage actor, conductor, comedian, director, producer, media writer, novelist, poet, artist and sculptor - a true all-around talent.

Since my early studio days, I held the unwavering belief that I would someday have the opportunity to meet or even collaborate with my ultimate idol, Tommy Steele.

During the early 1970s, Tommy happened to own a modest West London recording studio known as Recorded Sound, located just minutes away from Pye Studios on Bryanston Street.
In my quest for an encounter with him, I often dropped by to visit a friend who worked there and to enjoy a cup of coffee, all in the hope that fate would eventually bring me face to face with Tommy in his studio. I longed for the chance to meet the man I had once aspired to be like.
Sadly, two years passed without so much as a glimpse of the elusive Mr. Steele, let alone the opportunity for a handshake.

In the early 70s I was working at De Lane Lea in Wembley when, as luck would have it, a two-day weekend booking materialised to record the music for a Tommy Steele TV special. I immediately went after securing the job as engineer. Unfortunately, the television company adhered to stringent union regulations that dictated only their own engineers could handle the recording sessions.

Despite not having any work obligations that particular weekend, I made a conscious decision to linger around the studio's restaurant, hoping for an opportunity to cross paths with Tommy Steele himself. But much to my disappointment he never made an appearance during those sessions.

It was during the 90s that fate would bring me into contact with Tommy's daughter, Emma Steele. She booked a session at my studio, KD's, to record a couple of tracks. At the time our son Nathan was working alongside me and due to their similar ages, he and Emma quickly formed a close friendship.

Two anxious days passed before Tommy, her father, finally graced the studio with his presence. It was a momentous occasion for me, as I had waited nearly 40 years to meet the man I deeply admired. I was truly overwhelmed.

The initial days had been dedicated to laying down the backing tracks and now it was time for Emma to record her vocals.

Tommy, puffing on a massive cigar, occupied a seat at the end of the control room desk, assuring everyone that he wouldn't intervene or utter a word while his daughter sang.

From the moment Emma began singing the first few lines, Tommy sprang from his chair as if jolted by electricity, urgently calling for the talkback mic button.

He proceeded to provide Emma with a series of instructions about her performance, repeatedly leaping from his seat like a child on a seesaw. This pattern persisted throughout the entire vocal session.

It was evident that Emma felt somewhat inhibited by her father's presence and constant interference. In fact, I believe everyone had grown a bit weary of his involvement. Yet, for me, having Tommy's mere presence in the studio made the session exceptionally memorable.

Throughout the following week, I was fortunate to have multiple opportunities to engage in one-on-one conversations with Tommy.

Finally, I seized the moment to express my gratitude and explain how he had shaped all my dreams and aspirations during my youth. Tommy shared his deep love for the recording studio environment, mentioning that he had once owned one himself. To his surprise, I mentioned that I had probably spent more time at his studio than he had.

During one of our chats, I played him a rare stereo mix of his 1958 hit single, "Nairobi." He found it fascinating because he had previously only heard the mono version. When the music had finished playing, he turned to me and casually remarked, "You know, that only cost about a shilling to make."

In response, I said jokingly, "Oh! You recorded it twice then?" Despite his characteristic cockney smile and the occasional squint, it seemed that Tommy didn't quite see the humour in that comment.

Over the years, I had heard that Tommy wasn't particularly well-liked by many of the people he collaborated with. Some attribute this to his relentless pursuit of perfection, while others cite different reasons.

One anecdote I heard involved him being invited to a high-stakes celebrity card game at the Dorchester Hotel in London's West End.

Whether it was luck or skill, Tommy won the first hand, which involved a substantial pile of cash. To everyone's astonishment, he scooped up his winnings, expressed gratitude for the game and promptly left, denying anyone the chance to recoup their losses.

During his time in *Singing in the Rain* at the London Palladium, rumours circulated that he had been rather strict with a few members of the dance troupe. Legend has it that, in retaliation, they took matters into their own hands, quite literally, by peeing in the large water tank used to provide the rain in the "Singing in the Rain" solo dance routine. If he was going to upset them, they were going to be... well, you can guess the rest.

My preconceived notions of Tommy Steele and him being my idol, often left me feeling somewhat self-conscious in his presence. Our son, to the contrary, had no such reservations. To him, Tommy was simply Emma's dad – a person who could share amusing stories and delighted in performing card tricks. This perspective fostered a strong bond and camaraderie between Nathan and Tommy.

Back in a 1979 interview on "The Michael Parkinson Show," where he discussed his remarkable journey from the 2i's Coffee Bar to his accomplishments in the world of movies, Tommy also expressed his deep affection for Cooke's Pie and Mash shop.

So, during the session, when he offered to make the trip to South London to fetch takeaway from Cooke's, he affirmed his top position on my "all-time favourite pop idols" list. This gesture represented a true cockney feast and held a special place in our hearts.

Established in 1938, Cooke's was nestled in The Cut, just around the corner from Waterloo Station, making it a well-established location in South London and an integral part of its heritage. He truly embodied the spirit of a cockney hero.

Tommy possessed the art of spinning a captivating tale but didn't excel at listening to others' stories. In fact the star I had cherished all these years, the cockney lad who now savoured large cigars and possessed a couple of Picassos, had begun to fade. At this point in my career, I should have been wiser, recognising that the image a person projects to the public is often just that - an image. The reality can be quite different.

As the sessions drew to a close, I had fulfilled my desire to meet Tommy Steele, even though the experience proved to be more than disappointing. It's a reminder that sometimes, it's best not to meet your idols.

Several months passed when I received a call from Tommy, inquiring if I knew anyone who could collaborate with Emma to produce a couple of tracks. I suggested the producers she had previously worked with, but Tommy insisted on finding someone closer to Emma's age. Knowing that my son Nathan and Emma were of a similar age and got along well, I proposed Nathan as a potential collaborator, which Tommy enthusiastically accepted.

Nathan was highly skilled with computers and my studio equipment, so this project didn't require my direct involvement. They joined forces and created a couple of songs at the studio. Although I can't recall the fate of those tracks, what stuck with me was a phone call from Nathan one evening at Tommy's home in Richmond. Nathan was clearly having a blast, mentioning Tommy's plans to take him for a ride in one of his classic cars the next day.

During our conversation, Nathan asked me, "Dad, do we have a big house?" I replied, "Reasonably, why do you ask?" Nathan laughingly said, "Well, I'm calling you from Emma's apartment, which is located above Tommy's garage, where he houses his collection of classic cars. It's bigger than our entire house." It was at that moment that Nathan realised just how successful Tommy had become.

I had a flashback from when I was about five years old, I was watching Tommy Steele, for the first time, on a large cinema screen. Little did I know then that someday, our son would be calling me from his house.

In 2004, I caught Tommy Steele on a TV show where he was promoting the musical *Scrooge,* in which he was starring. His trademark smile, his unique way of speaking in a half-whispered voice, as if he was about to reveal a secret at any moment, had always charmed me. It was then that I realised I had never actually met Tommy Steele; I had only ever met Tommy Hicks.

Chapter 20

How to Sign an Exceptional Record Deal

Between 1978 and 1979, I invested approximately £15,000 of my own money into recording an album with an artiste I deeply believed in. Despite approaching several record companies, I couldn't find anyone who shared my enthusiasm for the project - until I crossed paths with my old friend and former manager, Dave Meyers.

When Meyers listened to the album, he was genuinely impressed and couldn't fathom why I hadn't garnered any interest from record labels. I explained that everyone I had approached had rejected it.
In response, he confidently declared, "You must be approaching this the wrong way. Give me six weeks and I'll secure you a deal that'll not only recover your investment but also get a release for the album."
Despite being aware of Dave's inclination to exaggerate, his captivating charm and enigmatic persona akin to Svengali made it difficult to resist him. Anyone who had ever been associated with him would attest to the same.
I must admit that the prospect of recouping my investment and finally seeing the product released was undeniably appealing.

Meyers proceeded to outline his strategy for securing the deal. He planned to make an initial investment of around £4,000. Once we secured an advance from a record company, his priority would be to recoup his investment first, followed by the repayment of my £15,000 investment.
After these initial repayments the artiste would receive the remainder of the advance and any further profits from sales would be divided as follows: half to the artist, with the remaining half split equally between Dave and me.

Dave's Meticulous Plan

- Meet with Polydor A&R Heads across Europe
- Play them two tracks and leave a cassette tape of the full album
- Tell them Polydor Germany boss loves the album and will ask for opinions soon
- Meet with Polydor Germany boss last - the deal maker

Dave arranged meetings with all the major European heads of A&R and promptly set out on his tour, starting in France and heading through Belgium, Netherlands and onto Spain. In each country he presented the songs to the A&R heads, eventually reaching Germany and the crucial meeting with the head of Polydor Germany and Deutsche Grammophon, Odo von Stein.
During this pivotal meeting, he played the tracks for Odo and shrewdly mentioned that every European PolyGram company expressed strong interest in signing the artist. He then pointed out the need for it to be a substantial record deal.
Meyers encouraged Odo to listen to the entire album and use the old-fashioned

telex system to contact all the European offices, to seek their reactions to the product.
A follow-up meeting with Dave was scheduled a few weeks later, allowing Odo time to reach out to the various PolyGram territories.
Odo followed Meyers' advice and contacted the A&R departments across Europe. Given that Dave had assured each of them that Odo held the album in the highest regard, these departments were eager not to disappoint their organisation's leader. Remarkably, every single A&R department responded to Odo's telex with detailed reviews, expressing their enthusiasm for the album and a strong desire to release it as soon as possible.

Dave returned to Germany for his second meeting with Odo to conclude the negotiations. Meanwhile, Meyers had another trick up his sleeve. He requested that I make a call to Polydor Germany while he was in the meeting with Odo, I was to pretend to be Clive Davis, the President of Arista Records in New York. My task was to contact Odo's secretary and convey that I had just spoken with Mr. Meyers' office in London who had told me he was currently in Germany meeting with Odo and that it was imperative that I speak to Mr. Meyers urgently.

Although it was a nerve-wracking concept, when the time came, I mustered the courage to dial Odo's office. In a terrible fake American accent, I carried out Meyers's instructions and insisted that the secretary interrupt the meeting and connect me with Dave immediately. To my astonishment, the next voice on the other end of the line was Dave himself. I inquired about the progress, but he disregarded my questions and continued down the phone with his script saying, "I really appreciate your interest Clive, but PolyGram has a deep appreciation for this artist. However, if we don't reach an agreement with PolyGram today, I'll get back to you promptly."
After the call, Meyers continued to inform Odo that Arista had intense interest in the project and had contacted his London office about a deal, only to be told that negotiations were already in progress in Germany, prompting the call.
Fearing the prospect of losing the album to the fictitious Clive Davis, Odo made a desperate move and offered $150,000 for a worldwide deal. Meyers skillfully negotiated the advance up to $200,000 and even kept the rights for the USA. It was an audacious plan executed to perfection.

After sealing the deal with PolyGram, our sights were set on securing a record deal in the USA. Given Arista's inadvertent influence in our previous success, we decided to offer them the first opportunity.
We managed to arrange a meeting with the actual Clive Davis in New York, who, unsurprisingly, had never heard of us or our album. Within minutes, it became apparent that he had no interest in our project. Despite his politeness, he called his secretary to direct us to his assistant, who displayed even less enthusiasm. Concluding that Arista was not the right fit for us, we left without further ado. Our next destination was CBS.

With our egos intact, we secured a meeting with Dick Asher, the president of CBS Records. We arrived at their reception at 9:45 a.m. For our scheduled 10 a.m. meeting. After signing in and affixing our badges, we were directed to a private elevator that whisked us straight to Asher's top-floor office at the CBS building. The elevator doors opened into a reasonably small office, where one of two secretaries greeted us. She explained that Mr. Asher would be running late and organised some coffee while we patiently waited for about an hour.

Finally, Dick Asher arrived. After his secretary briefed him on messages, she informed him that we had been waiting since ten to present an album we were interested in placing with CBS. He apologised for the delay, attributing it to his dental appointment where he had a tooth removed.

Sensing his potential reluctance to listen to our music at that moment, I suggested rescheduling for another time. To our surprise, he graciously declined this proposal and invited us into his office for coffee. Realising this might be our only opportunity to meet with him, we eagerly accepted his invitation.

His office exuded grandeur and, as he settled behind a vast desk, he enthusiastically shared insights about CBS, emphasising its prestige and the enduring careers of artistes such as Johnny Mathis, Barbra Streisand Andy Williams and Johnny Cash, who had all spent two decades or more with the company.

He then engaged us in small talk, inquiring about our impressions of New York and gradually steering the conversation toward our artiste and the music.

We provided a brief overview of our artiste and the PolyGram deal. Noticing the discomfort caused by his earlier dental appointment, we thought better than to make him listen to any album tracks.

Curious about the PolyGram deal, he inquired further. We explained that PolyGram had secured the album's rights for the world except the USA, embellishing the interest shown by Arista.

Amidst a flurry of phone calls, he persistently requested to hear our tape, which we initially declined. Despite our comfort in his opulent office, a sense of intimidation crept in due to his towering presence in the music industry.

As our refusal continued, his insistence grew. Eventually, we relented and handed over the cassette. He played about 45 seconds of a couple of tracks.

Following this brief audition, Dick expressed his interest in the product but raised a crucial concern. He asked if PolyGram owned the rights for Canada.

Dave confirmed, "Yes."

Dick responded, "Well, we can't sign it. Launching this act in the US would be costly and PolyGram would simply import the albums from Canada, reaping all the profits. How long is your deal with them?"

I answered, "Five years, but if you sign the artist, you'd still have at least 15 years remaining." He burst into laughter.

Shortly after, we exchanged handshakes and expressed gratitude for his time. As we departed, we carried with us a valuable lesson about the intricacies of the Canadian and USA border dynamics in the music industry.

Back in Germany

At PolyGram Germany, Hans Muller, appointed by Odo as the head of A&R, was our point of contact for the album's release.

Week after week, Hans would request various changes to almost everything we provided to PolyGram, including the artwork. He even suggested adding strings to most of the album and remixing it in the USA. His rationale for the American mixes was to enhance the album credits.

We invested a considerable sum in adding strings, featuring magnificent arrangements by ELO's Lou Clark. We then journeyed to my favourite studio in Nashville to complete the album's mixing.

After nearly a year of dedicated work, we finally had the finished product in hand. We organised a launch party at Legends, an upscale London nightclub and invited dignitaries from PolyGram.

The major issue we faced throughout the process was that despite the artiste's immense talent and youthful-sounding great voice, he unfortunately looked more like a 35-year-old lawyer. To avoid revealing this to the record company during the deal negotiations, we managed to keep anyone from meeting or seeing him. The front cover of the album featured a photograph of the artiste looking into a window, with the actual face smudged and the back cover showcased a painting with the artiste's name on a personalised number plate of a car.

Creating a promotional video for the launch party turned into a disaster, as there was no way to hide the fact that he was not an 18-year-old idol. The video screening was set up downstairs at the club. To prevent any PolyGram personnel from discovering the artiste's true age, Dave bribed the DJ to claim that the video facility was broken. We took turns ensuring that whenever PolyGram people were upstairs, the artiste remained downstairs and vice versa.

Around 2 a.m. someone announced, "At last, the video is now working." Dave rushed downstairs with another bribe and just as Michael Jackson finished on the screen, the DJ declared to the dance floor that the video had once again broken.

This strategy worked successfully until the end of the evening when the launch was over. Dave and I were waiting for a taxi in the doorway of Legends when Odo, along with a couple of people from PolyGram, joined us. While we were all chatting, the artiste also appeared. Although everyone was a bit tipsy, there was no way to avoid introducing everyone.

About two weeks later, Odo called Dave and asked when he could meet the artist. Dave replied, "You met him at Legends." Odo responded, "No, no, I only met his father." Oops.

Sadly within a few months, Odo left the company and was soon followed by Han's departure. Even though PolyGram had fully funded the advance, which we had spent on the extensive changes, the new executives showed no interest in an artiste they hadn't personally signed. Consequently, the album was shelved across all territories.

We inquired about the possibility of taking the album to another company and offering them an override, but this request was denied.

After all the emotional turmoil, time and investment, the album remained unreleased.

Chapter 21

Vic Maile Engineer/Producer

Throughout the years, Vic employed a plethora of unorthodox techniques across his impressive array of recordings which he both engineered and produced.

Unique Techniques

When Vic was recording his own material he would start the track with the bass drum sound, using an AKG 224E microphone covered in cloth, he then tapped the top of the mic with his finger to mimic a bass drum beat. He would then record the sound on quarter-inch tape. This laid the groundwork for the basic bass drum track. Typically, Vic would record around a minute's worth of material.

From that point, he carefully handpicked the most harmonious and perfectly timed eight bars, skillfully weaving them together. Next, he wound the tape around a 5-inch plastic spool. Afterward, he guided the tape across the playback heads of the quarter-inch tape machine, pressing the play button and capturing it on the multitrack recorder. This ingenious method yielded an impeccably synchronised loop of the bass drum, providing a foundation of rhythmic precision. With the loop established, Vic's true expertise came into play. He applied equalisation and compression to sculpt the sound, yielding an astonishing bass drum tone that was now ready for integration into the multitrack recording. This innovative method of tape looping for instruments left a lasting impression on me, marking the first instance I had witnessed such a technique in action. It's intriguing to note that many years later, I would come across information indicating that "The Bee Gees" had played a pioneering role in loop recording during the production of their album *Saturday Night Fever*.

While many engineers tended to employ gentle compression, used to reduce a signal's dynamic range - that is, to reduce the difference in level between the loudest and quietest parts of an audio signal, Vic had a more unconventional approach. He harnessed them not merely for their effects but as tools to craft distinctive sounds.

For instance, let's consider a cymbal with its typical splash sound. Rather than settling for the expected, Vic would push boundaries. He'd create a loop using a few cymbal crashes and then devote considerable time to experimenting with the compressor. By skillfully pushing the compressor to its extreme thresholds, he ventured into uncharted sonic territory, ultimately producing remarkably unique percussion sounds that went far beyond the cymbal's conventional tonal range.

More unconventional percussive tones were produced by employing a guitar. The guitar strings were strummed exclusively in a downward direction, with the right hand resting above the neck, not actively shaping a chord but rather positioned in a way that produced a rhythmic vamping sound.

To achieve piano percussion, he would drape a humble cloth over his fingertips and then press any lower to middle piano string. Simultaneously, he struck the corresponding key on the keyboard in perfect harmony with the bass drum's beats. This ingenious technique seamlessly blended the bass drum with harmonic richness, ushering in a unique musical dimension.

When recording bands and finalising the drum track, Vic adhered to a steadfast routine: he'd request the drummer to execute an overdub, using a barely open hi-hat and striking it in tandem with each snare beat. This meticulous approach guaranteed that the snare sound resonated with a distinct, sharp and pristine quality, setting it apart in its crispness and character, although not quite to the same extent as the recording of the Dr Feelgood album *Stupidity*.

When it came to handclaps, Vic had a distinctive technique: he would use two empty wooden U67 Neumann microphone boxes, clapping them together and subsequently layering the overdubbed recordings a few times. This meticulous process yielded an incredible consistent handclap sound.

This hallmark technique left its mark on numerous of Vic's productions, particularly notable in tracks like Tom Robinson's "2-4-6-8 Motorway." The resonance of this rock-solid handclap sound became a defining characteristic of his work.
On this recording you can also hear Vic's profound fondness for slide guitar. Once more, his approach was to transform every element into an evocative effect, surpassing the realm of commonplace sounds.

The Juke Box

One evening, I was hanging out at Pye with Vic when a mutual friend of his, Dave, paid us a visit. Dave struck me as a polite and softly-spoken individual. Our conversation was fairly casual with music being the central theme. After Dave left, my curiosity got the better of me and I inquired about Dave's involvement in the music industry. Vic grinned and revealed, "He's Screaming Lord Sutch." I was taken aback. This was the very same person who, in the 1960s, was known for his horror-themed stage performances. He often donned the persona of Jack the Ripper, arriving at gigs in a hearse or even inside a coffin. His acts included theatrical elements like the simulated dismemberment of a baby doll with splattered fake blood - a precursor to the shock rock theatrics later embraced by artistes like Arthur Brown and Alice Cooper. Interestingly, when Alice Cooper adopted similar elements, Sutch replaced the doll with an effigy of Alice.
Vic had collaborated with Sutch on a single titled "Gotta Keep A-Rocking" and together, they produced a live album called *Hands of Jack The Ripper*. This live recording was done by the Pye Mobile unit and featured an impressive line-up including Keith Moon on drums, Noel Redding on bass and Ritchie Blackmore on guitar. It was truly an extraordinary assembly of musicians for the rhythm section.

Around this time Vic bought a wonderful vintage dial-up selector jukebox from me, for a sum of £35.00. It was only on arriving at his Ruislip maisonette it became clear; the jukebox had no way of fitting through the front door. We tried it at every angle to no avail, the whole debacle could have been straight out of the Bernard Cribbins song "Right Said Fred."

The reality was inescapable: this hefty jukebox had no intention of making its home with Vic so there was no alternative but to load it back into the van, Vic reluctantly placed the £35 back into his wallet. I decided not to take it back home but to store it at the studio back in Wembley until I found another buyer.

A few weeks later Vic was recounting the tale of our jukebox misadventure to Dave and it turned out that Dave was more than eager to take the jukebox off my hands. He promptly offered me £60.00 and settled the payment on the spot. Having lost the sale to Vic I was happy to acquaint my wallet with another sale of the jukebox.

Curious about the delivery details I inquired when he would like to receive it. His response was simple and noncommittal: "I will let you know." Approximately two months passed without a word from Dave. Frustrated by the silence, I took the initiative to call him at home and address the matter of the jukebox.

Dave's answer took me aback once again. He apologised, stating, "Sorry Kenny, my mum said I can't have it in the house." Thus, the journey of the jukebox took yet another twist. In the end, I managed to sell it for £75 to Malcolm Jackson, the proprietor of Jackson Studios, which allowed me to pay £60 to Dave concluding the jukebox's nomadic adventures.

Vic and I departed Pye Studios around the same period to embark on new opportunities at separate studios. My initial assumption was that this transition might lead us to grow apart. Surprisingly, the opposite occurred and our bond strengthened further. We found ourselves collaborating frequently at De Lane Lea studios. Additionally, weekends became occasions for us to connect on a more personal level. Vic and his future wife Lesley enjoyed many memorable dinner parties with Sue and me. These shared experiences not only deepened our professional relationship but also fostered a genuine and lasting friendship.

Bronze Records

By the mid-1970s, whilst under the management of another close friend, Stuart Taylor, who took on the role of guiding my career as a producer. Stuart's efforts led me to securing production opportunities with several record labels.

I proposed to Vic that he connect with Stuart to explore potential opportunities with various record labels - an idea he embraced.

Before long, Stuart had introduced Vic to Gerry Bron, owner of Bronze Records, resulting in Vic's production of the single "Yeah Right" for the band Girlschool. This marked the beginning of a successful productive collaboration, leading to two additional singles, "Emergency" and "Nothing to Lose," along with the album *Demolition*.

Vic's next notable project for Bronze Records was producing the album *Ace of Spades* for Motorhead, a recording that took place from August 4th to September 15th, 1980. It's worth noting that during that era, the standard producer royalty percentage was around two percent. I recall Vic advocating for three percent during negotiations. I asked him whether the effort was truly worth fighting for that additional one percent. Vic's response stuck with me: "Well, that one percent is actually an extra 50 percent for me."

From then on, I learned the importance of holding out for that little extra, understanding how seemingly minor percentage points could translate into substantial gains.

Jackson's Studio

Vic's choice of studio was Jackson's in Rickmansworth This was a rather unimpressive place, with an ageing Neve console But I was reminded of my first encounter with Studio 2 at Pye in 1969, which despite its worn appearance, had played host to the recording of numerous 1960s music luminaries.

It's worth noting that, Sun Studios in Memphis was situated at the rear of a shop, Joe Meek produced his hits in his apartment above a shop on Holloway Road and Buddy Holly's early classics were captured at Norman Petty's studio in Clovis, New Mexico - a facility that would seem prehistoric when compared to the likes of Sun Studios and Holloway Road.

Ultimately, it is the skill of the engineer and the artistic prowess of the recording musicians that shape the studio's sonic character, regardless of the facilities' appearance.

Vic was the unsung hero behind Jackson's triumphs; his dedication and expertise were the driving force behind the hits he masterminded during these sessions.

At Home with Vic

One of our regular gatherings with Vic was on a Saturday night. Sue and I would arrive at Vic's house for dinner along with Vic's partner Lesley, his Revox tape machine would invariably be humming in the corner, having been playing 1950s rock 'n' roll all morning and afternoon. Come the evening, the mood transformed with a change to movie soundtracks such as *South Pacific* or *Seven Brides and Seven Brothers*.

I asked Vic, "Can you imagine the reaction of Motorhead or Dr Feelgood if they walked in and caught you playing "Gonna Wash That Man Right Out Of My Hair" at full blast?"

Vic's response was his trademark gentle smile, never taking offence.

Vic and I were inseparable, our conversations revolving around our mutual love of music. We'd share tracks we were currently working on or introduce each other to artistes we held in high regard. But not every evening unfolded flawlessly.

I recall one incident shortly after Vic and Lesley had settled into their bungalow in Ivor, Bucks. Despite it being a bungalow, there was an additional upstairs room which served as their dining area. During a meal involving a meat fondue, Vic's attempt to add more oil resulted in him setting fire to the fondue set. In a frantic bid to douse the flames, he grabbed the entire setup and raced downstairs, inadvertently spreading burning oil throughout the house. Sue, Lesley and I hurriedly followed Vic, quenching the fiery trail. A major disaster was averted, but Vic's hands bore the scars of that incident. Suffice it to say, from that day on fondue was off the menu.

In late 1977, Vic and Lesley joined us for dinner at our home. During the meal, I fervently praised a track I'd heard on the radio that week. "Vic, you'll adore it - it encapsulates everything you cherish in a pop song. It's titled "2-4-6-8 Motorway."
In his characteristically modest manner, he responded softly, "Oh, um, I produced that."
The song has remained a cherished favourite of mine ever since. I once questioned him about a pronounced guitar bleep at 2:07 in the recording and why he opted to retain it. It turned out he hadn't even noticed it until I pointed it out. From then on, he'd jestingly find anomalies in my recordings and bring them to my attention. To this day, that bleep catches my ear.
Regrettably, Vic didn't live to witness the 1989 BBC Christmas special of Only Fools and Horses entitled *"The Jolly Boys Outing,"* featuring "2-4-6-8 Motorway." Undoubtedly, he would have been immensely pleased, as the show held a special place in his heart.

Health Issues

During the early 1980s Vic fell victim to Guillain–Barré syndrome, an ailment characterised by swift muscle weakness due to the immune system attacking the peripheral nervous system. Whilst he was ill, I made bi-weekly visits to the hospital where Vic was confined. He found himself virtually paralysed from the neck down. On these visits, I would assist him by offering biscuits and reading chapters from books about rock 'n' roll. As I discovered more about the ailment, I came to understand that there existed no definitive cure.
Curiosity led me to ask Vic, "How long have they indicated this might persist?"
With unwavering composure, he responded, "For however long it takes."
Six weeks passed before Vic finally left the hospital, embarking on a gradual journey towards complete recuperation.

Over the course of the following years, Vic encountered several health issues, all of which he approached with the same composed and calm character. During this period, Vic made the decision to quit smoking his potent non-filtered Senior Service cigarettes and also chose to abstain from drinking. He did, although derive some enjoyment from smoking the odd Jamaican Woodbine.
On June 9th, 1989, shortly after his return from a trip to the USA, I paid a visit to Vic at his home in Marlowe. While sipping on coffee and sharing stories about his travels, Vic casually broached the topic of his will. He inquired if I would be willing to serve as a witness, emphasising that this was merely an item on his "to-do" list. I was happy to do so. We also agreed to reconvene for a lunch outing in a few weeks' time.
Throughout the ensuing weeks, we engaged in several phone conversations and on Thursday, July 13th, we solidified our plan to meet at a familiar pub in Denham

Village. A prelude to our forthcoming gathering occurred on Monday, July 10th, when Vic contacted me to confirm the meeting time.

The very next evening, I received a call from Lesley, delivering the sombre news of Vic's passing earlier that day. In a state of shock and emotional distress, my recollection of the conversation remains somewhat fragmented. I do recall inquiring about the cause of Vic's passing, wondering if it had been due to a heart attack.
Lesley shared that, in fact, Vic had been informed approximately six weeks prior that he had cancer and his time was limited. Learning this left me overwhelmed with a mixture of sadness and anger, primarily directed towards Vic for not having confided in me about his condition.
In a candid conversation, I approached Lesley and questioned why Vic hadn't informed me about his condition. I considered him such a dear and close friend. She revealed that Vic was well aware of the significant challenges and stress that Sue and I were navigating during that period, particularly with the recent loss of my brother and a multitude of other difficulties. Out of consideration and care, Vic had chosen not to burden us further by sharing his own health struggles. The sign of a true friend, my wonderful friend Vic Maile.

On July 18th, in Amersham, Buckinghamshire, a cremation ceremony was conducted in honour of Vic. The day was illuminated by radiant sunshine and brought together a significant gathering of friends, family and fellow artists who had gathered to show their respect. They all shared in each other's sorrow, mourning the loss of a truly remarkable individual.

From those early days at PYE until his sad passing at the age of 45, Vic was one of my and Sue's closest friends and we miss him to this day.

Chapter 22

A Few Gems I Picked Up Along the Way

Barry Gibb and Blue Weaver

While collaborating during the production of the *Saturday Night Fever* soundtrack. Blue Weaver, co-founder of the Welsh rock band Amen Corner, had an extensive musical career, contributing to projects with renowned artistes such as Family, T-Rex, Lou Reed, Alice Cooper, Chicago, Stephen Stills, The Osmonds, Stevie Wonder, Art of Noise, Duran Duran, The Damned, and Swing Out Sister.

Blue Weaver joined the Bee Gees and remained with them from 1975 to 1980. One late night in the studio while working on a song for the *Saturday Night Fever* soundtrack, Barry Gibb and Blue Weaver were in the studio, when Blue experienced some discomfort due to an ongoing health issue. This prompted Barry to offer to take him to the local hospital.

On arriving in the out-patients department and before he could see a doctor, a standard questionnaire form had to be completed by a nurse.

She started the questions by asking name, date of birth and medical history. When she got to the question, "Have you ever been a practising homosexual?" Barry couldn't resist speaking up saying, "Practising? He's got it perfect."

Roy Orbison

During a British tour, Roy used a pickup band. A pickup band consisted of local musicians you could easily "pick up" instead of bringing your own, saving money and avoiding red tape.

Many musicians on the road indulge in pre-show drinks. In this particular band the piano player was the leader of that particular pack.

One night before the show, the entire band, except the piano player, left the bar to take their positions on stage. As the curtain rose to a thunderous applause, the band noticed the piano player hurrying from the wings to his instrument just as Orbison made his stage entrance. Before striking the first chord, the piano player regrettably threw up all over the piano. Orbison, acknowledging the situation, turned to the audience and simply said, "Mercy!"

Diana Dors

Originally named Diana Fluck, she was frequently referred to as the British Marilyn Monroe. She even appeared on the cover of the legendary Beatles album, *Sgt. Pepper's Lonely Hearts Club Band*.

Following her passing in 1984, she posthumously gained acclaim as a cherished national treasure. When once asked about her birth name, she humorously remarked, "They requested that I alter my name. I assume they were concerned that if my actual name, Diana Fluck, were prominently displayed in lights and one of those lights happened to malfunction..."

I was working on a session in Studio Two at Pye alongside Dave Hunt and the producer Miki Dallon. Miki was collaborating on an album with the artiste Don Fardon when Diana Dors dropped in to see Don.

During a break in the recording, Diana shared a fabulous tale from her early days. She recounted that after returning to England from Hollywood many years prior, she received an invitation to her hometown of Swindon for a ceremony where the mayor would honour her achievements in the movie industry. The mayor's intended introduction was, "We are here today to welcome back from Hollywood and honour a truly unique star. The world knows her as Diana Dors, but to us, she will always remain our very own, Diana Fluck."

At this point in the story, Diana, rising from her chair for emphasis, continued; The mayor, was slightly nervous about making an obvious mistake and the speech actually went like this "We are here today to welcome back from Hollywood and honour a truly unique star. The world knows her as Diana Dors, but to us, she will always remain our very own, DIANA CLUNT."
We all collapsed with laughter, it was clear that Diana relished sharing this story. Over the years I have read various accounts of this story, where the nervous character has changed from a mayor to a vicar or an MP, so I wonder about the veracity of the claim. It doesn't really matter if Diana fictionalised the event; it's a great story.

Little Richard

While performing at Hamburg's legendary Star Club in 1962, Little Richard received a proof of his new album cover. After gazing at the photograph of himself on the front cover, he tossed the sleeve across the room, declaring, "This is shit, I's much prettier than that."

Clem Cattini

Clem is a notable English rock & roll drummer. His musical journey started at the 2i's Coffee Bar in Soho. Later he joined Johnny Kidd & the Pirates, contributing his drumming talents to their successful track "Shakin' All Over".

He also became the preferred drummer for Joe Meek, participating in sessions for artistes such as John Leyton and Don Charles. Eventually he co-founded the Tornados in 1961 and his drumming skills graced their chart-topping international hit "Telstar".

Beyond being a most sought-after session musician, Cattini, as the drummer for the Tornadoes, was notably depicted by James Corden in Nick Moran's film, *Telstar: The Joe Meek Story*. Amazingly Clem holds a spot in the Guinness Book of Records. It is for his drumming on the most UK number one singles. Ironically, he lost track of the exact count, as he moved from studio to studio, sometimes participating in up to four sessions a day, often unaware of the artiste or song he was contributing to.

In addition to his drumming prowess, Clem's sense of humour is another of his delightful qualities. This aspect of his personality is evident in his collection of anecdotes from the golden age of recording, which not only showcases his razor-sharp wit but also adds to his overall charm.

Revered for his witty storytelling prowess, he can regale you for hours on end with captivating tales from his years of session work.

On a session for Dick Rowe, a segment in the middle of the song demanded a succinct break with a distinctive drum fill. At the correct spot Clem played a wonderful drum fill, easily and without hesitation.

Nevertheless, Dick was not entirely satisfied with Clem's initial attempt, prompting him to request a retry. This process was repeated multiple times as Dick's contentment continued to elude him, leading to several more takes.

After each take the tape would stop and with Dick's voice resonating through Clem's headphones via the talkback microphone he would hear "Clem, Clem - play it with more magic, a hint of enchantment, make it truly magical."

After enduring several versions of these enigmatic and vague calls for greater magic, poor Clem found himself teetering on the edge of exasperation. So, at the next drum break, he struck the snare drum, flung his drumsticks into the air and screamed at the top of his lungs.

"ABRACA FUCKING DABRA!"

Clem was booked to play on significant orchestral recording at Abbey Road Studios. With orchestral recordings, the string section, due to their slow attack during bowing always appear to be just a little behind the beat. After several rehearsals the engineer announced over the talkback "Let's go for a take – is everyone happy with their headphone balance?" Clem looked up and replied "All is fine but could you make the strings a little quicker in the cans?" - Much to the irritation of the now very pissed-off string players.

Whilst I was setting up the microphones on Clem's drums, a fellow musician shouted over to him, "Cattini, you've got a bloody big head!" Without missing a beat, Clem replied, "No matter how big my head is, it'll always fit in your mouth."

Dick Rowe

During most of the Decca Studios recording sessions the esteemed Dick Rowe held the reins as producer.

Renowned for his role as the head of A&R at Decca Records, Rowe gained notoriety for his decision to pass on signing up The Beatles, it is rarely mentioned that he did sign The Rolling Stones, Van Morrison and The Moody Blues amongst many other successful artistes.

I had the pleasure of collaborating with Dick on several occasions and found him to be an amiable and genuinely kind individual.

During a recording session for the hit song "Diamonds" with bass player Jet Harris and drummer Tony Meehan, Dick expressed dissatisfaction with a particular drum part. Over the talkback mic, he instructed Tony, saying, "When you reach the bridge, change the hi-hat rhythm and play eighth notes."

He proceeded to describe the rhythm with words like "tish tish tish tish." But as soon as Tony began playing the hi-hat alone without other instruments, it became challenging to discern the beat's starting point. Dick then remarked, "That's fine, but you're doing it on the off-beat; you should be doing it on the on-beat."

Of course, it was impossible to determine where the off-beat and on-beat were in isolation.

On another occasion, while remixing a track, Dick asked the engineer to increase the volume of the orchestra's strings.

The engineer explained that the strings were 'tacet' at that point, meaning they were silent. Dick humorously responded, "Alright, can you turn the 'tacet' up then?"

By the mid-70s, Dick had adopted an image reminiscent of the legendary American record producer Jerry Wexler. He sported a beard, donned a hat and even smoked a pipe. As a producer, Dick was known throughout the industry for his occasional mishaps during recording sessions. During one such recording with a large orchestra, a member of Dick's entourage in the control room suggested, "Dick, I think that sounds out of tune," during a practice run-through. Dick immediately hit the talkback mic to halt the run-through and told the conductor, "Stop, stop, stop... it's out of tune." The conductor, perplexed, asked, "Where?" After a moment's pause and a puff on his pipe, Dick pointed into the recording room where the orchestra was playing and replied, "In there."

Chris Thompson

Chris joined Manfred Mann's Earth Band in 1976 as the lead vocalist. With the band, he recorded a reworked version of Bruce Springsteen's song, "Blinded by the Light." This rendition quickly became a hit, reaching number one on Billboard's Hot 100 and securing Top 20 chart positions in various other countries.

In 1979, while Chris was touring Europe with The Earth Band, he received an intriguing opportunity. He was asked to fly to New York to perform the lead vocal for "If You Remember Me", the theme song to the movie *The Champ* and it would forever hold a special place in his heart. So, between shows Chris hopped on Concorde and flew from London to New York.

Arriving at the airport, he headed straight to the recording studio to work with producer Richard Perry.

They were on such a tight recording schedule, Chris decided to stay in the vocal room throughout the session, receiving directions from Perry who was in the control room. As Chris sang his heart out, he couldn't help but notice Perry repeatedly ducking under the mixing desk out of view. Eventually it became apparent that Perry was trying to hide that fact he was taking phone calls during the recording.

Undeterred, Chris remained the consummate professional and continued to deliver a stellar performance. Unbeknown to Chris there was an even bigger surprise to come. Towards the end of the song, he witnessed a young woman entering the control room, this mysterious lady proceeded to throw a cape over Perry and began cutting his hair in the middle of the session.

Chris successfully completed the vocal recording and, afterwards, returned to Europe to re-join the band for their next live gig. Meanwhile, Richard Perry emerged from the studio with a fresh cut and blow-dry, looking quite lovely.

The Acoustic Strawbs

In 2001 Dave Cousins, along with the talented performers, Dave Lambert and Brian Willoughby made up the band The Acoustic Strawbs.
I recorded their album, *Baroque and Roll*, and it was a delightful project to be a part of.
During recording, the three guitars were always recorded live, straight to tape and often the lead vocal was captured at the same time completing a totally live performance.

Dave Cousins, while a passionate musician, could occasionally bring an intense atmosphere into the studio. Whenever things felt a bit too serious, I'd inject a bit of humour with a line or two to restore a more cheerful and relaxed ambiance. Interestingly, Dave was the only one who couldn't tell if I was being sarcastic or genuinely humorous; my intent was always to bring some humour.

For one particular song Dave pulled a banjo from the case, tuned it and, to everyone's delight, played it absolutely beautifully.
When he finished, he casually remarked, "You know, that's the first time I've played the banjo in 30 years." I couldn't resist saying, "Surely, it must be longer than that!"

During the recording of "Not All the Flowers Grow." A song which reflects on the Aberfan tragedy. Dave grew increasingly frustrated with each take. until finally he declared, "I just can't sing this song right now. I have to be in such a down and miserable mood to perform it."
I said down the talkback mic into the headphones, "Dave I have an idea, come back into the control room and I'll play you the previous track we recorded."

Miller Anderson and Jon Lord

Miller Anderson, a Scottish guitarist and vocalist, has remained at the forefront of rock music for over three decades. He has collaborated with numerous influential musicians and been a member of notable bands like the Keef Hartley Band, Savoy Brown, T. Rex, Mountain, The Spencer Davis Group and groups led by Deep Purple's Jon Lord, as well as folk-rock artiste Donovan. One of his best-known albums is titled *Bluesheart*.

During the recording of the *Bluesheart* album, Miller Anderson's old friend, Jon Lord, joined the studio to contribute some Hammond organ to a couple of tracks.

Jon, the original keyboard player and co-founder of Deep Purple, encountered a setback when it was discovered that the organ's volume pedal was broken.

Undeterred and always practical, Jon requested some masking tape and a couple of thin wooden sticks. With these improvised tools, this elegant and jewellery-adorned figure headed for the organ. He soon found himself lying on his back, rolling around under the organ while emitting grunts, groans and a few choice words. This process continued for about 15 minutes, after which he rose triumphantly and declared, "Alright, that's got it fixed!"

Appreciative of Jon's resourcefulness, I extended my gratitude, saying, "Thank you for coming. Miller mentioned how skilled you are with Hammonds. If you could leave your contact details at the reception, I'll contact you if the organ ever needs fixing again."

Fortunately for me, Jon was also renowned for his great sense of humour.

A Special Dinner Guest

Anthony Newley being a big star himself, had a list of friends that would read like a who's who of showbiz. He once told me about the time Warren Beatty visited London. Peter Sellers, a close friend of Tony's, had offered to arrange a female dinner companion for Warren. On the appointed evening, Peter picked up the phone and called Warren, saying, "I have a '10' for you tonight, my dear fellow."

Warren Beatty was pleasantly taken aback when Peter arrived at his hotel to drive him to the restaurant and introduced Princess Margaret as his dinner companion. After their meal Sellers bid farewell to the pair.

Tony went on to tell me that Princess Margaret invited Beatty back to her home, where they found themselves in a grand room with a piano and a roaring fire in the hearth. Princess Margaret insisted that Beatty stand by the piano while she treated him to a brief recital.

Her performance concluded with a deceptive cadence, with the Princess's hands leaving the piano and landing on Warren's private parts. With a twinkle in her eye, Princess Margaret asked Beatty if he had enjoyed her musical performance. Beatty's response to her question reportedly led to an evening marked by a series of crescendos.

The following day, Warren phoned Peter Sellers and said, "Thank you for the wonderful dinner and by the way, that was no 10; that was an 11."

Studio Booking

A client once phoned the studio, requesting a one hour booking to record 45 minutes of music. The studio's booking manager responded humorously, "I assume you don't plan to listen to the entire playback, then." Indeed, the world of studio bookings encounters all sorts of requests.

TV Jingles

Many recording engineers will readily admit that working on radio or TV jingles can be quite challenging. It's not the fault of the artistes, voice-over talents, musicians, or writers; it's often the advertising agency staff who present the real challenge.

Typically, agencies would send three or four staff members, each with their own strong opinions on how the final product should sound. Finding a harmonious meeting of minds was a rare occurrence.

Like most engineers at Wembley, I had my fair share of these miniature commercials or persuasive radio messages. One evening, as I watched TV, I realised that every advertisement during the commercial breaks had been recorded by me and the memories of the turmoil from each recording session came rushing back. From that point on, I did my utmost to make myself unavailable for jingle work.

If, by some unfortunate turn of events, I found myself booked for a jingle session, my only survival strategy to keep me sane was to inject a bit of humour into the chaos.

On one occasion, I was tasked with recording a Persil detergent ad. The music went relatively smoothly, but then the voice-over artiste arrived.

As I attempted to follow the simultaneous directions from all the agency staff and coax the best performance out of the obliging professional, I noticed that the word Persil was causing a popping sound on the microphone. I had already attached a pop shield to the mic to address this issue, but the popping persisted.

I asked the voice-over artiste to shift his head slightly to the side to avoid blasting the microphone with the spoken "P." This adjustment didn't immediately solve the problem and chaos erupted among the producers. They reacted as if it were the end of the world, with voices clamouring:

"What are we going to do?"

"Oh my God! This is terrible."

"This isn't working at all, what's the solution?"

In an attempt to maintain my composure, I assured them, "It's not a problem; I can easily fix this." The control room fell silent, with everyone hanging on my next words. I suggested, "Instead of saying 'Persil,' why doesn't he say 'Dreft' or 'Daz'?"

This was when I discovered that humour wasn't a strong suit among the clients. To everyone's relief, on the next run-through, the voice-over artiste put less emphasis on the problematic "P," and suddenly, everyone was ecstatic.

Bumming Around Europe

I knew a guitarist who was travelling through Spain on vacation and performing a few gigs to earn some spending money. He would locate a bar, set up his gear and sing whatever the audience requested.

One night, as the gig neared its end, a beautiful young German girl approached the stage and boldly said, "Take me home." In a hushed tone off the mic, he replied, "I won't be finished for another 30 minutes." To his surprise, she responded, "No, I meant, "Take me home, country roads."

Charlie Katz - Fixer and Booker for Sessions Players

During one session, a saxophone player arrived late and explained his tardiness by blaming it on the Woolwich ferry being delayed. Charlie Katz, a well-known session fixer, said, "How dare you come to my sessions by boat!"

On another occasion during one of Charlie's sessions, a cellist failed to show up. Concerned, Charlie asked his secretary to call the cellist and inquire about the delay. His secretary returned with the sad news that the cellist had passed away the night before. Charlie's somewhat self-centred response was, "Why does everything always happen to me?" This story is courtesy of Alan Hawkshaw's book *The Champ: The Hawk Talks*.

Tangerine Studios

This was a small studio, which nestled in the heart of North London. While not the most famous recording facility around, it was well priced and had adequate facilities. Tangerine was leased by my friends, Dave Meyers and John Worsley.

Although this studio operated smoothly, it did contend with a rather peculiar challenge - it shared a party wall with a working bingo hall situated just behind it. Surprisingly, this unusual setup led to issues during recording sessions, but not in the way you might expect.
There were no complaints from the bingo hall's passionate blue-haired patrons about not hearing their favourite bingo calls, such as "two little ducks" or "two fat ladies." Oddly, no one ever mentioned disruptive drum solos, screeching guitars, or thunderous bass lines from the studio side either.
In fact, it was quite the opposite. Dave Meyers often had to venture into the bingo hall before recording sessions, make his way to the stage and turn down the volume on the bingo caller's microphone to ensure a peaceful recording environment.

One memorable incident occurred during a vocal overdub session with Wayne Fontana of Wayne Fontana and the Mindbenders fame. Wayne was in the recording room, standing confidently in front of the microphone, headphones on, pouring his heart into the song.
Halfway through the track, he halted his singing so the engineer stopped the tape. Wayne's voice came over the microphone to the engineer, "Hey, I can't hear what I'm doing! Please can you turn my voice up and the bingo down?"

Recording Studios Myth Buster

Tangerine Studios once had the honour of hosting a young prince from the Middle East who had booked a session to record a religious document. Everything appeared to be proceeding smoothly and the young prince, along with his entourage, left the studio content with the recording.

The original master tape, as part of standard practice, was scheduled to undergo

editing then sent to an address in central London.
Unfortunately, the following day, a shocking discovery was made – the quarter-inch master tape was entirely blank.
The tape had been mistakenly overwritten the previous night when someone had used it as an echo reel tape. A common practice during that era meaning that tape was constantly in record mode acting as a delay for the echo plate signal.
Meyers, recognised the gravity of the situation and devised a clever plan. He dispatched the young tea boy to deliver a blank reel of tape to the awaiting client in London and patiently awaited the client's call.
When the client phoned to express their understandable frustration at receiving a completely blank tape, Dave calmly replied, "I'll investigate and get back to you." Sometime later, he made the return call, explaining that he had taken action against the young lad who had been entrusted with the delivery. He explained the tea boy had opted to save money by travelling on the underground train instead of taking a taxi, despite being provided with cab fare. Unfortunately, the strong magnetic forces generated by the underground train's engines had erased the tape. This story reverberated around the music business.
Following this incident, for many, many years, no one dared to risk transporting magnetic recording tapes on the underground unless the tapes were meticulously wrapped in layers of tin foil.
Knowing this story well, I never had any issues carrying tapes on the underground.

Don't Cash That Cheque

Despite having slightly waned in popularity, a prominent artiste continued to maintain a loyal fan base. To express his appreciation to his dedicated supporters, he offered them a unique opportunity: if they sent him a £15 cheque, they would secure a copy of his forthcoming limited-edition album. By the time all the cheques were processed, the artiste sent each fan a personal cheque along with a typed message, regretfully explaining that the album would not be produced as planned at this time. As anticipated, the autograph on the cheque was a cherished keepsake for fans, prompting them to frame it rather than cash it.

Flat Or Sharp?

A very well-known singer overdubbing his vocal on to a music track said, "I can't sing to this, the track is flat". Some ten minutes later he said, "No it's not flat, it's sharp." A few minutes later he said, "No it's not flat or sharp, it's somewhere in between."

Chris Farlowe

In 2003, I found myself in the role of producer and engineer for the artiste Chris Farlowe during the production of his album, *Farlowe That!*
The band responsible for laying down the tracks was Chris's regular live backing group, known as "The Norman Beaker Band."
It didn't take me long to realise that working with Chris could be quite

challenging. His temperament was rather unpredictable and he always insisted that his opinions were both correct and final, even when he was mistaken. Consequently, the album ended up taking much longer to complete than initially anticipated.

The backing tracks were relatively straightforward, but recording the lead vocals presented more difficulties. Once the recording phase was finished, I was tasked with mixing the album.

When Chris came to the studio to listen to the final playback, he had issues with virtually every track. He suggested we needed to redo the guitar and sax solos, which I strongly disagreed with as I believed there was nothing wrong. This would have added several more weeks to the project unnecessarily.

After spending a considerable amount of time with Chris, I realised that arguing the point was futile. So, I decided to take a different approach. I explained to him that he could hear a minor tuning issue that the average ear could never detect. I assured him that he had a rare gift - perfect pitch and what he could hear, others could not. To everyone's relief, he readily accepted my explanation.

Several months later, I received a phone call from the immensely talented Norman Beaker. He jokingly said, "Kenny, I can never forgive you for that 'perfect pitch' story you made up. Since then, at the end of every gig, Chris insists, 'You were out of tune tonight,' and I tell him I wasn't. He just responds, "Don't argue with me, I have perfect pitch". Sorry Norm.

The Studio Lounge & Bar

It was an ordinary working day at CTS Studios in Wembley when two individuals clad in brown overalls, brandishing clipboards, casually strolled into the lounge area. They approached Lawrence, the bar manager, and confidently informed him that they were there to collect the pool table for re-covering, assuring him that a replacement would be delivered later in the day. Without any reason to doubt their story, Lawrence gave them the green light to proceed with the removal of the pool table. Gathering a group of staff members to assist, they embarked on the challenging task of carrying this bulky and unwieldy item out of the establishment.

After an arduous journey through a lengthy corridor and down a steep flight of stairs, they finally arrived at the reception area, where the imposing glass doors leading to the main exit posed an insurmountable obstacle. It soon became evident that the table was far too large to pass through the doors.

To overcome this unexpected predicament, we all went to great lengths, dismantling the alarm system and, with considerable effort, removing the doors from their hinges. Undeterred, the collective effort of all present continued as they worked together to hoist the table onto the awaiting truck. With their mission accomplished, the two men drove away with the table securely loaded.

Later that day, Lawrence decided to call the leasing company to inquire about the expected arrival of the replacement pool table. To his dismay, the leasing company had absolutely no knowledge of any order related to re-covering, replacement, or maintenance for the pool table. It became painfully clear that these two audacious individuals had simply walked in and swiped a valuable pool table and to make matters worse, they had received the unwitting assistance of

everyone present.
Talk about sheer audacity, they had some balls - ours!

Barry Mason

Barry Mason, an exceptionally accomplished lyricist with numerous gold and platinum discs to his name, has left an enduring legacy in the music industry. His lyrical genius has graced the compositions of artistes such as Tom Jones, The Drifters, Rod Stewart, Perry Como and Barbra Streisand to name but a few.

Among Barry's notable achievements stands the monumental success of "The Last Waltz," famously performed by Englebert Humperdinck. In a delightful story, Barry told of an encounter during the song's chart-topping days. While at a club, he found himself in the men's room alongside a gentleman who was whistling the melody of "The Last Waltz." Unable to resist the temptation, Barry said, "I wrote the lyrics to that song." To his surprise, the gentleman turned to Barry and replied, "I'm not whistling the fucking lyrics."

Chapter 23

Epilogue

Farewell

In 2009, I said goodbye to an industry that had changed beyond recognition and one I no longer held a passion for. This decision was accompanied by the heartache of losing so many dear friends and colleagues. Studios such as De Lane Lea/CTS and Pye were replaced by apartment buildings, and KD's in Chiswick underwent a change into residential flats. Studios were closing down rapidly, as the music scene shifted towards kids recording on computers, bypassing the necessity of a large studio. While this may have democratised music creation, I couldn't shake the belief that a computer merely imitates, unable to authentically create or encapsulate the essence of a musician's soul.

The Fifties

The emergence of rock 'n' roll heralded a seismic shift in the musical landscape, signifying far more than just a new genre. It marked a cultural revolution, drawing in a diverse array of music enthusiasts and sparking a wave of excitement and energy unlike anything seen before.
The arrival of rock 'n' roll brought with it a fusion of musical styles, blending elements of rhythm and blues, country, gospel and jazz into a dynamic and electrifying sound. Its infectious rhythms and catchy melodies and rebellious spirit captivated audiences of all ages, transcending traditional boundaries and resonating with the collective consciousness of a generation hungry for change and expression.
Moreover, rock 'n' roll served as a catalyst for social transformation, challenging existing norms and breaking down barriers of race, class, and gender. It became a symbol of youth rebellion and freedom, empowering individuals to embrace their individuality and challenge the status quo.
In essence, the arrival of rock 'n' roll was a transformative moment not only in music but also in society as a whole, leaving an indelible mark on the cultural fabric of the 20th century and beyond.

The Sixties

During this era, the music industry experienced a remarkable surge in record sales, propelled by the release of iconic albums like "Beatles for Sale" and "With the Beatles." What was particularly notable about this period was the phenomenon of albums driving sales without relying on the release of singles. Instead, fans were enticed to purchase entire albums to experience a cohesive collection of music.
Take, for example, "Beatles for Sale" and "With the Beatles," both of which captivated audiences despite lacking any standalone singles. This underscored the enduring appeal and influence of The Beatles, as fans eagerly snapped up these albums to immerse themselves in the band's latest musical offerings.

Furthermore, the strategy of releasing singles separately from albums, as seen with tracks like "Help" emerging from the album of the same name, added to the allure of owning complete albums. Fans knew that purchasing an album meant gaining access to exclusive tracks not available as singles, such as "I'm Down," "Can't Buy Me Love," "I Feel Fine," "She's a Woman," and "Paperback Writer." This incentivised consumers to invest in albums for a comprehensive musical experience.

In response to the growing demand and changing consumption patterns, record labels embraced a variety of formats, including singles, LPs (long-playing records) and EPs (extended plays). This diversified approach catered to different preferences and budgets, providing fans with value for their money while simultaneously boosting overall sales across the industry.

Overall, this era exemplified the symbiotic relationship between artistes, record labels and consumers, where innovative marketing strategies and diverse formats converged to fuel a period of unprecedented growth and enthusiasm in the music industry.

By the end of the 60s the music industry was experiencing an electrifying period of experimentation. The Beatles had already shattered conventional recording norms with ground-breaking tracks such as "Strawberry Fields" and "I Am The Walrus," along with their iconic album "Sgt. Pepper's Lonely Hearts Club Band." This era captivated a generation, propelling the industry to new heights and birthing music legends who continue to inspire us today.

The music business was experiencing an explosive growth, captivating an entire generation with its magnetic allure. It was a time when dreams could come true, and anyone with a passion for music had a chance to make their mark. This dynamic era was poised to create music heroes and legends who would stand the test of time, continuing to be cherished and loved by generations to come. The industry's magic was undeniable and its influence on culture and society was unparalleled, forever shaping the course of music history.

The Seventies

During this era, record companies recognised the immense potential of emerging artistes and demonstrated a willingness to invest significantly in their development. This investment went beyond just funding initial recordings; it encompassed a strategic approach to supporting artistes over the long term, with a focus on nurturing a dedicated fan base for sustained success.

One key aspect of this support was the commitment to funding the creation of multiple albums. Rather than expecting immediate returns or focusing solely on short-term gains, record companies understood the importance of allowing artistes the creative freedom and time to evolve their sound and craft over multiple releases. This approach not only helped artistes refine their skills and develop their artistic identity but also allowed them to build a deeper connection with their audience over time.

Moreover, record companies recognised the importance of cultivating a loyal fan base as the foundation for long-term success in the music industry. They understood that sustainable careers were built on more than just hit singles or fleeting trends; they required a strong and engaged community of supporters who would continue to champion the artiste's work for years to come. To this end, record companies invested in marketing and promotion efforts aimed at building awareness, fostering fan engagement and cultivating a sense of loyalty among listeners.

Overall, the significant investments made by record companies in emerging artistes during this era reflected a broader understanding of the music industry's dynamics and the importance of fostering talent for sustained success. By supporting artistes over the long term and prioritising the development of a dedicated fan base, record companies played a crucial role in shaping the trajectory of emerging careers and laying the groundwork for lasting impact in the music landscape.

The Eighties

During this period, a notable shift occurred in the music industry landscape, with lawyers and accountants assuming central roles alongside artistes and record labels. This transformation was driven by a relentless pursuit of profit, wherein financial considerations increasingly shaped decision-making processes to benefit both industry professionals and record labels.

One significant consequence of this shift was the demand for albums to feature a minimum of six potential hit singles. This requirement had profound implications for the sales dynamics of individual singles. As albums became viewed as comprehensive packages designed to maximise revenue potential, the emphasis shifted away from the standalone single as a primary revenue generator.

Instead, singles evolved into promotional tools strategically deployed to drive album sales and enhance the overall commercial success of an artiste's catalogue. This strategic shift meant that singles played a diminished role in contributing to industry revenue compared to previous eras. After all, why purchase a single when consumers could acquire an entire album containing all the forthcoming singles, along with additional content and cohesive artistic statements?

This shift in consumer behaviour not only impacted the sales metrics of singles but also underscored the changing dynamics within the industry. Record labels and industry professionals adapted their strategies to align with the evolving preferences and consumption patterns of audiences, leveraging albums as the primary revenue driver while using singles as supplementary promotional vehicles.

Overall, this era marked a pivotal moment in the music industry's evolution, as financial considerations and profit motives reshaped the traditional paradigms governing the production, distribution, and consumption of music. The strategic emphasis on albums containing multiple potential hits reflected a concerted effort to maximise revenue streams and capitalise on the commercial potential of artistes' catalogues in an increasingly competitive marketplace.

The Nineties

The 1990s witnessed a major transformation, largely shaped by the rapid rise of the internet. Initially, major corporations and record labels underestimated the profound impact this technological advancement would have on their traditional business models.

However, the emergence of the internet sparked a seismic shift in the way music was consumed, particularly among youthful enthusiasts.

One of the most significant developments during this time was the proliferation of file-sharing platforms, which allowed users to freely exchange music files online. This phenomenon democratised access to music and empowered listeners to explore a vast array of artists and genres with unprecedented ease. However, it also posed a significant challenge to established revenue streams for record labels, as unauthorised file sharing led to substantial losses in sales revenue.

Despite the growing threat posed by online piracy, it took some time for record companies to fully grasp the internet's potential and adapt their strategies accordingly. Initially caught off guard by the rapid pace of technological change, record labels struggled to establish control over online sales channels and mitigate the impact of unauthorised file sharing on their bottom line.

Eventually, as the magnitude of revenue loss became undeniable, record labels began to take proactive measures to reassert control over the distribution of music online. This involved developing new business models and partnerships to monetize digital content effectively while also implementing stricter measures to combat piracy and protect intellectual property rights.

Overall, the rise of the internet in the 1990s represented a paradigm shift in the music industry, challenging established norms and reshaping the way music was produced, distributed and consumed. While initially disruptive, this period of technological upheaval ultimately stimulated innovation and paved the way for the digital transformation of the music industry in the years to come.

The New Millennium

The turn of the new millennium witnessed the meteoric rise of television talent competitions, captivating audiences around the world and thrusting celebrity judges into the spotlight. These shows, often showcasing aspiring singers, dancers and entertainers, provided a platform for eager young performers to showcase their talents and potentially launch their careers in the entertainment industry.

Nevertheless, it's essential to recognise that the emergence of television talent competitions represented a departure from the traditional paths to fame taken by artists like Bob Dylan, The Beatles, and The Rolling Stones.

These legendary artistes achieved their status through a combination of talent, perseverance and innovation, without relying on the structured format and mass exposure offered by television shows.

Indeed, the trajectories of such artistes were shaped by a different cultural landscape, one characterised by grassroots movements, live performances and word-of-mouth. Their journeys to stardom were marked by artistic experimentation, cultural significance and a deep connection with their audience, factors that transcend the confines of a televised talent competition.

While television talent competitions undoubtedly offer aspiring artists valuable exposure and opportunities, it's worth acknowledging that they represent just one pathway to success in the music industry. The legacies of these legends serve as a reminder that true artistic greatness often lies in authenticity, originality and a willingness to defy conventional norms in pursuit of creative expression.

Throughout the 2000s, a wave of fresh talent emerged, captivating a new generation.
The proliferation of digital platforms has democratised access to the world, enabling individuals to reach audiences and attain significant success with the simple push of a button. This accessibility has liberated artists from the arduous grind of touring and performing gigs nationwide. Moreover, it has shattered the traditional barriers imposed by a select few major record labels. In the past, artists faced demoralising rejections from these labels, but today, they hold the reins of their own destiny. Record companies now actively pursue artists who have cultivated their own following and achieved independent success.

Lastly

Reflecting on my journey, I consider myself incredibly fortunate to have experienced what many would call the golden era of an extraordinary business. I'm filled with gratitude for the opportunity to have been a part of such a dynamic and ever-evolving industry, where creativity knows no bounds and the pursuit of excellence knows no limits.
Throughout my career, I've had the privilege of meeting and working with incredible individuals who have left an indelible mark on the music industry and popular culture as a whole.
Elvis Presley, The Beatles and Michael Jackson stand out as once-in-a-lifetime talents whose influence transcends generations. Their ground-breaking contributions to music not only redefined genres but also set the standard for excellence in performance, innovation and cultural impact. Witnessing their rise to fame and witnessing, first-hand, the fervour and adulation they inspired among fans worldwide has been truly awe-inspiring.
Yet, even as these legendary artists cemented their places in music history, each era continued to produce its own crop of global pop sensations. From Madonna to Beyoncé, from Prince to Rihanna, the music industry has consistently churned out remarkable talents who have captivated audiences with their artistry, charisma and ability to push boundaries.

Today's younger generation, immersed in the vibrant and ever-evolving landscape of music, may not always fully grasp the rich history that precedes them in the industry. But they continue to pursue their dreams with unwavering passion and dedication, often idolising the musical inspirations that resonate with them on a deeply personal level. While the terms and conditions of the music business may have undergone significant transformations over the years, one fundamental truth remains unchanged: music has the power to inspire, provoke emotion and capture the collective imagination of us all.

This simple yet profound statement underscores the essence of music as a form of self-expression that defies conventions, challenges norms and transcends boundaries.

Regardless of the era or the prevailing trends, the essence of music remains rooted in its ability to connect people, evoke emotion and spark change. Whether it's the raw energy of punk rock, the introspective lyrics of folk music or the infectious rhythms of pop, music has the power to unite us in shared experiences and transcend the limitations of language, culture and geography.

For countless young kids today, lacking the insights of past industry pioneers, their journey is fuelled by imagination and idol-inspired dreams. While the terms and conditions may have changed, one thing remains ever constant;"

'There Ain't No Rules In Rock 'n' Roll

INDEX

Acoustic Strawbs, The 211
Adrian Kerridge 53
Alan Florence 19, 53
Alan Perkins 30
Alan Sizer 91, 103
Albert Agras 87, 88, 93, 94, 100, 109, 110
Albert Grossman 89
Alisha's Attic 168, 170, 171
Andrew Heath 98, 99
Andy Robin 125, 126, 127, 128
Anthony Newley ... 168, 179, 180, 181, 182, 183, 184, 185, 186, 187, 188, 189, 190, 191, 192, 212
Augie Meyers 136, 137, 138, 139, 140, 141, 145, 146, 149, 150
Barry Gibb 207
Barry Murray 19, 20
Beatles 7, 10, 11, 49, 77, 79, 83, 86, 107, 165, 207, 209, 218, 219, 221, 222
Beggars Banquet 98, 99, 102
Ben Matthews 108
Ben Nesbit 77, 80
Beth Hannah 79, 80, 81
Bev Bevan 64, 65, 133
Bill Haley 24, 39, 40, 91, 113, 114, 115, 117, 119, 121, 122
Billy Ocean 48, 168
Bing Crosby 68, 69
Blake Edwards 111, 112
Blue Weaver 207
Bob Dylan 88, 89, 136, 221
Bob Young 23, 24
Bobby Hart 69, 70
Brian Eden 9, 44
Brian Eno 92
Bronze Records 103, 104, 203
Camey Doucet 161
Caroline Boyce 75
Charlie Katz 214
Chicago 31, 32, 207
Chris Farlowe 215
Christy Lee 79, 81
Chuck Berry 113, 119, 120, 168
Clem Cattini 8, 208
Cleo Laine 108
Cliff Williams 44
Clive Davis 198
Colin Blunstone 95
Colin Hankins 102, 103, 104, 105
Cozy Powell 95, 173
Creedence Clearwater Revival 141
CTS Studios 53, 60, 61, 62, 216, 218

Dag Häggqvist 139, 144, 150
Danny Saxon 168, 169, 170, 171
Dave Cousins 211
Dave Hunt 12, 16, 17, 19, 24, 49, 53, 54, 76, 208
Dave Lawson 103, 104
Dave Meyers 45, 46, 47, 48, 197, 214
Dave Miller 24, 39, 40, 41, 42, 43, 116, 121, 122
Dave Robinson 106
Dave Siddle 49, 50, 51, 53, 54, 59, 60
David Carradine 66, 67, 68
David Sutch 95, 202
De Lane Lea 15, 49, 53, 58, 59, 60, 61, 73, 78, 88, 94, 103, 105, 115, 121, 134, 193, 203, 218
Deep Purple 49, 59, 85, 211, 212
Deodorovic Smith 82
Derek Lawrence 85
Derek Taylor 77
Diana Dors 207, 208
Dick Asher 198, 199
Dick Lewzey 60
Dick Plant 53, 64, 65
Dick Rowe 209
Different Fur Studios 142
DJ Fontana 156
Don Airey 95
Don Arden 62, 65, 66, 80, 81
Donald Sutherland 94
Doors, The 33
Dorothy Squires 27, 28
Doug Sahm 138, 141, 142, 143, 144, 145, 146
Dougie Clifford 141, 142
Dougie Dudgeon 177, 178
Dr Dolittle 184
Dr Feelgood 28, 82, 83, 204
Dusty Springfield 95, 168
Elaine Page 46
Electric Light Orchestra 64, 65, 80, 130, 131, 132, 133, 200
Elvis Presley 7, 39, 75, 113, 117, 118, 119, 147, 150, 154, 156, 165, 193, 222
Errol Brown 86, 87, 88
Fame Studios 117
Francis Rossi 21, 23, 24, 130
Frank Gorshin 183
Fred Astaire 68, 69, 193
Gary Moore 95
Gary Numan 97, 98, 99, 100, 101
George Curry 44
George Michael 81, 107, 108
Georgios Panayiotou 105
Gerry Bron 103, 104, 105, 203
Gigi Garner 109, 110

Gina Fratini	187, 188, 189, 191
Grace Newley	184, 185, 187, 188, 189, 190, 191
Grant Santino	96
Harvey Hinsley	87, 88
Henry Mancini	108, 109
Henry Spurway	125, 126, 127, 128
Hercules The Bear	125, 126, 127, 128
Hot Chocolate	85, 86, 87, 88, 96, 117
Howard Barrow	19, 20, 27
Ian Kimmet	89
J. Edgar Hoover	113
Jack Fishman	26, 27, 39, 63, 83
Jackson's Studio	204
Jacquelyn Fusco	89, 90, 91
James Garner	109, 111, 112
Jeff Lynne	64, 65, 66, 131, 133
Jerry Foster	154, 156
Jerry Lee Lewis	80, 113, 120, 168
Jess Conrad	8
Jim Webb	75, 76, 77
Jimi Hendrix	28, 36, 49
Joe Sun	137, 146, 148, 149, 150, 151, 152
John Lennon	9, 10, 85, 86, 139, 179
John McCloud	19, 24
John Richards	60, 62, 65, 108, 109, 111
John Schroeder	19, 22
John Sebastian	32, 91
John Smyth	43
John Worsley	45, 46, 47, 214
Johnny Dankworth	108
Jon Lord	211
Jordanaires, The	156
Joshua Logan	84
Julie Felix	87
Ken Dodd	59
Kevin Metcalf	63
Kinky Friedman	152, 153
Koffee n Kreme	79, 80, 81
Kris Kristofferson	31, 37
Lance Ellington	79, 80, 81
Larry Bartlett	19
Laurie Jay	168, 169
Lee Marvin	83, 84
Les Charles	45, 46, 47, 48
Little Richard	80, 113, 208
Lou Clark	65, 80, 130, 131, 132, 133, 200
Louie Austin	53
Louis Elman	53, 60, 62, 63, 64, 77, 78, 80, 135
Mal Gray	114, 115
Margaret Wilson	89

Mark Philips	110
Martin Birch	53, 54, 58, 59, 60
Martin Mills	98
Marvin Hamlisch	63
Mary Hopkin	87
Max Clifford	126, 127, 128
Michael de Albuquerque	64, 65
Micky Most	87, 88
Miki Dallon	11, 12, 17, 24, 208
Miller Anderson	211
Mo Foster	95
Monkees, The	69, 70
Moonies, The	129
Motorhead	28, 203, 204
Mungo Jerry	19
Music Centre, The	62, 63, 68
Neville Crozier	28, 30, 33, 35, 37
Nick Austin	98
Nigel Olson	76
Nostromo	102, 104, 105
Odo von Stein	197, 199, 200
Pat Godwin	17, 18, 44, 51
Patrick Malynn	114, 115, 122, 123
Paul Gardiner	100
Paul White	170
Peanut	16, 17, 18, 43, 44, 45, 48, 49
Pete Townsend	29
Peter Green	168, 173, 174, 175, 176, 177, 178
Peter Harris	53, 60, 101, 134
Peter Sellers	190, 212
Peter Wilson	68
Pickettywitch	19, 24
Porter Wagoner	120, 154
Portsmouth Sinfonia	92, 93
Princess Margaret	59, 212
Pye Mobile	19, 28, 30, 202
Queen	54
Rafe McKenna	78, 79
RAK Records	87, 88
Randy VanWarmer	89, 91
Ray Dorset	20
Ray Prickett	19
Ray Randall	95
Rex Harrison	184
Richard Hartle	70
Richard Perry	210, 211
Richard Tandy	65
Rick Parfitt	130
Ringo Starr	10
Robert Johnson Songbook	174, 178

Robert Lemon	103
Robert Stigwood	80, 81
Robin Cable	76, 77
Rock Hudson	110
Ron Foulk	37
Ronnie Harwood	117
Roy Budd	26, 63
Roy Orbison	130, 152, 207
Rudolf Huber	125
Ry Cooder	141
Scotty Moore	156
Sean Burke	100
Shakin' Stevens	118
Sham 69	78, 79
Shawn Randoo	92
Sigourney Weaver	103
Sir Douglas Quintet	136, 137, 138, 139
Small Faces	28, 80
Sonet Records	114, 116, 117, 118, 136, 139, 156, 158
Sonnie Rae	106, 107
Splinter Group	173, 174, 175, 176
Status Quo	19, 21, 22, 23, 130
Stiff Records	106, 107
Stuart Taylor	94, 95, 96, 97, 98, 99, 130, 173, 175, 203
Sue Denton	24, 41, 56, 58, 81, 105, 107, 111, 123, 124, 132, 133, 144, 163, 164, 165, 184, 185, 186, 187, 188, 189, 190, 191, 203, 204, 205, 206
Tangerine Studios	47, 214
Teo Macero	30, 31, 35, 36
Terry Evennett	19
Terry Yeadon	54
Thin Lizzy	59
Thomas Hicks	193
Tim Rice	25, 26
Tommy Boyce	69, 70, 71, 72, 73, 74
Tommy Steele	7, 190, 193, 194, 195, 196
Tony Bridge	102
Tony Carey	30, 37
Tony Hatch	80, 81
Tony Wilson	85, 86, 87, 88, 89, 90, 91, 92, 96, 117
Tornados, The	8, 95, 98, 136, 208
Tubeway Army	97, 98
Vic Maile	19, 28, 29, 30, 32, 33, 34, 35, 37, 82, 201, 202, 203, 204, 205, 206
Vinnie Fusco	89
Walter Hale	120, 154
Warren Beatty	212
Wham	107, 108
Who, The	28, 29, 34, 98
Yoko Ono	10, 86

Printed in Great Britain
by Amazon